TEACHING SPEECH COMMUNICATION
IN THE SECONDARY SCHOOL

TEACHING SPEECH COMMUNICATION
IN THE SECONDARY SCHOOL

WILLIAM D. BROOKS
GUSTAV W. FRIEDRICH
Purdue University

HOUGHTON MIFFLIN COMPANY · Boston
Atlanta · Dallas · Geneva, Ill. · Hopewell, N. J. · Palo Alto

TO
GRACE
AND
ERENA

ACKNOWLEDGMENTS

A book cannot be written without the contributions and assistance of many others. In the writing of this book we were especially grateful to the following people for their excellent critical readings and suggestions: Dorothy Higginbotham, Southern Illinois University; Wayne Minnick, Florida State University; Jud Newcomb, University of South Florida; Marcella Oberle, California State College at Los Angeles; Ed Pappas, Wayne State University; and Bobby Patton, University of Kansas. Our sponsoring editors and editorial supervisors at Houghton Mifflin provided inspiration to begin the project and encouragement as we progressed. Very special acknowledgment is due to our wives, Grace and Erena, for their assistance in typing the several drafts of this book and for the substantial psychological and intellectual contributions they made to it.

CONTENTS

PREFACE

Teaching Speech Communication in the Secondary School is intended primarily as a textbook for college students who are preparing to teach speech in the secondary school, and secondarily as a reference book for student teachers and teachers in the field. Its purpose is to enlarge the number and quality of understandings and behaviors available to the teacher as options in managing the teaching-learning situation. It is the authors' hope that this book will help the student acquire a broad range of teaching skills applicable to speech communication.

Recognizing that effective teaching may well be both a science and an art, this book not only attempts to help the student acquire specific teaching skills, but also encourages him to become an artistic manager of the learning situation. A model that includes the basic components of the teaching-learning system provides the framework for developing an effective classroom experience.

Parts One and Two focus directly on the classroom teaching-learning situation. Chapter 1 identifies the goals of secondary school speech education, as well as the goals of teacher education in speech communication, and describes the speech curriculum of the secondary school and the nature of the basic speech course. A model of the teaching-learning process explains the systems approach to teacher education in speech. Chapter 2 presents the case for behavioral objectives (one element of the model mentioned previously) and includes guidelines for writing and evaluating objectives, using examples of two taxonomies of types of learning.

Another element of the model, capabilities of students, is the subject of Chapter 3. Chapter 4 focuses on teaching strategies and skills. It explains in detail the most important instructional skills and provides guidelines for acquiring proficiency in these skills. Chapter 5, lesson planning, requires that the teacher know his students' capabilities and that he know and use instructional strategies and skills (the third element of the model) to create a plan for teaching and learning which will result in the attainment of the learning objectives.

Chapter 6, concerning discipline, achievement, and mental health in the classroom, explains the interacting relationships of these elements and includes tested principles for improving them.

Part Two is concerned with the fourth and fifth components of the model, evaluation and feedback. Chapter 7 deals with a primary area of evaluation in speech classes—evaluating and grading speech performances. Chapter 8 is a comprehensive chapter on teacher-made tests. Chapters 9 and 10 focus on two methods by which the teacher may secure feedback helpful in evaluating the teaching-learning situation. The topics of Chapters 9 and 10 are metacommunication and systematic observation. Various systematic classroom observation systems are presented in Chapter 10.

The four chapters constituting Part Three include a reference file of assignments and resource materials (books, films, etc.) for interpersonal communication, public speaking, drama and oral interpretation, radio and television. Chapter 13 (drama) and Chapter 14 (radio, television, and film) are included for two reasons: (1) Although most introductory courses in communication in the secondary school do not include units on these subjects, some do; (2) use of this resource file is not limited to the basic course only.

Part Four includes three chapters treating professional concerns outside the classroom. Chapter 15 presents a description of the typical student-teaching experience through discussions of the roles of university coordinator, supervising teacher, and student teacher with guidelines for the student-teaching experience. Chapter 16 provides information about the professional organizations and publications most relevant to the needs of the speech communication teacher. The final chapter of the book discusses in detail cocurricular speech activities such as debate, drama, speech contests, legislative assemblies, and speakers bureaus.

In the final analysis, the speech communication teacher manages an entire, highly complex system, and this task requires careful observation, accurate judgment, and creative decision making. By presenting the best in recent theory and research on instruction in the framework of a systems approach, the authors hope teachers will be challenged to explore and test a wide variety of strategies to improve their teaching ability. To aid them in achieving this goal, the beginning of each chapter includes a list of behavioral objectives toward which the student's attention and energies should be directed as he studies that chapter.

W.D.B.
G.W.F.

TEACHING SPEECH COMMUNICATION
IN THE SECONDARY SCHOOL

ONE

A RATIONALE FOR
TEACHER EDUCATION IN
SPEECH COMMUNICATION

Technological changes and social changes are impinging on society at an ever increasing rate, necessitating modification of current educational practice as well as the development of totally new understandings, intellectual skills, and behaviors. It is the function of our schools to provide them.

During the past few years there has been an intensive search for better ways of conducting the entire educational enterprise. Terms such as non-grading, team teaching, flexible or modular scheduling, programmed learning, and computer-assisted instruction have become part of our everyday vocabulary; yet there is every reason to believe that these innovations will accomplish little until we have developed teachers skilled in their use. That we are not yet doing so is suggested by a recent study published by the American Association of Colleges for Teacher Education, which argues that one of the major causes of educational failure is defects in the education of teachers (AACTE, 1969). Consequently, reform in the training of teachers for today's schools is a national imperative.

To meet the need of the times and be genuinely effective, a program for teacher education in speech communication must have two basic goals. First, it must provide the prospective teacher with an understanding of the contributions that speech education makes to secondary school students. In other words, it must make him cognizant of the general goals to be achieved. Second, it must provide him with the means of helping secondary school students achieve these general goals. For example, it must suggest ways of

OBJECTIVES

1. Identify the goals of teacher education in speech communication.
2. Identify the goals of speech education.
3. Describe the speech curriculum of the secondary school.
4. Describe the content of the basic speech course in the secondary school.
5. Identify the major components of the teaching-learning process as represented in the COSEF model.
6. Explain the implications of viewing teaching-learning as a process.
7. Explain the teaching-learning process in terms of a systems approach.
8. Identify the types and ingredients of systems.
9. Identify and explain the universal principles of general systems theory.

assessing student capabilities, of structuring the teaching-learning process, of presenting material, and of assessing the results. Let us now examine the general goals of speech courses.

GOALS OF SPEECH EDUCATION

THE SECONDARY SCHOOL SPEECH CURRICULUM

An understanding of the goals of speech education in the secondary school in the United States can best be achieved by looking at the development of the speech curriculum. The secondary school speech curriculum, as composed of credit courses, was almost nonexistent before the 1930's. During the thirties speech courses began to be organized and offered for credit, but their growth was slow. By 1939 the percentage of secondary schools offering one speech course or more for credit ranged from none in some states to 15 percent in Pennsylvania. It was not until the fifties that surveys began to reveal a significant number of schools offering speech courses for credit, with some indication that the major growth occurred in the years immediately following World War II. For example, Knower reported in 1950 that 44 percent of the secondary schools in Ohio offered speech for credit. Other studies in the late fifties and early sixties reported that speech was offered by 47 percent of the secondary schools in Illinois, by 51 percent of those in South Dakota, by 56 percent in Michigan, 54 percent in Washington, and 45 percent in Nebraska, Arizona, and Kansas. In general, the proportion of secondary schools offering speech for credit increased from zero to 15 percent in the late thirties to approximately 50 percent in the late fifties and early sixties. Surveys in 1967, 1968, and 1969 indicate that 80 to 90 percent of American secondary schools are offering speech for credit (Brooks, 1969, p. 281).

In the larger schools, the speech curriculum has developed from a single basic course into a four-course program consisting of a basic course (general in nature), a course usually called Advanced Speech or Speech II, a course in drama, and a debate course. A few secondary schools offer additional courses with titles such as Speech Arts, Radio, Drama II, Forensics, Discussion, College Preparatory Speech, Persuasion, Business Speaking, Interpersonal Communication, Parliamentary Procedure, Logic and Reasoning, and Salesmanship.

THE BASIC COURSE

The basic speech course in American secondary schools usually is titled Speech, Speech I, or General Speech. General Speech is an appropriate title because the content of the course is general. This finding is common to the more than forty state and area studies Brooks reviewed in 1969. The basic speech course contains several separate units including informative speaking, persuasive speaking, drama, listening, choral reading, voice and diction, delivery, discussion, parliamentary procedure, and debate. An examination of current textbooks (see Table 1) reveals similar content in all. It is significant that most of the units are concerned with platform or public speaking.

If we were to generalize about the goals of speech education from the content of the high school speech curriculum, we would have to conclude that the aim is to produce proficient public performers. Fortunately, one trend that is now beginning to emerge is the addition of nonplatform types of communication to the content of the basic course. For example, increasing emphasis is being placed on principles of communication that apply across the various types of communication including dyadic, interpersonal, small-group, and mass communication. Units on listening, semantics, persuasion, and discussion are being taught in progressive speech courses. The trend has received support from the Conference on Intercultural Communication

TABLE 1   *Analysis of content of eleven leading high school texts*

	A	B	C	D	E	F	G	H	I	J	K
Conversation	x	x	x	x	x	x	x	x	x	x	x
Information informative speech	x	x	x	x	x		x	x			
Verbal tools for expression	x	x	x	x	x	x	x	x	x	x	x
Physical tools, body delivery	x	x	x	x	x	x	x	x	x	x	x
Voice and diction	x	x	x	x	x	x	x	x	x	x	x
Choral reading	x		x	x	x	x	x	x		x	x
Persuasive speaking	x	x					x		x	x	x
Parlimentary procedure	x	x	x	x	x	x	x	x	x	x	x
Discussion	x	x	x	x		x	x	x	x	x	x
Debate	x	x	x	x	x	x	x	x	x	x	x
Radio/television	x	x	x	x	x	x	x	x	x	x	x
Drama	x		x	x	x	x	x	x	x	x	x
Speeches for special occasions	x	x	x	x	x		x	x	x	x	
Special difficulties	x										
Audience analysis	x	x					x	x			
Listening		x	x	x	x	x	x	x	x	x	x
Organization of a speech	x	x	x	x	x	x	x	x	x	x	x
Speechmaking in free society				x							
Storytelling				x	x	x		x	x	x	
History of speech		x		x			x			x	
Total	16	15	14	17	14	13	17	16	14	16	13

A. Lyman M. Fort and Edward E. Markert, *Speech for All* (Boston: Allyn & Bacon, 1966).

B. Margaret Painter, *Ease in Speech* (Boston: D. C. Heath, 1962).

C. John V. Irwin and Marjorie Rosenberger, *Modern Speech* (New York: Holt, Rinehart and Winston, 1966).

D. Wilhelmina G. Hedde, William N. Brigance, and Victor Powell, *The New American Speech* (Philadelphia: J. P. Lippincott, 1963).

E. Francis Griffith, Catherine Nelson, and Edward Stasheff, *Your Speech* (New York: Harcourt, Brace & World, 1960).

F. Paul Brandes and William Smith, *Building Better Speech* (New York: Noble & Noble, 1962).

G. E. F. Elson and Alberta Peck, *The Art of Speaking* (Boston: Ginn, 1966).

H. Harlen Adams and Thomas Pollock, *Speak Up!* (New York: Macmillan, 1964).

I. Charles Masten and George Pflaum, *Speech for You* (Evanston, Ill.: Row, Peterson, 1965).

J. Karl Robinson and Charlotte Lee, *Speech in Action* (Chicago: Scott, Foresman, 1965).

K. William Lamers and Joseph Staudscher, *The Speech Arts* (Chicago: Lyons & Carrahan, 1966).

(1968), the New Orleans SAA-USOE Conference (1968), the Department of Public Instruction of Wisconsin (1967), and several speech educators in journal articles or textbooks (Irwin and Rosenberger, 1966, pp. 4–5; Ratliffe and Herman, 1969, pp. 45–49).

It is hoped that this new emphasis will make the goals of speech education what, in the authors' opinion, they ought to be—helping individuals develop their communication abilities to the fullest possible extent for several types of situations: marital communication, social communication, on-the-job communication, conference and committee work, as well as public speaking.

METHODS OF ACHIEVING THE GOALS

Methods of achieving the goals of speech education will be developed in this text within the framework of a teaching-learning model. This model is based on the assumption that teaching-learning is a complex process that must focus on student learning rather than on teaching. Before outlining the model, however, some implications of the underlying assumption will be explored.

TEACHING-LEARNING: A COMPLEX PROCESS

Berlo (1960, p. 24) has described process in this way:

> If we accept the concept of process, we view events and relationships as dynamic, on-going, ever-changing, continuous. When we label something as a process, we also mean that it does not have a beginning, *an* end, a fixed sequence of events. It is not static, at rest. It is moving. The ingredients within a process interact; each affects all of the others.

Communication is a process. Learning is a process. Teaching is a process. Each consists of events, factors, and parts that are meaningless when isolated; or, stated positively, the parts of each process can be understood only as they are analyzed and described according to their relationships to all other relevant events and factors in the process.

That teaching-learning is a process has important implications for the prospective teacher. For example, it would be inconsistent with the concept of process to believe that a *single* formula, a *single* method (lecturing, for example), or an *absolute* set of rules would enable one to be an effective teacher. Given the fact that teaching-learning is a complex process, there can be no short, absolute answers. Depending on the particular combination of variables, a given method may be highly salient at one point in the teaching-learning process and of little importance in another situation. Cultural orientation, values, motivation, learning style, past school experience, instructional strategy, and interpersonal relationships are just a few of the elements that interact in the teaching-learning process to influence educational outcomes.

In other words, the individual learner, the classroom, the teacher, the school, the community, each is a system composed of subsystems; and together they form a higher system. A teacher, then, is a systems manager— a person who formulates a teaching-learning strategy and uses feedback throughout the process to judge its success, to discover weaknesses or causes of failure, and to make the necessary adjustments in the system on a rational basis. The ability to operate in such a manner implies that the teacher understands that teaching-learning is a process; it implies that the superior teacher is one who has a large pool of instructional strategies and resources available as options to be used in the education process; and it implies a flexibility in the best behavioral science sense.

A SYSTEMS APPROACH

In the past few years the systems approach has been applied to the educational process with apparent success. It has been utilized because planned intervention in a complex process having several interactive forces (systems) is preferable to an unorganized approach or a rigidly static approach. Management systems seek to achieve organized integration and orderly interrelations of the major components of complex processes. Knowledge of the interrelationships and interactions among components is more important than knowledge of each element alone. It is necessary for decision makers (such as speech teachers) to achieve an organized integration of all those salient components in the classroom that influence learning. General systems theory provides an approach to this end.

The essential characteristics of a system have been identified as (1) organized and orderly, (2) made up of components and relationships among components, (3) functioning as a whole because of the interdependence of its parts, and (4) existing to accomplish a goal or goals. Systems have been classified as natural or man made. Solar systems and the human organism are examples of natural systems. Man-made systems are organizations (schools, speech classrooms) devised by man rather than found in a natural state. Systems may be open or closed. If there is no importation or exportation of information, energy, physical materials, etc., the system is closed. If there is an exchange of materials or information between the system and its environment, the system is open. All living systems are open. They are characterized by the exchange of information and energy with their environment and by the achievement and maintenance of steady, homeostatic states. Speech communication classrooms are man-made, open systems. They have component parts that interact upon each other to influence the whole of the teaching-learning system or process.

Boulding (1956) conceptualized general systems theory as a framework on which to hang the flesh and blood of particular disciplines and subject matters in an orderly body of knowledge. Von Bertalanffy (1956, 1963, p. 1) has said that there are principles which apply to all systems—open systems, closed systems, man-made systems, machine systems, subsystems, human systems, biological systems, and cultural systems. General systems theory is the set of universal principles that apply to all systems.

These principles provide bases for discovering and understanding how it is that certain wholes (systems and suprasystems) function, what their salient components are, how these components are interrelated, and how they may be influenced or controlled. These are precisely the things an effective speech teacher learns to do, and they are the skills that teacher-training programs must come to develop.

The four universal principles of general systems theory are: (1) The greater the degree of wholeness in the system, the more efficient the system. (2) The greater the degree of systematization, the more efficient the operation of the system. (3) The greater the degree of compatibility between system and environment, the more effective the system. (4) The greater the degree of congruence between system synthesis and system purpose, the more effective the system. Fromer (1969, p. 51) has summarized the role of the systems approach to education:

The world of education is currently undergoing a strong revolutionary movement. . . . Its most significant aspect is the current attention being directed toward the systems approach to designing and developing education and training. This is supported by many recent articles in journals . . . and by numerous recent books and manuals covering such topics as instructional systems, instructional objectives, instructional technology, etc.

Most of the procedures described and discussed in the current literature are based upon a general systems development model. They all include elements such as problem definition, statement of objectives, selection of methods and techniques for achieving the stated objectives, identification of appropriate content . . . development of measurement instruments to evaluate and diagnose the system's effectiveness, and a feedback control system to optimize system effectiveness.

Wholeness (the working together of the factors or subsystems), systematization (the tightness of the relationship of the parts of the system), compatibility (the relevance of the system and its goals to the environmental need), and congruence (how the working of the system fits the purpose of the system)—these are the guidelines or principles that are the basis of effective decision making in systems management. The role of a teacher is to manage a learning system. Thus the systems approach is being applied increasingly in teacher training and is the basic orientation of this textbook.

FOCUS ON STUDENT LEARNING

As pointed out earlier, the focus of this book is on student learning rather than on teaching. A good teacher, therefore, is defined as one who so manages the educational process under his charge that the result is efficient and significant learning—change in behavior—by the students. This means that the teacher must be more than a dispenser of information and opinions. He must be knowledgeable about variables such as instructional strategies, student capabilities, instructional objectives, evaluation, and feedback. His business is to manage and influence all these variables or systems so as to increase the probability of learning.

It may be that traditional education in the United States has emphasized the *transmission and storage* of information rather than the *acquisition and assimilation* of information and skills. With the former, there is a tendency to place the initiative on the teacher, who presents information which the student is expected to replicate. With the latter, however, the initiative lies primarily with the learner, who seeks information and skills because he views them as relevant to himself and his situations, present or expected. Whether or not the student will be motivated to take an active role in learning, however, will depend on his capabilities (interests, desires, goals, concerns, prior learning, etc.), on the objectives of the course (clarity, relevancy, attainability, etc.), on the instructional strategy (understood by the student, accepted by the student, etc.), and on the evaluation and measurement of progress. All these elements compose the instructional system. It is the management of this entire system for which the teacher is responsible.

When one teaches from a systems approach, he becomes concerned about how the student is to get from where he is to where he wants to be. Too many teachers ignore entirely the need to discover where students are. They begin where *they* are, making no attempt to relate the learning process to the students. An instructional systems approach causes the teacher to be aware of the total process—to be concerned with what he is doing in terms of its effect upon the goal of the course: behavioral change in students.

The systems approach is not new. For years effective teachers have learned by experience to handle all these elements in the learning situation. Such teachers have become skilled artists in handling it. They understand and influence the learning process. However, it is easier to learn anything purposefully than accidentally; consequently, this text focuses directly on a systems approach.

To summarize, because teaching-learning is a complex process that focuses on student learning, the teacher must be concerned with student capabilities, instructional objectives, selection of appropriate teaching strategies, accurate evaluation, and monitoring of the system. These components can be integrated into a purposeful system, or model.

A TEACHING-LEARNING MODEL: COSEF

A teaching-learning model is used in this text for the following purposes: (1) to enable prospective speech teachers to relate the many topics treated in this text in a framework, (2) to encourage them to view teaching as a process composed of interactive elements, and (3) to provide them with a means of evaluating their teaching in terms of the total system. The teaching-learning model about which this book is organized is called COSEF. The letters represent the five basic elements with which a teacher of speech communication must concern himself in order to manage the learning situation: capabilities, objectives, strategies, evaluation, and feedback.

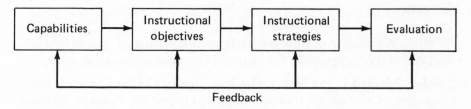

FIGURE 1   *COSEF: A teaching-learning model*

C – denotes the student's capabilities, both latent and manifest; where the student is now in terms of his knowledge, intellectual skills, and behavior. Who is the learner? What interests and abilities does he possess?

O – denotes the instructional objectives that have been selected as the outcomes to be expected from the completion of this specific speech course. Objectives describe where the student is to be at the conclusion of the course in terms of knowledge, intellectual skills, and behavior.

S – denotes the instructional strategies that are devised and used to provide productive learning experiences. Included in instructional strategies are such activities as giving speeches, reading textbooks, lecturing, discussing, preparing outlines of speeches, etc.

E – denotes evaluation. Evaluation in speech communication classes consists of more than paper-and-pencil tests and examinations. Speeches and other communication performances are evaluated and criticized by the teacher.

F – denotes feedback, the relating of the results (evaluation) to the various main components in the process so that adjustments and/or reinforcement may occur.

The elements included in this teaching-learning model are basic ones and have been identified by other names and in other patterns in models of teaching and/or learning proposed by scholars. For example, Glaser (1962, p. 6) proposed a teaching model composed of instructional objectives, entering behaviors, instructional procedures, and performance assessment. Others who have identified similar elements include DeCecco (1968), Stolurow and Davis (1965), Carroll (1963, 1965), and Amidon and Flanders (1963). But although the basic elements in the proposed model are not unique, their direct application to a methods book on teaching speech communication in the secondary school *is* unique.

REFERENCES

American Association of Colleges for Teacher Education. *Teachers for the Real World.* Washington, D. C.: National Education Association, 1969.

Amidon, Edmund J., and Ned A. Flanders. *The Role of the Teacher in the Classroom: A Manual for Understanding and Improving Teachers' Classroom Behavior.* Minneapolis: Amidon, 1963.

Amidon, Edmund J., and John B. Hough. *Interaction Analysis: Theory, Research, and Application.* Reading, Mass.: Addison-Wesley, 1967.

Berlo, David K. *The Process of Communication: An Introduction to Theory and Practice.* New York: Holt, Rinehart and Winston, 1960.

Bertalanffy, L. von. "General System Theory." *General Systems* 1 (1956): 1.

_____. "General Systems Theory." *General Systems* 7 (1962): 7, 1–12.

Boulding, K. A. "General Systems Theory: The Skeleton of Science." *General Systems* 1 (1956): 1, 17.

Brooks, William D. "The Status of Speech in Secondary Schools: A Summary of State Studies." *Speech Teacher* 18 (1969): 276–281.

Campbell, James Reed, and Cyrus W. Barnes. "Interaction Analysis: A Breakthrough?" *Phi Delta Kappan* 50 (1969): 587–590.

Carroll, John B. "A Model of School Learning." *Teachers College Record* 64 (1963): 723–733.

_____. "School Learning Over the Long Haul." In *Learning and the Educational Process,* edited by J. D. Krumboltz. Chicago: Rand McNally, 1965.

Crowder, Norman A. "On the Differences Between Linear and Intrinsic Programming." *Phi Delta Kappan* 44 (1963): 250–254.

_____. "The Rationale of Intrinsic Programming." In *Human Learning in the School,* edited by J. P. DeCecco. New York: Holt, Rinehart and Winston, 1963.

DeCecco, John P. *The Psychology of Learning and Instruction: Educational Psychology.* Englewood Cliffs, N. J.: Prentice-Hall, 1968.

Department of Public Instruction of Wisconsin. *Teaching Speaking and Writing in Wisconsin: Wisconsin Language Arts Project.* Madison: Department of Public Instruction, 1967.

Eriksson, Bo. "A Systems Approach to Educational Technology." *Educational Technology* 9 (1969): 62–69.

Fromer, Robert. "A Basic Difference Between Educational and Training Systems." *Educational Technology* 9 (1969): 51–52.

Gagné, Robert M. *The Conditions of Learning.* New York: Holt, Rinehart and Winston, 1965.

Glaser, Robert. "Psychology and Instructional Technology." In *Training Research and Education,* edited by R. Glaser. Pittsburgh: University of Pittsburgh Press, 1962.

Gordon, Jerome J. "A System Model for Civil Defense Training and Education." *Educational Technology* 9 (1969): 39–45.

Hall, A. D., and R. E. Fagen. "Definition of a System." In *Modern Systems Research for the Behavioral Scientist,* edited by W. Buckley. Chicago: Aldine, 1968.

Hilgard, Ernest R., and Gordon H. Bower. *Theories of Learning.* New York: Appleton-Century-Crofts, 1966.

Irwin, John V., and Marjorie Rosenberger. *Modern Speech.* New York: Holt, Rinehart and Winston, 1966.

Jamison, C., and J. McLeod-Guerton. "Two System Models for Educational Planning." *Educational Technology* 9 (1969): 7–17.

Knower, Franklin H. *Speech Education in Ohio.* Columbus: Ohio State University, 1950.

Miles, M. E., ed. *Innovation in Education.* New York: Teachers College, Columbia University, 1964.

Pressey, S. L. "A Simple Device for Teaching, Testing, and Research in Learning." *School and Society* 23 (1926): 373–376.

————. "A Third and Fourth Contribution Toward the Coming 'Industrial Revolution' in Education." *School and Society* 36 (1932): 934.

Ratliffe, Sharon A., and Deldee M. Herman. "The Status of Speech in High Schools in Michigan." *Speech Teacher* 18 (1969): 45–49.

Rouch, Mark A. "A System Model for Continuing Education for the Ministry." *Educational Technology* 9 (1969): 32–38.

Ryan, T. A. "Systems Techniques for Programs of Counseling and Counselor Education." *Educational Technology* 9 (1969): 7–17.

Sedlik, Jay M. "Diagnostic Pretesting of the United States Air Force Instructional Motion Picture: Theory and a Proposed Model." Ph.D. dissertation, University of Southern California, June, 1969.

Silvern, L. C. *Systems Engineering of Education I: Evolution of Systems Thinking in Education.* Los Angeles: Education and Training Consultants Co., 1968.

Skinner, B. F. *Behavior of Organisms.* New York: Appleton-Century-Crofts, 1938.

————. "Teaching Machines." *Science* 128 (1958): 969–977.

————. *The Technology of Teaching.* New York: Appleton-Century-Crofts, 1968.

Stolurow, Lawrence M., and Daniel Davis. "Teaching Machines and Computer-Based Systems." In *Teaching Machines and Programmed Learning, II: Data and Directions,* edited by R. Glaser. Washington, D. C.: Department of Audiovisual Instruction, National Education Association, 1965.

PART ONE   THE INSTRUCTIONAL PROCESS: DEVELOPMENT AND MANAGEMENT

Part One of this book focuses on the first three elements of the COSEF model: capabilities, instructional objectives, and instructional strategies and skills. If the teaching-learning process is to result in student learning, clear goals must be specified. Chapter 2, therefore, shows the speech teacher how to develop skill in selecting, writing, and using instructional objectives. Chapter 3 points out that instructional objectives often need to be modified to meet the student's entering behavior. Since instructional objectives that are realistic in terms of student capabilities are of little value unless the teacher has some idea of how to help students achieve them, Chapter 4 is devoted to various instructional strategies and skills for helping students attain specified objectives. Chapter 5 integrates the material in Chapters 2, 3, and 4 into a plan of action for the teacher through the use of resource units, teaching units, and daily lesson plans. The final chapter in Part One, Chapter 6, discusses the three interacting variables—discipline, achievement, and attitude—that play a major role in the speech communication classroom at the secondary level.

TWO

DEVELOPING
INSTRUCTIONAL OBJECTIVES

The broad goal of the teacher education program in speech communication represented in the COSEF model is to develop ways of bringing about major changes in the classroom behavior of teachers—and consequently in the behavior of students. Among the skills which it aims to develop in speech teachers are the selecting, writing, and using of behavioral objectives in classroom instruction. This chapter, in three major sections, deals with instructional behavioral objectives. The first section distinguishes explicit behavioral objectives from implicit nonbehavioral objectives and also identifies the important characteristics of meaningfully written behavioral objectives. The second section presents the types of learning for which behavioral objectives can be written. The third section presents the advantages of using behavioral objectives in teaching speech.

Instructional objectives should not be confused with educational objectives. *Educational objectives*, in this book, refer to the broad goals and values of education in general. Chapter 1 focused on such goals. Instructional objectives, on the other hand, have to do with the results of particular teaching procedures. Instructional objectives may be explicit or implicit, behavioral or nonbehavioral. Most instructional objectives used by speech communication teachers at this time are not explicit behavioral objectives, but implicit nonbehavioral ones. Unfortunately, many speech communication teachers write no instructional objectives of any kind. It is the aim of this book to encourage the use of explicit behavioral objectives in teaching speech.

OBJECTIVES

1. Translate educational goals or objectives into instructional behavioral objectives.
2. State the three criteria for a behavioral objective.
3. Classify sample objectives as behavioral or nonbehavioral.
4. Define and explain Bloom's three general types of learning.
5. Identify, explain, and differentiate Bloom's six types of cognitive learning.
6. Identify, explain, and differentiate Bloom's four types of affective learning.
7. Identify, explain, and differentiate Kibler, Barker, and Miles's four types of psychomotor outcomes that are especially relevant to speech communication.
8. Classify examples of learning outcomes as to general type of learning and specific level within the general type.
9. Identify and explain Gagné's classification system of types of learning.
10. Summarize and evaluate the major arguments for and against behavioral objectives.

CHARACTERISTICS OF BEHAVIORAL OBJECTIVES

A *behavioral instructional objective* is a statement (or statements) that identifies the expected terminal behavior of the students, describes the important conditions under which the behavior is expected to occur, and specifies the criteria which are acceptable as evidence that it has occurred.

In this definition *behavior* is anything observable by man or machine. It can be verbal or nonverbal—in short, any audible, written, or physical performance of a student. Thus, a behavioral objective is concerned with observable activity of a student. *Terminal behavior* is the behavior the student should be able to demonstrate upon completion of an instructional unit. Through observing the terminal performance of the student, the instructor infers the state of knowledge or skill. The *criterion* is the standard of performance by which the teacher measures the student's terminal behavior.

Implicit instructional objectives, as opposed to explicit ones, do not indicate how the student will demonstrate the fact that he has learned. They do not identify particular behavioral outcomes that will be taken as evidence that the objective has been achieved. *Meaningfully stated behavioral objectives* clearly communicate the teacher's *intent* to the student, or any other person. For example, if another speech teacher used an objective you wrote, and taught his students to perform in a manner consistent with what you intended by the objective, the objective would be a meaningfully stated one. The best way to write a clear objective is to use words that are open neither to misinterpretation nor to a wide range of interpretation. Particularly the *verb* in the statement must denote a measurable behavior. The following lists give examples of good and bad verbs:

Verbs Open to Many Interpretations	*Verbs Open to Few Interpretations*
know	write
appreciate	recite
understand	solve
really understand	construct
fully appreciate	list
believe	identify
enjoy	differentiate
have faith in	compare
	contrast
	name
	order

Typically, teachers use verbs such as "understand," "know," "appreciate," and "believe" in their objectives. But since the phenomena to which these statements refer are difficult to measure, the teachers are unable to determine objectively whether or not the goal has been attained. Take, for example, this implicit instructional objective: The student will know the principles of organizing a speech. What does the teacher mean by it? Is the student to be able to recite the principles, to identify the correct and incorrect uses of the principles in printed speeches, or to prepare a speech in which he correctly applies the principles? To know can mean many things. It should be understood that a teacher can use words such as "to know" in instructional objectives, but when he does he should indicate how he intends to sample the knowing. Unless he has described what the learner will be *doing* when demonstrating that he knows, he has said little in the objective. Thus the behavioral objective should describe the *terminal behavior* of the learner explicitly enough to prevent misinterpretation.

Consider the following objective: To develop an understanding of the speech mechanism. Although this might be an important objective, the statement does not indicate what the learner will be doing when he demonstrates that he has reached the objective. A more appropriate way to state this objective is: When the learner completes the program of instruction, he must be able to demonstrate his understanding by identifying by name each component of the voice mechanism.

The way to write a clear behavioral objective is to state your educational intent and then to modify the statement until it answers the question, What is the learner *doing* when he is demonstrating that he has achieved the objective?

Which of the following objectives is stated in observable performance terms?

1. To develop an appreciation of good speech
2. To write an outline of a speech according to the requirements for outlining described in our speech textbook

Only the second objective indicates what the learner will be doing. Although the first objective may be important, it is stated so vaguely that the intent is lost. It fails to communicate clearly the expected learning outcome.

A second important characteristic of a meaningfully stated behavioral objective is that it describe the *conditions* under which the behavior is expected to occur. Although the teacher may clearly indicate the terminal behavior that is to result from instruction, this may not be enough to prevent misunderstanding. Consider, for example, this objective: to conduct an effective informational interview to gather valid information. It describes a behavior that is expected as the result of units of instruction on interviewing but does not indicate the expected *qualities* or conditions of the interview.The objective must state the conditions under which the learner will demonstrate achievement of it. For example, in informational interviewing one might stipulate that the learner will be given twenty minutes to interview a person who is thoroughly familiar with a case problem and who will provide honest information as a reluctant interviewee (i.e., he will provide *only* that information requested).

Some phrases frequently used to state the conditions under which the learner must demonstrate his mastery of the objective are:

Given a list of . . .

Given a problem of the following class . . .

Given a dictionary . . .

Given access to recent periodicals . . .

Without the aid of references . . .

Without prior notice . . .

Before the classroom audience . . .

Given thirty minutes . . .

The following two questions can be used to identify the conditions that ought to be stated in the objective:

What will the learner be provided?

What will the learner be denied?

A good way to inform the learner of the conditions under which he will be expected to perform is simply to show him some sample test items. Many good teachers make it a practice to show students at least a page of sample test items so that the students understand the conditions under which they will be evaluated. In the same manner, some teachers use model outlines of speeches or cuttings from literature.

The third characteristic of a meaningfully stated behavioral objective is that it identifies the *criterion of acceptable performance*. If at least the minimum acceptable performance for the objective can be specified, a standard exists against which the instructional program can be tested. As a teacher, you are then able to determine whether your instructional strategies are successful in helping students achieve the instructional objective.

One way to indicate the lower limit of acceptable performance is to specify a time limit. In a speed test, in which students are allowed a specific amount of time to complete the examination, it is only fair to state the time limitation in the objective. In interviewing, the teacher might stipulate that within one hour after the interview the student will submit a written report of the information he has gained and that the report will be judged in terms of its comprehensiveness and accuracy.

Another frequent way of specifying a criterion of acceptable performance is to indicate the minimum number, percent, or proportion of correct responses the learner must make; the number of principles that he must apply in a given problem; or the number of principles, concepts, or characteristics that he must identify.

There are other ways of specifying acceptable performance, and the individual teacher will undoubtedly find some that are especially suited to the behavioral outcomes he expects.

In summary, the meaningfully stated instructional objective will (1) identify the terminal behavior, (2) specify the conditions under which the behavior will be demonstrated, and (3) indicate the criterion, or standard of performance—the level of performance which is acceptable as evidence that the objective has been achieved. Now let us take a look at the types of learning, or behavior, for which instructional objectives can be written.

TYPES OF LEARNING OR BEHAVIOR

Two of the best known systems of types of learning, or behavior, are Bloom's *Taxonomy of Educational Objectives* (1956) and Gagné's classes of behavior in *The Conditions of Learning* (1965). These two category systems have been found quite helpful to teachers who use behavioral objectives.

BLOOM'S TAXONOMY OF EDUCATIONAL OBJECTIVES

Bloom's taxonomy includes a range of educational outcomes and sample objectives chosen from a variety of subject-matter fields, each of which illustrates one of the taxonomy's classes. By using either Gagné's or Bloom's categories, one can test a course or unit to determine whether its only focus is on factual data and recall. Almost all units should include some objectives dealing with application of knowledge and with analysis.

Bloom and those who worked with him viewed learning as composed of three general types: cognitive, affective and psychomotor. Cognitive learning deals with intellectual abilities and skills, and it includes remembering, recalling, thinking, problem solving, creating, etc. It is the domain in which most of the work in curriculum development and test construction has taken place. It is the domain for which most behavioral objectives are written and which claims most of the teaching-learning activities and classroom time in schools.

The second general type of learning in Bloom's taxonomy is affective learning, which denotes interests, attitudes, values, and appreciations. While it is difficult to describe the behaviors associated with these learnings and to write behavioral objectives for them, many such objectives have been written successfully.

The third domain is psychomotor learning. Psychomotor skills are motor skills and perceptual motor skills involving gross bodily movements and finely coordinated bodily movements. Nonverbal communication, for example, involves gestures, facial expressions, and physical movement, all of which are muscle-mind activities, i.e., psychomotor skills. Of course, verbal communication also involves very fine, technical psychomotor skills. Bloom (1956, p. 7) stated, "We find so little done about it in secondary schools or colleges, that we do not believe the development of a classification of these objectives would be very useful at present." Since that time, however, Kibler, Barker, and Miles (1970) have formulated a set of subclassifications of behavior in the psychomotor domain, which appear later in this chapter. Their purposes for adding these subclassifications were (p. 67): "(1) to provide a framework for examining a variety of psychomotor objectives, and (2) to provide initial definitions for classes of psychomotor behavior."

Although some scholars see cognitive learning and affective learning as one inseparable domain, Bloom's division of learning into three types—cognitive, affective, and psychomotor—is followed in this book, primarily from an educational viewpoint. These are the pragmatic distinctions that teachers make in developing courses and units and in making up examinations. Moreover, such a classification system seems functionally sound for the teacher education program in speech communication developed in this text. The system helps the instructor develop a course of study that includes a wide range of types of learning. Speech teachers must be concerned with all these types of learning. Yet in the basic course in speech it is possible to cover twelve to fifteen topics in which all objectives and learning exist *at the level of facts only*. It is possible also for a teacher to ignore the factual data, principles, and concepts that students need in order to understand the behavior being taught and simply require that students give speeches. It is also possible to teach a speech course giving no attention to the development of critical evaluation skills. It is the authors' contention that all types of learning identified by Bloom in the cognitive domain, as well as all types in the affective domain, should be developed in the basic speech course in the secondary school. The taxonomy helps the teacher accomplish this goal.

COGNITIVE LEARNING

Bloom's cognitive domain comprises six major types of learning: knowledge, comprehension, application, analysis, synthesis, and evaluation. This is the hierarchical order of the different classes of objectives from simple learning to complex learning. Objectives in the simple classes are likely to be used to create the behavioral objectives in the higher classes since the integration of simple behaviors are the basis of more complex behaviors. Bloom (1965, pp. 18–19) has stated:

> Our classifications may be said to be in the form where behaviors of type A form one class, behaviors of type AB form another class, while behaviors of type ABC form still another class. If this is the

real order from simple to complex, it should be related to an order of difficulty such that problems requiring behavior A alone should be answered correctly more frequently than problems requiring AB. We have studied a large number of problems occurring in our comprehensive examinations and have found some evidence to support this hypothesis. Thus, problems requiring knowledge of specific facts are generally answered correctly more frequently than problems requiring a knowledge of the universals and abstractions in a field. Problems requiring knowledge of principles and concepts are correctly answered more frequently than problems requiring both knowledge of the principle and some ability to apply it in new situations. Problems requiring analysis and synthesis are more difficult than problems requiring comprehension.

Following is an abbreviated outline of the taxonomy for the cognitive domain of Bloom (1956) as adapted from the condensed taxonomy in the appendix.

1. Knowledge
   a. Definitions of terms
   b. Specific facts
   c. Conventions, usages, styles
   d. Trends and sequences
   e. Classification or categorization systems
   f. Criteria to be used in judging
   g. Principles and generalizations
   h. Theories
2. Comprehension
   a. Translation or paraphrasing
   b. Interpretation
3. Application
   a. Problem solving by using facts, principles, theories
   b. Predicting
4. Analysis
   a. Identifying parts or elements
   b. Identifying relationships of elements
5. Synthesis
   a. Production of unique communication
   b. Production of unique plan of operations
   c. Production of hypothesis
6. Evaluation
   a. Quantitative and qualitative judgments on the value or worth

    b. Using criteria as a standard for appraisal
    c. Comparing concepts, theories, or generalizations

The most frequently used category in instruction and testing is knowledge. Since schools are most concerned with the acquisition of knowledge, it is an important, basic type of educational objective. In many courses, however, it is the only class of objectives. Knowledge can be defined as recalling data, ideas, or phenomena in a form close to that in which it was originally encountered. The emphasis on recalling distinguishes it from understanding or applying. Knowledge is of little value if it cannot be used as an ability or skill. Yet it must be recognized that skills and abilities are grounded in knowledge.

Some knowledge is quite simple, such as the specific fact that the Lincoln-Douglas debates took place in Illinois. Other knowledge is more complex, such as the theory of cognitive dissonance. In the secondary school speech course, instruction and tests should include all levels. Knowledge is basic to all the other purposes of education since problem solving, thinking, and creating cannot be carried on in a vacuum. Moreover, it is generally held to be true that learning or behavior change in the affective domain is based upon knowledge. Thus interests are developed as the result of an increase in information; attitudes involving personal adjustment and the resolution of conflicts and anxieties are grounded in the recognition that accurate knowledge about oneself and others is necessary for growth.

It should be kept in mind that the acquisition of knowledge is important not for its own sake but rather for the development of other skills and behaviors.

Comprehension differs from knowledge in that one not only can recall information but can translate, paraphrase, and interpret it. The data have meaning in forms different from the form in which they were first received. Bloom (1965, p. 89) defines comprehension as follows: "Those objectives, behaviors, or responses which represent an understanding of the literal message contained in a communication. In reaching such understanding, the student may change the communication in his mind or in his overt responses to some parallel form more meaningful to him."

The student demonstrates comprehension by translating (putting the communication into another language, into other terms, or into another form of communication); by interpreting (recording ideas or making inferences, generalizations, or summarizations); or by extrapolating (making estimates or predictions, making inferences with respect to corollaries, implications, or consequences).

The third class of cognitive learning is application. Most of what a student learns should be applicable to problem situations in real life. Research shows that giving a person information provides no assurance that he can apply the information to problem solving. The possession of knowledge and the ability to apply it are not synonymous. That fact is extremely important in teaching speech communication. The speech student must learn not only to recall the principles of organizing or structuring a speech but also to structure it.

The fourth class of cognitive learning is analysis, a more advanced level than comprehension or application. Comprehension denotes grasping the meaning of data. Application is using appropriate data, principles, and generalizations to solve problems. Analysis means breaking down the material into its component parts in order to perceive the interrelationships.

Skills in analysis must be included in speech communication courses. Students need to develop the ability to distinguish statements of fact from statements of value; to identify transitions, supporting statements, hypotheses, and conclusions; to distinguish relevant from extraneous material; to see how one idea relates to another; and to find evidence of the speaker's techniques and purposes.

The fifth category is synthesis—the combining of elements and parts to form a whole. The performance resulting from synthesis is essentially a creative behavior. A speech prepared by a student is an example of synthesis.

The final type of cognitive learning is evaluation—making judgments about the value of a thing. It involves the use of criteria and may be either qualitative or quantitative. Evaluating makes use of all the simpler behaviors just discussed: knowledge, comprehension, application, analysis, and synthesis. What is added, according to Bloom (1956, p. 185), are criteria of values; and Bloom maintains that evaluation not only is an end product of the other cognitive learnings but is also a major link with affective behavior such as liking, enjoying, appreciating, and valuing.

AFFECTIVE LEARNING

Affective objectives involve feelings, emotions, interests, attitudes, appreciations, and values. It is not unusual to find such objectives in speech courses, although they are generally stated in implicit, nonbehavioral terms and are seldom measured objectively.

The categories of affective objectives are ordered hierarchically as are those of the cognitive domain. The categories are arranged along a continuum from low or little internalization to high internalization. The categories, as adapted from Krathwohl, Bloom, and Masia (1964, p. 95), are:

1. Attending
   a. Awareness
   b. Willingness to receive
2. Responding or interested in
   a. Complies or obeys
   b. Willingly responds
   c. Enjoys, has zest for
3. Valuing (attitudes)
   a. Believes (accepts the attitude or value)
   b. Makes a commitment
4. Organizing a value system

One seldom sees instructional objectives dealing with attention. Such concerns are usually included in the instructional strategy. Teachers use visual aids, films, bulletin boards, animation, graphs, and charts to create an awareness of the topic being studied. Krathwohl (1964, p. 99) says that "awareness is the bottom rung of the affective domain and is almost a cognitive behavior."

The second category, responding, best describes interest objectives. Teachers often have the objective (whether they write it or not) of the student's developing sufficient interest in or commitment to the subject that he will seek out the activity again to gain satisfaction. Three levels of responding have been identified. At the lowest level, the student complies or responds because he is required to do so. With greater internalization he is interested to the point of responding willingly (the element of resistance in the first level is replaced with a willingness). There are a large number of educational objectives in this category. At the third level of responding, not only is the student willing, but his responding behavior is accompanied by feelings of satisfaction, pleasure, zest, enthusiasm, and enjoyment.

The third class of affective objectives is valuing. Two levels of valuing are identified. The lower level is belief: The student accepts the value or attitude. (Attitude implies a valuing, positively or negatively, of some behavior, phenomenon, or object.) At this level, although the belief is not firmly established, the student is perceived by others as holding the belief or value, and he is willing to be identified as holding it. At the higher level of valuing, the student makes a strong emotional commitment to the object, group, phenomenon, etc. (e.g., loyalty to a group or cause). He increases his involvement with it and seeks to convince others. This level of valuing is not unusual in the effective speech communication classroom. Underlying these values and attitudes are aroused needs and drives, which strongly motivate students to engage in this level of behavior. An example of a behavioral objective of this nature in the affective domain is:

> After completing the instruction in open–closed mindedness (reading assigned materials, engaging in the activities and "experiencing situations," and completing the assignments), the student will give evidence of his preference for open-mindedness by: listening carefully when others are talking, insisting on hearing more than one opinion or viewpoint on a controversial issue, being willing to change his ideas when new evidence or additional evidence is presented, and being willing to give consideration to ideas which differ from his own.

A final category in the affective taxonomy is organizing or assimilating attitudes and values into a system. Certainly, this is an important category in speech communication. One of the desired outcomes of the speech communication course is the student's development of a value or attitude system toward his own communication and the communication of others about him. Students encounter situations to which several values are relevant, and thus there is a need for the organization of communication attitudes and values into a system. Communication courses need to include objectives that encourage the student to engage in comparative evaluations of beliefs, attitudes and values. Speech communication teachers want to know whether comparative evaluation of values has taken place, and they look for evidence that the student has developed evaluative judgments of such concerns as freedom of speech, responsibility in speech, and ethics in advertising and political campaigning. An organizing objective requires that the student bring together a complex of values, sometimes disparate ones, and order them into a relationship with one another. The ordered relationship should be a harmonious and internally consistent one. An example of an organizing affective objective for a speech communication student, as indicated above, is the development of a philosophy of freedom of speech and responsibility of speech.

Teachers have had difficulty evaluating the affective areas of learning. The instructional objectives which appear in curriculum guides and teachers' manuals are usually vague and contain words open to several interpretations (or, more accurately, misinterpretations)—words such as "feel," "understand," and "appreciate" rather than specific words such as "write," "construct," and "differentiate." Yet progress is being made, and banks of excellent affective instructional objectives will soon be available.

PSYCHOMOTOR LEARNING

Unlike the cognitive and affective objectives, the psychomotor objectives
are not organized hierarchically. Kibler, Barker, and Miles (1970, pp. 68–75)
provide a classification of psychomotor behaviors rather than a taxonomy.
The classification has four subdivisions: gross bodily movements, finely
coordinated bodily movements, nonverbal communication behaviors, and
speech behavior. An abbreviated outline of the psychomotor domain follows:

1. Gross bodily movements
   a. Movements involving the upper limbs
   b. Movements involving the lower limbs
   c. Movements involving two or more bodily units
2. Finely coordinated movements
   a. Hand-finger movements
   b. Hand-eye coordination
   c. Hand-ear coordination
   d. Hand-eye-foot coordination
   e. Other combinations of hand-eye-ear movements
3. Nonverbal communication behavior
   a. Facial expression
   b. Gestures
   c. Bodily movement
4. Speech behavior
   a. Sound production
   b. Sound-word formation
   c. Sound projection
   d. Sound-gesture coordination

GAGNÉ'S CLASSIFICATION SYSTEM OF TYPES OF LEARNING

DeCecco (1968, p. 52) maintains that Gagné's system is more useful than
Bloom's for distinguishing various performances and establishing the
necessary learning conditions for achieving those performances. Gagné's
classes of behavior are given in his book *The Conditions of Learning* (1965).
As in Bloom's taxonomy, Gagné's eight types of learning range from the
simple forms to the complex. Gagné refers to the eight classes as learning
types, but his emphasis is on the observable behavior or performance that
results from these types of learning. The eight classes are signal learning,

stimulus-response learning, chaining, verbal association, multiple discrimination, concept learning, principle learning, and problem solving.

Signal learning is essentially classical conditioning as studied in detail by Pavlov. The student acquires a conditioned response to a given signal. The learning is involuntary. The classical example is the salivation of the dog upon hearing a bell which he has learned to associate with food.

In *stimulus-response learning* (sometimes called operant conditioning), the learner associates a rewarded response with the stimulus, causing him to operate on his environment.

Chaining could be called skill learning of a nonverbal type in which two or more stimulus-response units are combined to produce the skill.

Verbal association is the chaining of verbal units. The lowest level of verbal association is naming an object. Such a verbal chaining has two links: the object and the name for it. Verbal association may take place without actually seeing a physical object. Verbal association may also be the chaining of two words—for example, a German word and its English equivalent.

Multiple discrimination learning is learning in which different responses must be associated with the appropriate stimulus for each, when the stimuli are similar and might be confused. Learning to call each student by his or her correct name is multiple discrimination learning on the part of the teacher.

Concept learning is identification of the characteristics of a phenomenon, characteristics which are abstract qualities of the stimulus phenomenon. Concepts are learned through language.

Principle learning is that which relates two or more concepts. A principle is an expressed relationship between two or more concepts.

Problem solving is the use of principles to solve a problem. The solution to a problem can be referred to as a higher-order principle, i.e., the product of combining two or more principles.

One way to use Gagné's classification system of types of learning or Bloom's taxonomy is to prepare a grid in which the instructional units, topics, or areas to be studied in a course are listed on one axis and the levels of learning are listed on the other axis. Behavioral objectives can then be written for each topic at each level of learning. (For an example of this, see Chapter 3.)

This chapter has pointed out the importance of specifying instructional objectives in the teaching-learning system, thus emphasizing learning outcomes rather than content. To teach content because it is there rather than because it is relevant to developing desired learner competencies is to weaken the course. By concentrating on behavior competencies as a basis for designing instruction, the teacher will find that several advantages are likely to result. Students and parents want demonstrable performance against goals. As White (1969, pp. 595–596) has pointed out, "The press for performance . . . is the real revolution in our schools today." Parents and students, as they become increasingly sophisticated, are less interested in goal statements "about maturity, love of learning, cooperation, responsibility, and enjoyment" of the course and are more interested in goals that are precise, definable, and measurable. Parents and students are moving toward rational educational management. "This involves the ability to state educational goals clearly, to institute systematic ways of measuring progress toward them, for public reporting of that progress, and reconsideration of goals and strategies based upon the data."

ADVANTAGES OF USING BEHAVIORAL OBJECTIVES

The importance of using operationalized objectives (behavioral objectives) has been stressed repeatedly by many persons including Mager (1962), Cogswell (1966), Churchman (1968), DeCecco (1968), Loughary (1968), Pfeiffer (1968), and Ryan (1969). One advantage is that they provide guidance for instructional planning. When clearly defined objectives are lacking, it is difficult for the teacher to select appropriate and efficient materials and methods. Instructional activities are sometimes carried out *with no objective in mind.* Clearly defined objectives are easily remembered, and teachers can design instructional strategies that are directly relevant. As Mager (1962, p. 3) argues:

> After all, the machinist does not select a tool until he knows what operation he intends to perform. Neither does a composer orchestrate a score until he knows what effects he wishes to achieve. Similarly, a builder does not select his materials or specify a schedule for construction until he has his blueprints (objectives) before him. Too often, however, one hears teachers arguing the relative merits of textbooks or other aids of the classroom versus the laboratory, without ever specifying just what goal the aid or method is to assist in achieving. I cannot emphasize too strongly the point that an instructor will function in a fog of his own making until he knows just what he wants his students to be able to do at the end of the instruction.

Before the teacher prepares instruction, chooses materials, and selects media machinery and methods, it is important that he know and state his objectives—where he is headed.

The second advantage of behavioral objectives is that they provide a base for evaluating the efficiency of an instructional unit—they enable the teacher and the student to know when the student has gotten there, i.e., when he has learned what he is supposed to have learned as a result of the instruction. Tests are supposed to indicate to the student and the teacher the degree of the student's achievement of course objectives. But unless the objectives have been clearly defined and used as focal points for instruction, tests may be irrelevant, unfair, and useless. Teachers cannot select or construct appropriate test items when they cannot identify *explicitly* what they are trying to enable the students to do. Moreover, when students do not know *explicitly* what the objectives of instruction are, they are likely to find tests frustrating and irrelevant.

A third advantage of using behavioral objectives pertains to the student rather than the teacher. The student is often unable to make even an approximate statement of what the teacher is trying to explain to him or what he is trying to learn. When he is merely exposed to large amounts of content and kept busy with activities without clear-cut objectives, he has no basis for directing his efforts or for assessing his progress toward relevant achievement. His judgment may differ greatly from that of the instructor, and this may result both in his inability to prepare for evaluation situations and in embarrassment at examination time. The goals of instruction—specific knowledge and skill objectives—must be defined and communicated to the student to help him better direct his own attention and efforts. Mager and McCann (1961) used three groups of learners who were being trained for a particular task. In one group, the instructor selected and arranged the content of the unit. In the second group, the students selected and arranged the content. In the third group, Mager and McCann wrote and presented to the students a detailed list of behavioral objectives. The third group of learners then instructed themselves by whatever procedures they desired. The training time for the third group was 65 percent less than that for the other groups, with no loss in achievement. Thus learning appears to be greatly enhanced by the teacher's doing nothing more than giving students a list of behavioral objectives.

Additional empirical support is found in a study by Walbesser and Carter (1968), who report that pupils can obtain extremely high levels of performance when provided with behavioral objectives. Similar findings have been reported by Miles, Kibler, and Pettigrew (1967, pp. 25–26). When students know what they are to learn, what behavior they are to acquire, and what specific achievement they are to demonstrate at the end of a unit of instruction, according to a study by Harrison (1967), they can assume a high degree of responsibility for their own learning and can better measure their own progress toward achievement. They do not have to guess what is expected of them, and they do not question the purpose of a learning activity. Vague objectives impede learning.

The practice of providing students with explicitly stated instructional objectives is not widespread. Few teachers have been trained to write behavioral objectives, and doing so is a time-consuming task. However, the time spent in writing and communicating behavioral objectives to students is time well spent. With clear objectives in view and performance criteria identified, the learner knows which activities are relevant to his success. Too many students spend more of their time in playing the game of getting grades from the teacher than they do in learning. The need to communicate clearly the expected outcomes of instructional units is apparent, and behavioral objective seems to be the most efficient vehicle for doing this.

There have been arguments against the use of explicitly stated instructional objectives. Ebel (1963) has maintained that education is concerned with the development of processes as well as products. Gagné (1965, p. 6) answers the argument by citing and evaluating two implicit objectives: (1) the student should acquire a developing awareness of the magnitude of the solar system and the universe; and (2) the child should become increasingly confident in extemporaneous oral expression:

It is difficult to know what to say about such statements except that they are weasel-worded. Why is it not possible to say exactly what one wants the student to do in showing his awareness of solar system magnitudes? Why is it not possible to state what kind of extemporaneous oral expression one expects the child to perform? The answer may be, of course, that the latter kind of objectives can indeed be stated, but not all students will attain them. Unfortunately, this is probably true under present circumstances. It would be good, though, if we could amend the statement to read: "not all students will attain them *with the same speed.*" Then they would still remain objectives which any intelligent person could identify, rather than descriptions which if not deliberately hedging are at least ambiguous.

A second argument against using explicit instructional objectives is that they emphasize conformity and stifle critical judgment, creative innovation, and adaptive behavior on the part of the student. DeCecco (1968, p. 40) responds:

This position, often defended with notable passion and dedica-
tion, contains many uncritical assumptions about the psychology of

learning in general and about problem solving in particular. . . .
First, why cannot we define critical judgment, creative innovation,
and adaptive behavior explicitly as one or more concrete alternatives the individual may choose in hypothetical situations? Second,
does evidence support the assumption that critical judgment,
creative innovation, and so on are not based on previously acquired
performances and, therefore, cannot result in new performances
which can be described in explicit terms? Finally, to claim that the
acquisition of knowledge and performances result in slavish conformity to the past presumes a uniformity of achievement which no
teacher or school has ever produced or recorded, given the initial
variations in the entering behavior of their students. Furthermore,
this claim ignores the well documented observation that those individuals who make creative contributions in the sciences and the
arts are those who are the most knowledgeable about their fields.

In view of the advantages of behavioral objectives over nonbehavioral,
general, and abstract ones, this text advocates the use of behavioral
objectives.

SUMMARY

This chapter has identified the essential characteristics of behavioral
objectives and has explained in detail Bloom's and Gagné's taxonomies of
types of learning. In addition, the four types of psychomotor learning
outcomes, as described by Kibler, Barker, and Miles, have been discussed.
Finally, the major arguments for and against the use of behavioral objectives
have been presented.

REFERENCES

Allen, Dwight W. *Model Elementary Teacher Education Program*. Washington, D. C.: U. S. Department of Health, Education and Welfare, 1968.

Baker, Eldon E. "Aligning Speech Evaluation and Behavioral Objectives."
Speech Teacher 16 (1967): 158–160.

Bloom, Benjamin S., ed. *Taxonomy of Educational Objectives, Handbook I:
Cognitive Domain*. New York: David McKay, 1956.

Byers, Burton H. "Speech and the Principles of Learning." *Speech Teacher* 12 (1968): 136–140.

Churchman, C. W. "Humanizing Education." *Center Magazine* 1 (1968): 90–98.

Clevenger, Theodore, Jr., "Some Factors Involved in Classroom Procedures for the Acquisition of Verbal Concepts." *Speech Teacher* 15 (1966): 113–118.

Cogswell, J. F. "Instructional Management Information Systems." In *Man-Machine Systems in Education,* edited by V. W. Loughany, pp. 93–106. New York: Harper and Row, 1966.

DeCecco, John P. *The Psychology of Learning and Instruction: Educational Psychology.* Englewood Cliffs, N. J.: Prentice-Hall, 1968.

Dickson, George E. *Educational Specifications for a Comprehensive Elementary Teacher Education Program.* Washington, D. C.: U. S. Department of Health, Education, and Welfare, 1968.

Dressel, P. L. "Are Your Objectives Showing?" *National Education Association Journal* 44 (1955): 297.

Ebel, Robert L. "The Relation of Testing Programs to Educational Goals." In *The Impact and Improvement of School Testing Programs,* Part 2 of the 62nd Yearbook of the National Society for the Study of Education, pp. 28–44. Chicago: University of Chicago Press, 1963.

Gagné, Robert M. *The Conditions of Learning.* New York: Holt, Rinehart and Winston, 1965.

Gruner, Charles R. "Behavioral Objectives for the Grading of Classroom Speeches." *Speech Teacher* 17 (1968): 207–209.

Harrison, G. V. *The Instructional Value of Presenting Explicit versus Vague Objectives.* Santa Barbara: California Educational Research Studies, University of California, 1967.

Johnson, Charles E.; Gilbert F. Shearron; and A. John Stauffer. *Georgia Educational Model Specifications for the Preparation of Elementary Teachers.* Washington, D. C.: U. S. Department of Health, Education, and Welfare, 1968.

Kibler, Robert J. "Developing Behavioral Objectives for Undergraduate Speech Instruction." Paper read at Speech Association of America Convention, Denver, 1963.

Kibler, Robert J.; Larry L. Barker; and David T. Miles. *Behavioral Objectives and Instruction.* Boston: Allyn and Bacon, 1970.

Krathwohl, David R.; Benjamin S. Bloom; and Bertram B. Masia. *Taxonomy of Educational Objectives, Handbook II: Affective Domain.* New York: David McKay, 1964.

Loughary, J. W. "Instructional Systems: Magic or Methods?" *Educational Leadership* 25 (1968): 730–734.

Mager, Robert F. *Preparing Instructional Objectives.* Palo Alto, Calif.: Fearon, 1962.

Mager, Robert F., and J. McCann. *Learner-Controlled Instruction.* Palo Alto, Calif.: Varian, 1961.

Miles, David T.; Robert J. Kibler; and L. Eudora Pettigrew. "The Effects of Study Questions on College Students' Test Performances." *Psychology in the Schools* 4 (1967): 25–26.

Pfeiffer, J. *New Look at Education: System Analysis in Our Schools and Colleges.* New York: Odessey Press, 1968.

Ryan, T. A. "Defining Behavioral Objectives." Paper read at Presession on Systems Approach in Counseling and Counselor Education, American Educational Research Association meeting, Los Angeles, February, 1969.

Schalock, H. Del, and James R. Hale. *A Competency-based, Field-centered, Systems Approach to Elementary Teacher Education.* Washington, D. C.: U. S. Department of Health, Education, and Welfare, 1968.

Southworth, Horton C. *A Model for Teacher Training for the Individualization of Instruction.* Washington, D. C.: U. S. Department of Health, Education, and Welfare, 1968.

Sowards, G. Wesley. *A Model for the Preparation of Elementary School Teachers.* Washington, D. C.: U. S. Department of Health, Education, and Welfare, 1968.

Walbesser, Henry H., and Heather Carter. "Some Methodological Considerations of Curriculum Evaluation Research." *Educational Leadership Research Supplement* 26 (1968): 53–64.

Wood, Barbara Sundene. "Implications of Psycholinguistics for Elementary Speech Programs." *Speech Teacher* 17 (1968): 183–192.

THREE

ASSESSING
STUDENT CAPABILITIES

If you achieved the goals established for Chapter 2, you now possess some skill in selecting, writing, and using behavioral objectives. Let us assume that you are teaching a unit on public speaking, that you have decided to include the topic: "The Use of Evidence," and that your behavioral instructional objective for this topic is:

> Given a three-page typewritten speech, in thirty minutes you are to identify, in writing, and then apply tests of evidence to one example of each of the five types of evidence (example, comparison, statistics, testimony, visual aids). A minimum standard of performance would be to apply the four major criteria for evaluating evidence (discussed in class) to each example.

Having specified your objective, the question for you as a teacher now becomes, What do I know about the students' capabilities for achieving this objective? Two independent aspects of this question are the focus of this chapter: (1) How much of the material to be learned do the students already know? (2) Do the students have the prerequisite behavioral capabilities to understand the instruction?

OBJECTIVES

1. Describe the differences between the two types of student capabilities: objectives the students have already achieved and prerequisite behavioral capabilities.
2. Describe a rationale for ascertaining which objectives students have already met.
3. Describe the differences between en route and terminal objectives.
4. Describe the differences between a formal pretest and an informal pretest.
5. Define and differentiate between the types of prerequisite behavioral capabilities: mental, physical, and environmental.
6. Describe at least five differences in behavioral characteristics between students twelve to fifteen years old and students fifteen to eighteen years old.
7. Describe five ways of assessing the prerequisite behavioral capabilities of students.

WHAT IS ALREADY KNOWN

No doubt most of you can cite numerous examples of facts and principles which you learned and relearned to exhaustion. Perhaps it was certain facts in American history. Or the principles of outlining and organization. Or the types of evidence and reasoning. Whatever it was, it should be obvious to you that the total number of pupil hours so misspent is staggering. This duplication of effort results from teachers' failure to assess what is already known. One purpose of ascertaining capabilities of students, therefore, is to eliminate teaching knowledge and skills which they already possess. The first component of an assessment of student capabilities, then, is a pretest.

In constructing a pretest, the teacher must first list the en route objectives that lead to the terminal objectives, for it is as important to assess student performance on these as on the terminal objectives. Such information not only enables the teacher to decide where to start instruction but often indicates a need of individualizing instruction or of organizing groups of students with similar competencies. To illustrate how this might be done for the terminal objective cited earlier for the topic "The Use of Evidence,"

Table 1 presents an abbreviated grid in which the instructional topics to be covered are listed on the horizontal axis and the levels of Bloom's cognitive taxonomy on the vertical axis. While exploring this grid (which can be very profitable), keep in mind that the order in which the en route and terminal objectives are listed does not determine instructional sequence. How one makes such decisions will be covered in a later chapter on instructional strategy.

After the en route and terminal instructional objectives have been specified, one can develop either a formal or an informal pretest. For example, the teacher can construct multiple-choice items that present actual examples of different types of supporting material and ask the students to select the label that best describes each example. Or he can ask the students to define briefly the various types of evidence (e.g., hypothetical example, literal analogy, descriptive statistic, testimony, etc.). Since a detailed description of how the items in a formal pretest should be constructed is contained in Chapter 8, this subject will not be discussed further in this chapter.

It is not usually necessary, however, to administer a formal pretest. If the probability is low that the students are familiar with the specified objectives, it may be wiser and less time-consuming to conduct an *informal* pretest. The teacher simply asks the students several informal questions to determine what they know about the objectives. Or he may create a setting in which he observes the relevant behaviors.

Whichever approach he decides to use—formal or informal—the important point is that he pretests. Without pretesting, the danger is great that the students already know much of what he wants them to learn. Classroom time is far too valuable to be wasted in this manner. After making such an assessment, the teacher usually will find it necessary to modify his instructional objectives by adding some, discarding some, and adjusting some.

PREREQUISITE BEHAVIORAL CAPABILITIES

The second part of assessing student capabilities is ascertaining prerequisite behavioral capabilities, those capabilities which determine a student's overall ability to achieve the instructional objectives. The list of prerequisite behavioral capabilities will be more comprehensive than the corresponding list of terminal and en route performances because it will include mental, physical, and environmental conditions related to the task at hand. For example, mental prerequisites might include appropriate levels of reading ability, writing ability, intelligence, emotional adjustment, and social

TABLE 1 *The use of evidence*

Topics / Taxonomy	Evidence	An arbitrary but useful list of types of evidence					
		Example	Comparison	Statistics	Testimony	Visual aids	Tests of evidence
Knowledge	To be able to state a definition of evidence	To be able to state definitions of the three types of examples	To be able to state definitions of the two types of comparison	To be able to state definitions of the two types of statistics	To be able to state a definition of testimony	To be able to state definitions of the five types of visual aids	To be able to state four major criteria for evaluating evidence
Comprehension	To be able to classify instances of evidence as a type						
Application	To be able to recognize situations which require evidence						
Analysis	To be able to identify instances of evidence in the text of a speech						
Synthesis							To be able to use evidence (that passes the tests) in a speech
Evaluation							To be able to apply tests of evidence to the text of a speech

adjustment; physical prerequisites might include appropriate levels of
vision, auditory perception, dominance and laterality, and general health;
and environmental prerequisites might include nutrition, parent-child
relationships, and peer influences. Whether a list of prerequisite behavioral
capabilities should include a particular factor depends solely upon its
relevance to the en route and terminal objectives specified.

Since it would be a burdensome, if not impossible, task to list all the
relevant prerequisite behavioral capabilities, the teacher—after specifying
the terminal and en route instructional objectives—should list only those
which he considers most germane to the task at hand and then through
formal or informal means ascertain whether the students possess them.

A good preparation for assessing prerequisite behavioral capabilities is
to gain a general understanding of the behavioral characteristics of secondary
school students. The National Council of Teachers of English Curriculum
Commission has provided a summary of some of the more important
characteristics:[1]

Physical, Mental, and Emotional Characteristics	Language Characteristics
Level: 12–15 Years	
1. Go through a period of rapid growth and development, making many new adjustments necessary (many girls are approximately a year ahead of boys in physical and organic maturity).	1. Desire to have fun, a fact which manifests itself in language expression related to sports, amusements, and humorous situations; develop increased maturity in interests through clubs and teamwork; show interest in language activities related to animals, adventure, mystery, collections, and explorations, but resist tasks requiring lengthy application; girls show interest in sentiment and romance.
2. Undergo internal changes involving heart, gland, and bone structure; the heart grows faster than do the arteries,	2. Desire to be interesting is manifested in the individual's pursuit of his own welfare, and in human relationships,

thus causing a strain on the heart and often conflicts and emotional upsets.

3. Need emphasis on good posture; possess relatively poor coordination; often feel they do not "belong"; evidence marked concern and interest in their accelerated growth and changing bodies, and take increasing pride in personal appearance.

4. Have wide intellectual interests as a group but growing specializations of interest on the part of the individual; are more capable of intellectualizing their own experiences than at earlier levels but often are hampered by their emotions; are alert, active, and curious about everything; want facts; are still interested in firsthand experiences but are increasingly capable of learning vicariously.

5. Often feel socially insecure and may compensate by making themselves conspicuous in one way or another hoping for group approval; are more interested in approval, but need and desire adult support at times; desire to understand themselves, to be interesting, and to have freedom with security; experience anxiety over financial, social, and family insecurity; desire satisfying vocational experiences for immediate needs and for building for the future.

with increasing social sensitivity to reaction of individuals and group in language situations.

3. Desire to understand and express themselves through dramatization and imaginative thinking; show wide variation in educational attainment; desire to realize their capacities as shown in their attempts to understand personal abilities and to seek interests that will fulfill their recognized language needs.

4. Desire to become informed and to discuss ideals by which men live (manifested in hero worship); and express a challenging mental attitude toward social problems, and a concern about right and wrong.

5. May display marked aggressiveness in speech and a tendency toward constant argumentation; show a liking for parliamentary procedures; enjoy hobbies involving use of much technical knowledge and skill and employ a more logical approach to solving problems; establish habit of reading periodicals and books related to interests; experience a need to express a new awakening to beauty.

Level: 15–18 Years

1. Reveal great individual differences in intelligence, scholastic achievement, background, and interests; increasingly wide variations in groups of older children because of the additional years of living and differing experiences.

1. Reveal great variations in degrees of development in the various language arts; a small percentage have developed the ability to write creatively, but a greater number probably have powers that are undeveloped; often show reluctance in sharing their production; manifest far less difference in reading interests between sexes than between individuals; exhibit a wide range in ability in various aspects of language power; an individual may be skillful in one or more abilities (as reading and speaking) and immature in aspects of others (as skill in spelling or punctuation in writing); range from almost total inadequacy to a successful degree of fluency in oral expression; increase in writing skills as their thinking becomes more clarified; acquire skill in discriminative use of many types of instructional materials.

2. Complete their physical changes and have grown-up-looking bodies; require adequate food, sleep, and precaution against fatigue; are aware of physical characteristics of themselves and others; admire physical vigor and courage; tend toward awkwardness; become concerned about sex, pair with the opposite sex, as well as go in crowds.

2. Extend language experiences in the treatment of mature problems, including relationships among persons, sexes, economic classes, races, political parties, nations, and periods of history; boys seek fiction and talk about physically vigorous and morally courageous heroes; girls enjoy romantic stories.

3. Have strong feelings for their

3. Increase in power to think to-

group; are extremely sensitive to the opinion of the group; give importance to the gang and seek its approval and acceptance; remain inherently conservative as to group pattern; become increasingly aware of the importance of cooperation with others in classroom and school activities; have strong feelings of loyalty.

gether in large groups (whole classes), to share opinions, and to reach a common feeling and understanding; are so preoccupied with radio and television programs, and with activities, pleasures, and friends that it is necessary that all reading and expression suggested by the school be meaningful to them in order to compete successfully for their out-of-school time; are willing to use their specific talents for the group (e.g., postermaking, lettering, running machinery, writing verses, planning programs); cooperate because of group loyalty.

4. Have considerable feeling of insecurity; may replace lack of assurance and security by rowdyism; often cover shyness and sensitivity by apparent indifference; often indulge in conspicuous behavior and employ various other devices for gaining attention.

4. Make considerable use of slang and swearing in their speech since it serves not only to furnish a form of expression for their emotions, but also to attract attention of adults and to show belongingness in their own group; are interested in dramatics for personal satisfaction and to gain status within the group.

5. Are growing increasingly independent of parents and other adults; resent domination; respect adults without feeling dependence on them; are curious about people in the adult world and seek vocational guidance.

5. Desire intensely to gain information on their special interests, so are easily led toward becoming good readers; appreciate the importance of vocational success and are willing to master necessary language skills and adult standards; many delight in expressing opinions, very often in a critical way; are

willing to "sharpen" their powers of discrimination to select from many sources those literary experiences including books, periodicals, music, radio programs, plays, etc., which best fill their needs.

6. Have intense emotions and sensory impressions; subordinate intellectual drives to emotional and social needs; are uncertain or questioning with regard to values, particularly in respect to such areas as meaning of life and nature of success; desire insight into themselves; seek understanding of self, asking: "What am I like as an individual? Why am I as I am? Why do I do as I do?"; frequently alternating between self-reliance and self-distrust.

6. Have begun to see remote goals and are willing to go through experiences and practices in language even though tedious, because of the values anticipated in successful accomplishments; develop interest in becoming informed as to human relationships and issues; enjoy the beautiful in nature, literature, and human beings; strive to acquire beauty for themselves as a means of securing favorable reaction, as expressed in words from the group.

Knowing the general characteristics of adolescents, however important, is not enough for the teacher of speech communication; he must also get to know his students as individuals. A good way to start is to examine the cumulative record of each student, usually kept on file in the office of the principal. This task can be done before school begins. These records generally provide valuable information on the student in terms of the mental, physical, and environmental conditions (e.g., scholastic record, test results, health record, family data, and anecdotal reports filed by other teachers) that may affect his ability to learn the objectives the teacher established for his course. A handy method of using this information is to record it on the inside of an 8½ x 11 manila file folder.

At times you will find that the cumulative record does not contain the information you need, such as the sorts of speech performances in which the students have engaged, whether any students are hampered by speech impediments, and which students suffer from speech anxiety. When this is the case, you will need to devise either an informal or formal approach to obtaining this information (ascertaining prerequisite behavioral capabilities).

Methods that have proved useful include: (1) the autobiographical form or letter which asks the student about background, interests, and training; (2) the autobiographical speech in which the student elaborates on topics suggested by the teacher; (3) private conferences with each student; and (4) carefully devised tests to measure capabilities in such areas as voice and articulation, listening, and speech anxiety. An excellent instrument for measuring communication-bound anxiety in secondary school pupils is reported in the November, 1970, issue of *Speech Monographs*.

SUMMARY

This chapter has focused on the C of the COSEF model by examining two independent aspects of assessing student *capabilities*. First, it explained the necessity of a formal or informal pretest so that time will not be wasted in teaching knowledge and skills which students already possess. Second, it stressed the fact that a teacher needs to ascertain whether students possess the prerequisite behavioral capabilities—mental, physical, and environmental—which determine whether or not they will be able to achieve the instructional objectives. Performing these two types of assessment usually leads the teacher to modify his instructional objectives by adding some, discarding others, and adjusting some. He thus ends up with instructional objectives that are realistic in terms of student capabilities. Since such instructional objectives are of little value unless he has some idea of how to help students achieve them, Chapter 4 discusses the S in the COSEF model—instructional strategies and skills.

REFERENCES

Balcer, Charles L., and Hugh F. Seabury. *Teaching Speech in Today's Secondary Schools*. New York: Holt, Rinehart and Winston, 1965.

Commission on the English Curriculum of the National Council of Teachers of English. *The English Language Arts in the Secondary School*, pp. 16–20. New York: Appleton-Century-Crofts, 1956.

DeCecco, John P. *The Psychology of Learning and Instruction: Educational Psychology*. Englewood Cliffs, N. J.: Prentice-Hall, 1968.

McCroskey, James C. "Measures of Communication-bound Anxiety." *Speech Monographs* 37 (1970): 267–277.

Popham, W. James, and Eva L. Baker. *Systematic Instruction*. Englewood Cliffs, N. J.: Prentice-Hall, 1970.

FOUR

INSTRUCTIONAL STRATEGIES
AND SKILLS

Chapter 2 was devoted to developing skill in the selection, writing, and use of instructional objectives, and Chapter 3 showed that such objectives often need to be modified to meet the student's entering behavior. However, even realistic instructional objectives are of little value unless the teacher has some idea of how to help the student achieve them. Therefore, this chapter will focus on *instructional strategies* and *instructional skills*. The term "instructional strategies" denotes structural approaches which are devised and used to provide productive learning experiences, e.g., lectures,

OBJECTIVES

1. Describe the differences between instructional strategies and instructional skills.
2. List four nontechnical instructional strategies (books, lectures, discussions, and resource people), and describe potential uses for each.
3. List five technical instructional strategies (audiovisual aids, programmed instruction, simulations and games, computer-assisted instruction, and mediated self-instruction), and describe potential uses for each.
4. List eleven audiovisual aids (television, video tape recorders, audio tape recorders, record players, motion picture projectors, slides, filmstrips, overhead projectors, opaque projectors, bulletin boards, and chalkboards), and describe potential uses for each.
5. Describe five important instructional skills (establishing objectives, establishing strategy, using questions, using exposition, and using reinforcement).
6. Describe six guidelines for improving questioning skills (clear purpose, variety, preciseness, directing technique, probing technique, and encouragement of students' initiation of questions).
7. Describe the three-step process required for establishing objectives and strategy (attention, comprehension, and acceptance).
8. Provide questions which illustrate each of Bloom's six types of cognitive process (knowledge, comprehension, application, analysis, synthesis, and evaluation).
9. Describe the three-step process required for using exposition (attention, comprehension, and acceptance).
10. Describe the three categories of reinforcement (acceptance of student's feeling, praise or encouragement, and acceptance or use of student's ideas).

discussion, films, simulation, and computer-assisted instruction. The term "instructional skills," on the other hand, denotes specific teacher behaviors in employing instructional strategies, e.g., *asking questions* about a film or *using reinforcement* during a discussion.

Because of the complex relationships among variables in the teaching-learning process and the present state of man's knowledge about these relationships, few generalizations regarding strategies of teaching speech communication in the secondary school have solid empirical support. The purpose of this chapter, therefore, is not to tell you how you should teach but rather to provide a summary of possible instructional strategies and skills which you should consider using and *testing*.

INSTRUCTIONAL STRATEGIES

A brief description of instructional strategies is presented under two major headings—nontechnical and technical—although some overlap between the two categories is unavoidable. Instead of providing lengthy, specific guidelines for the use of each technique, this chapter gives a list of readings at the end to help you apply the various strategies in your teaching.

NONTECHNICAL STRATEGIES

BOOKS

With paperback books, reprint series, and a photocopy machine in the library, today's teacher is tempted to teach his course without a textbook. While such an approach provides flexibility, a variety of points of view, and an opportunity to maintain maximum interest, it has disadvantages. The task of integration can require so much time that it restricts the use of the class period. With a well-chosen textbook the teacher may rely on his students' obtaining a basic understanding of the content and subject matter through reading, thus freeing him to vary his procedures in the classroom.

If you decide to use a textbook, it is important to choose one that will help you meet the objectives of the course. Some questions that will help you decide on a text are: What is the professional competency of the author? What is the author's speech communication philosophy? Does the textbook fit the course requirements? Is the subject covered adequately? Is the book readable? Does the textbook provide useful teaching aids? Is the book well manufactured? A good place to begin the search for a textbook is in the book review section of the major speech communication journals: the *Speech Teacher,* the *Quarterly Journal of Speech,* and the *Journal of Communication.* Also, Table 1 in Chapter 1 of this book summarizes the contents of twelve leading speech communication texts for the secondary school. If you locate a book which you think might help you meet the objectives of your course, write to the publisher for a copy. Most publishers will provide an "examination copy" free of charge. One point to remember: the perfect textbook does not exist.

THE LECTURE

The popularity of the lecture method is probably derived from the conception of the teacher's primary goal as the *transmission and storage* of information rather than the *acquisition and assimilation* of information and skills. It is interesting to note that the lecture took its name from the religious teacher of the Middle Ages, the *lektor*. Whatever the origin, no instructional strategy is more overused, and as a result, the authors are tempted to suggest a moratorium on it. This is impractical, however, as the lecture is eminently well suited to a number of purposes. When material judged necessary for student consumption is not readily available or requires frequent updating, a lecturer can explore those points which he feels are pertinent and can do so succinctly and precisely. A lecturer can synthesize bodies of material that threaten to overwhelm his students; he can provide a framework within which students can organize their learning. But you should not allow the lecture to become a security blanket. Before using it, take the time to analyze your objectives and determine whether the lecture is the best way of meeting them.

DISCUSSION

McKeachie (1969, p. 37) suggests that the discussion technique is particularly appropriate when the instructor wants to do the following:

1. To use the resources of members of the group
2. To give students opportunities to formulate applications of [the principles being discussed]
3. To get prompt feedback on how well his objectives are being attained
4. To help students learn to think in terms of the subject matter by giving them practice in thinking
5. To help students learn to evaluate the logic of and evidence for their own and others' positions
6. To help students become aware of and to formulate problems which necessitate information to be gained from readings or lectures.
7. To gain acceptance for information or theories counter to folk-lore or previous beliefs of students
8. To develop motivation for further learning

Discussion in the classroom takes many forms. Some discussions are primarily group problem solving; others are gripe sessions or pep meetings; some provide practice in integrating and applying information gained from textbooks or lectures. The teacher's role will vary according to the purpose of the discussion, hence it is in discussion teaching that special training of teachers is most often needed. Most classroom discussions can be classified as developmental—that is, the purpose is to develop a concept and its implications or to solve a problem—and specific skills are needed for managing such discussions (starting the discussion, asking questions, appraising group progress, and overcoming resistance). An excellent introduction to discussion techniques is provided in *Problem-solving Discussion and Conferences: Leadership Methods and Skills* by N. R. F. Maier (1963), listed at the end of this chapter. Before moving to the next section, it is worth noting that one form of discussion, the buzz group, can be used profitably in conjunction with the lecture. By splitting the class into small subgroups (buzz groups) and having these groups discuss particular problems, the teacher can increase the involvement of the students.

RESOURCE PEOPLE

The term "resource people" includes such diverse strategies as student panels, student reports, peer group instruction, guest lecturers, field trips, and team teaching. These strategies, when used properly, supplement the resources of the teacher and add variety to classroom procedures. While most of these strategies are familiar to you and are easy to apply in the speech communication classroom, peer group instruction may not be. The teacher who uses this strategy teaches his students the criteria for evaluating communication. In a structured environment, he assigns the students partial responsibility for conducting their own speech communication class. The form of this responsibility varies, but it usually consists of having the students apply the criteria they have learned in order to make a realistic evaluation of various classroom communication performances.

A recent innovation in the guest lecturer strategy is the telelecture. Although it has rarely been used at the secondary level, the telelecture features a guest who cannot visit the school but is willing to devote some time to a dialogue with a remote class. The guest telephones the class, and his voice is amplified over loudspeakers; usually equipment is available for members of the class to talk directly with him. The guest's picture may be projected on a screen, thus helping to make his presence felt. The whole procedure is a flexible, convenient, and economical way of providing students an opportunity to talk directly and informally with persons whose actions and ideas are shaping our world.

TECHNICAL STRATEGIES

AUDIOVISUAL AIDS

The teacher who wishes to supplement his teaching resources with audio-visual aids will find a wide variety from which to choose. During the past ten years *television* has probably received more attention in education than any other medium. Research and development activity in educational television, commercial programming for education, and closed-circuit television have generated many innovative approaches to learning. Unfortunately, most secondary schools have used these innovations little if at all. An explanation, perhaps, lies in the fact that the programs do not lend themselves to flexible use. They are shown only at certain times, and in a series of programs the sequence is usually fixed.

With the advent of relatively inexpensive *video tape recorders,* however, television is becoming more flexible and hence more widely used. The video tape recorder (television tape recorder) is a device for recording pictures on tape much as audio messages are recorded on an audio tape recorder. Programs can be dubbed from a television set and then played back for students at a convenient time. Thus the student is provided with on-the-spot viewing of everything from contemporary speakers and their audiences to commercial advertising at a time when the teacher decides such viewing is most advantageous. If, for example, the teacher wants his class to analyze the communication involved in television commercials, he can dub several of them and play them back for his class. In addition, the video tape recorder can be used to tape live events, such as students engaged in various com-munication activities. The tape can then be played back for analysis and improvement of communication skills.

The inexpensive *audio tape recorder,* mentioned above, allows the teacher to make available to his students commercially recorded materials ranging from the speeches of such figures as Churchill, Roosevelt, Kennedy, and Stevenson to old radio programs such as "The Shadow," "Suspense," and "Tom Mix." In addition, the teacher can easily make audio tapes which suit his educational objectives; for example, student performances may be taped and then played back for self-analysis and self-improvement of speech communication skills. The recorder can also be used to illustrate the principles of good communication. If the teacher wishes to discuss basic principles of speech organization, for instance, he might develop a tape recording which presents the principles with adequate illustration.

While not as flexible as either the audio or video tape recorder, *record players* are available in most, if not all, secondary schools and can be used profitably in the speech communication classroom. Available records provide music, books, events of historical significance, speeches, poetry, and even entire courses of study. A teacher could, for example, illustrate the concept of style by playing a popular song as sung by two different recording artists.

Another device which found early favor in educational circles and has since been revived is the *motion picture projector*. In the past few years the development of eight-millimeter film has increased the usefulness of the motion picture projector by providing less expensive film, cameras, and projectors.

The *slide* has also proved useful in education. The two-by-two-inch slide, which uses film from the standard thirty-five–millimeter camera, provides an inexpensive way for the teacher to present many types of material.

While somewhat less flexible than the slide, the thirty-five–millimeter *filmstrip* (a series of still pictures on a strip of thirty-five–millimeter film) is often less expensive to produce and reproduce.

More adaptable to the speech communication classroom yet relatively inexpensive is the *overhead projector*. It casts large ten-by-ten transparencies on a screen at a high level of illumination so that a room need not be darkened. A special feature is that it enables the instructor to face his class as he works with the unit, for projection takes place over his shoulder. The projected image appears vertically behind him, but he sees and works with a horizontal image on the unit in front of him. The overhead projector is a versatile unit, for materials can be prepared in advance. In addition, overlays (information on transparent sheets of acetate placed one above the other) can be used. Thermofax and other copier machines make such transparencies directly from books, magazines, and drawings. Information can be presented in a predetermined sequence or altered if necessary during a presentation.

Somewhat less useful is the *opaque projector*. While it can be used to enlarge materials from books and magazines, photographs, charts, and diagrams, the image is less sharp than that of filmstrips, slides, and overhead transparencies. In addition, because the system depends on reflected light rather than incident light, the projector must be used in darkness, making note taking relatively impossible.

Obviously, any discussion of audiovisual aids would be incomplete without mention of the *bulletin board* and the *chalkboard*. Probably the oldest and most readily available of all visual aids, they are often taken for granted and not used to greatest advantage. When used well, they both can contribute to the teaching-learning process. The bulletin board, for example, can display current items (differing reviews of a current movie), contrasts of past with present (gestures in elocution books compared to current gestures), special days (Lincoln's birthday), cartoons and humor (long-winded, after-dinner speaker), outstanding work (the best speech outline), and announcements, assignments, and agenda.

PROGRAMMED INSTRUCTION

While programmed instruction can take many forms, all have three essential features: (1) the material is broken down into small steps, or frames; (2) frequent response is required of the student; and (3) each response the student makes elicits immediate confirmation if it is right or correction if it is wrong. The three main approaches to developing programmed instruction material are linear, branching, and adjunct autoinstruction. It should be noted, however, that most applications are not pure types; the three are often combined to meet instructional needs.

Linear programs, developed by B. F. Skinner, require that all students respond to each frame in the program and primarily use constructed (fill-in) responses. Branching programs, developed by Norman Crowder, require that the student proceed through the program until he makes an error, which branches him to supplemental materials providing remedial instruction. This type of program primarily uses multiple-choice responses paired with directions to the next frame. In adjunct autoinstruction, developed by Sidney L. Pressey, students respond to auxiliary or review programs after they have been exposed to expository materials. Typically, such programs are inserted into traditional textbooks. Of particular importance to the speech communication teacher is the fact that such varied subjects as speech organization and outlining, specific speaking assignments, parliamentary procedure, debate, phonetics, listening, and oral interpretation all have been taught by this method through use of different program formats.

SIMULATIONS AND GAMES

Simulations and games are among the most recent innovations in instructional strategies. They involve a miniature representation of a large-scale system or process; macroprocesses are reduced in scale and complexity so that a teacher or student may manipulate the model of reality when he cannot manipulate reality itself. Often such simulations and games are computerized; many of these have been devised in areas such as politics, economics, education, opinion formation, decision making, and administration.

While few simulations have been devised specifically for speech communication, many of those developed in other areas are readily adaptable and can be used to enhance the learning process in this area. Coleman's (1962) model of high school behavior is a case in point. In the game of "High School," each player takes the role of a high school student. Parents and teachers are represented through calculations prepared by those who designed the game. Players make both long-term and daily choices of activities, and they also decide which persons' judgments they will heed. As these decisions are made over an extended period of time, the consequences gradually unfold. Results are reported to the players, who may use the knowledge of previous outcomes in making future decisions. Help in finding other simulations and games is provided at the end of this chapter. In addition, it is always possible for the speech communication teacher to develop his own game to meet specific educational objectives.

COMPUTER-ASSISTED INSTRUCTION

While the use of computers has now become rather commonplace, their use as adjuncts to instruction at the secondary level appears to be rare and largely experimental. With increased availability of computers, however, their aid in instruction could become widespread, serving a variety of purposes. In the current experimental programs, individualized instruction is usually provided by a student console, consisting of a typewriter connected to a computer and a small electronic screen. The student communicates with the computer by using one of a series of command keys or by typing answers to problems which appear on the screen. The screen itself exhibits information from one of two sources: (1) a programmed series of slides, with random access by each student; or (2) an electronic blackboard showing instructions printed out by the computer, responses typed by the student, and reactions of the computer to the correctness of responses.

The computer could also be used in examinations, to provide the teacher and the student with nearly instantaneous reports on the student's total performance. In addition, computers could provide detailed diagnostic reports on individual student performances, enabling the teacher to prescribe study activity for each student on an individual basis. Test items could be evaluated and improved in a similar way.

MEDIATED SELF-INSTRUCTION

The self-instructional laboratory provides the space and materials necessary
for each student to learn at his own rate the concepts and the information
or skills for a given course. In mediated self-instruction, a student attends
self-study sessions of his own volition, where materials are presented to him
by some combination of audiovisual aids and programmed instruction.
Say, for example, the topic is "Speech Organization." The student goes
to a study carrel, where he finds a tape recording which presents speech
organization principles with illustrations. As he listens to the tape, frequent
breaks occur; during these he is asked to engage in various exercises set
forth in the programmed materials laid out in front of him. This is followed
by a video tape presentation of a speech, which he is asked to outline. A
slide then presents the outline of the speech.

INSTRUCTIONAL SKILLS

Educational researchers have expended a great deal of energy comparing
instructional strategies in terms of their impact on the teaching-learning
process. Not only has this effort failed to uncover any superior instructional
strategy at any grade level, but it is now felt that teaching is so amazingly
complex that a search for the best instructional strategy is not productive.
As a result, researchers have turned to isolating instructional skills (elements
of teacher behavior) which are applicable across various instructional
strategies, an approach which has proven somewhat more productive than
the former one. The remaining portion of this chapter, therefore, focuses on
five instructional skills which are considered important for the teacher of
speech communication: establishing objectives, establishing strategy, using
questions, using exposition, and using reinforcement.

It will not be enough, however, for you to read about these skills. To
apply them skillfully in your teaching, you must practice using them. One
approach that provides this opportunity is microteaching. Microteaching,
as developed by Allen (1969) and his staff at Stanford University, is basically
a scaled-down version of teaching. The teacher presents a single idea or
concept to a small number of students (usually three to ten) for a short time
(usually five to seven minutes but sometimes as long as twenty-five
minutes). This scaled-down lesson reduces some of the complexities of the
teaching experience and allows the teacher to concentrate on specific teaching
skills. The teacher is often video-taped while teaching a "micro-lesson"

and thus receives immediate feedback as to the strengths and/or weaknesses of the presentation. A more detailed description of microteaching is contained in *Microteaching* by Allen and Ryan (1969), listed at the end of this chapter.

ESTABLISHING OBJECTIVES

The teacher of speech communication should strive to communicate his objectives in such a way that students clearly understand them, that is, so that each student understands what he is to do, the conditions under which he is expected to do it, and what evidence will be accepted as proof that he has done it. But this is not enough. If students are to achieve the objectives, they must also be committed to them, both cognitively and attitudinally. Establishing objectives, therefore, is a three-step process: attention, comprehension, and acceptance.

Focusing attention involves both external and internal factors. External factors include activity or movement, reality, proximity, familiarity, novelty, suspense, conflict, humor, the vital, change or variety, intensity, repetition, definiteness of form, and concreteness. All these factors can and should be used by the teacher of speech communication. At the same time, however, what will get and hold attention is affected by two internal factors: the attention habits and the personal interests of the student. Therefore, it is important that the teacher of speech communication know his students well.

The basic methods of aiding comprehension have no doubt already been covered in other speech communication classes. In helping students to comprehend objectives, the teacher must state them precisely—the goal of Chapter 2—and organize them under a limited number of main points. These points should be arranged in a sequence that is both logical and appropriate *for the students.* When presenting the objectives, it is usually wise to provide a summary of them first and then utilize various devices to make them both interesting and clear: Show the student how the things you are talking about resemble what he already knows, give examples, include human interest material, vary the mode of presentation, and use familiar memory devices such as repetition, formulas, slogans, and key words. Whenever possible, supplement oral presentation with written handouts, which allow the student to review the objectives as he is trying to achieve them.

It is possible for the student to attend to and comprehend your objectives but remain uncommitted to them. You can aid his acceptance of them if you remember certain basic learning principles. Student acceptance is enhanced under the following conditions (adapted from a list by Canfield, Low, and Mullin, 1965, p. 41):

1. When the student is allowed to respond actively in the learning situation
2. When the purposes of the student and those of the teacher are sufficiently similar for him to perceive the relationship.
3. When the material to be learned is meaningful to the student
4. When the student can see some possibility of succeeding in the learning task he is attempting
5. When the student experiences success in a learning task
6. When the student has opportunities for and assistance in the discovery of facts, relationships, and generalizations
7. When the student has an opportunity to practice his learnings immediately, frequently, and in varied situations

ESTABLISHING STRATEGY

What was said about establishing objectives applies equally to establishing strategy. It is not enough that the student understand the teacher's reasons for structuring the learning environment in a certain manner; he must also have confidence in that strategy and commitment to it. Therefore, it is necessary that the teacher gain the student's attention, help him to comprehend the strategy, and win his acceptance of it. This matter is every bit as important as establishing objectives; for unless the student understands why he is to watch a particular film or why he is to work through a programmed unit on forms of support, he is unlikely to receive maximum benefit from the strategy.

USING QUESTIONS

Sixty years ago, Stevens (1912) estimated that four-fifths of the typical school day was taken up with questioning activities. He found that a sample of secondary school teachers asked a mean number of 395 questions per day. Frequent use of questions by teachers has also been found in recent investigations. Current estimates indicate that from two-thirds to four-fifths of the secondary school day is taken up with questions.

But what about the quality of the questions? To use questions effectively as a teaching device, well developed skills are needed; yet few teachers have had instruction in either the theory or the art of asking questions. Most teachers have developed their questioning techniques through trial-and-error experiences in the classroom and as a result do not use questions to their best advantage. Because skill in the use of questions is too important to be developed on a trial-and-error basis, the remainder of this section discusses guidelines for improving questioning skills.

CLEAR PURPOSE

To improve your question-asking skills, it is important that you first determine the purpose for asking the question. Unless you have a specific purpose clearly in mind, it will be impossible to select the most appropriate type of question, and you will waste a great deal of time.

VARIETY OF QUESTIONS

While educators generally agree that teachers should emphasize the development of students' skills in critical thinking rather than in learning and recalling facts, research over the last fifty years indicates that teachers' questions have emphasized facts. About 60 percent of teachers' questions require students to recall facts; about 20 percent require students to think; and the remaining 20 percent are procedural (Gall, 1970, p. 713). A good starting point for changing this situation is to learn to classify questions in terms of Bloom's taxonomy of cognitive objectives. This classification system, based on six types of cognitive processes required to answer questions, is illustrated below (adapted from Clegg et al., 1969, pp. 8–9):

Category	Key Words	Typical Question Words or Sentences
1. **Knowledge** Any question, regardless of complexity, that can be answered through simple recall of	Remember	1. Name. 2. List; tell. 3. Define. 4. Who? When? What?

previously learned material, e.g., Would you please list the components of the Wiseman-Barker Communication Model?

5. Yes or no questions. Did . . . ? Was . . . ? Is . . . ?
6. How many? How much?
7. Recall or identify terminology.
8. What did the book say . . . ?

2. **Comprehension** Questions that can be answered by merely restating or reorganizing material in a rather literal manner to show that the student understands the essential meaning, e.g., Can you give an example of what Monroe means by the "Visualization Step" in his "Motivated Sequence"?

Understand

1. Give an example.
2. What is the most important idea?
3. What will probably happen?
4. What caused this?
5. Compare. (What things are the same?)
6. Contrast (What things are different?)
7. Why did you say that?
8. Give the idea in your own words.

3. **Application** Questions that involve problem solving in new situations with minimal identification or prompting of the appropriate rules, principles, or concepts, e.g., Suppose you wanted to give a speech on love. Where would you look for information?

Solve the problem

1. Solve.
2. How could you find an answer to . . . ?
3. Apply the generalization to . . . .

4. **Analysis** Questions that require the student to break an idea into its component parts for logical analysis: assumptions, facts, opinions, logical conclusions, etc., e.g., What reasons did

Find the logic

1. What reasons does he give for his conclusions?
2. What method is he using to convince you?
3. What does the author seem to believe?
4. What words indicate bias or emotion?

President Nixon give to support his conclusion?

5. **Synthesis** Questions that require the student to combine his ideas into a statement, plan, product, etc., that is new for him, e.g., Please diagram your own model of dyadic communication.

6. **Evaluation** Questions that require the student to make a judgment about something using some criterion standard for making his judgment, e.g., How do you think Bill did as a discussion leader?

Create

Judge

5. Does the evidence given support the conclusion?
1. Create a plan . . . .
2. Develop a model . . . .
3. Combine those parts.

1. Evaluate that idea in terms of . . . .
2. For what reasons do you favor . . . ?
3. Which policy do you think would result in the greatest good for the greatest number?

PRECISE WORDING

The question must be stated precisely and in such a way that it is clearly understood *by the students*. They should never be puzzled about what is being asked. Adapting the question to the level of the students requires previous planning as well as quick adaptation in the classroom situation.

DIRECTING QUESTIONS

As a general rule, it is best to direct the question to the entire class, pause to allow comprehension, and then select the student who is to respond. This stimulates each student to think about the question; thus learning is more apt to take place for everyone, not just for the student who is called on. Exceptions to this guideline would include cases in which you wish to recapture a student's attention or to involve a student who does not ordinarily respond. In the former case, you might state the student's name to gain his attention and then ask him the question. The intent is not to embarrass him but simply to return his attention to the topic at hand. In the case of the student who does not ordinarily respond because of shyness, the alert teacher will either wait and ask him a question when he knows the student is well prepared or ask him a general question for which there is no incorrect answer. The objective is to provide a situation in which it is almost impossible for the shy student to fail.

PROBE QUESTIONS

Sometimes it is not satisfactory to accept only the first answer to a question. The teacher may either want to elicit additional information or to clarify the response. In a situation such as this, the teacher can use one of the following techniques:

1. Silence: a wait of fifteen to twenty seconds on the part of the teacher to encourage the student to elaborate on his original response
2. Encouragement: remarks, nonverbal noises, and/or gestures which indicate that the teacher accepts what has been said and wishes the student to continue speaking
3. Echo: an exact or nearly exact repetition by the teacher of the student's words
4. Reasoning: a question asking the student to justify his response
5. Direct clarification or elaboration: a direct request for explanation or more information
6. Confrontation: a question presenting the student with an inconsistency between two or more of his statements or between one of his statements and the statement of an authoritative source

STUDENT INITIATION OF QUESTIONS

Houston (1938, p. 28) observed eleven junior high school classes and found that an average of less than one question per class period was initiated by students. More recent studies confirm this low incidence of student questions. This seems to reflect a teacher-centered rather than learner-centered philosophy of teaching. Teachers of speech communication should encourage students to ask questions of each other and to make comments on what has been said. When a question is addressed to the teacher, instead of supplying the answer he would do well to reflect the question to other students in the class. If the low incidence of student-initiated questions seems to be due to students' lack of skill in asking questions, the teacher should focus on developing this skill in them.

USING EXPOSITION

The basic process for using exposition is the same as that for establishing objectives and strategy: attention, comprehension, acceptance. Other speech communication courses should have provided you with the principles of preparation and presentation which you will need in order to use exposition well. Additional techniques can be found in a number of sources listed at the end of this chapter. It is obvious that your oral instruction in the classroom requires effective speaking. Your goal should be to provide a model of public communication. This endeavor is well worth the great amount of effort it requires, for, as Becker (1949, p. 39) discovered, secondary school students rank "clear explanations based upon sound organization" highest in a list of the most significant components of the speech characteristics of superior teachers.

USING REINFORCEMENT

Teachers have long been aware of the value of reinforcement in the learning process. Too frequently, however, they fall into the habit of reinforcing only those students who are already doing well or of employing only a few reinforcing techniques from the full range available. Using the Flanders (1970) system of interaction analysis, this section suggests and illustrates three categories of reinforcement.

ACCEPTANCE OF FEELING

This category consists of teacher behaviors which accept and clarify an attitude or the feeling tone of the student in a nonthreatening manner. These behaviors do not imply a value judgment. Thus the teacher responds to both positive and negative feelings with verbal and nonverbal behaviors which imply "I understand" or "I know how you feel." With this neutral approach, the teacher is able to help the student discuss emotional reactions objectively and prevent them from inhibiting learning.

PRAISE OR ENCOURAGEMENT

This class consists of teacher behaviors which carry the value judgment of approval. Teachers have so thoroughly internalized the notion giving approval is a reinforcer that exclamations such as "Right!" "Good!" and "O.K." are used with such frequency that pupils are likely to ignore them. Genuine praise usually goes beyond one-word expressions. Nonverbal behavior is also important: a smile or nod to show enjoyment or satisfaction; vocal intonation or inflection to show approval and support. Praise and encouragement should not be reserved only for those who need it least.

ACCEPTANCE OR USE OF STUDENTS' IDEAS

The final category consists of teacher behaviors which clarify, build, or develop ideas suggested by a student. Since evidence indicates that such behaviors are associated with above-average content achievement and positive student attitudes toward content and the teacher, it is important that the teacher work on this skill.

SUMMARY

This chapter has focused on the S of the COSEF model by examining instructional *strategies* and instructional *skills*. Instructional strategies were covered under two major headings: nontechnical strategies and technical strategies. Nontechnical ones include books, lectures, discussions, and resource people (student panels, student reports, peer group instruction, guest lecturers, field trips, team teaching, and telelectures). Technical strategies were divided into audiovisual aids (television, video tape recorders, audio tape recorders, record players, motion picture projectors, slides, filmstrips, overhead projectors, opaque projectors, bulletin boards, and chalkboards), programmed instruction, simulations and games, computer-assisted instruction, and mediated self-instruction. Potential uses of the various strategies were discussed in terms of the speech communication classroom.

The chapter next focused on instructional skills—those elements of teacher behavior which apply across various instructional strategies. Five such skills were identified and discussed: establishing objectives, establishing strategy, using questions, using exposition, and using reinforcement.

What this chapter has attempted to do, then, is to provide a summary of possible instructional strategies and skills which you as a speech communication teacher should consider using and *testing*. The next chapter, "Lesson Planning," examines a framework for organizing the first three elements of the COSEF model (capabilities, objectives, and strategies and skills) into a plan of action in your speech communication classroom.

SELECTED SOURCES ON INSTRUCTIONAL STRATEGIES (INCLUDING REFERENCES)

BOOKS

Klopf, Donald W. "The High School Basic Speech Text." *Quarterly Journal of Speech* 29 (1970): 78–82.

Rousseau, Lousene. "How to Choose a High School Speech Text." *Speech Teacher* 17 (1968): 27–29.

Teague, Oran. "Selecting a Speech Textbook." In *Speech Methods and Resources: A Textbook for the Teacher of Speech*, edited by Waldo W. Braden, pp. 469–480. New York: Harper & Row, 1961.

THE LECTURE

Highet, Gilbert. *The Art of Teaching*, pp. 89–107. New York: Vintage Books, 1950.

McKeachie, Wilbert J. *Teaching Tips: A Guidebook for the Beginning College Teacher*, pp. 22–36. Lexington, Mass.: D. C. Heath, 1969.

DISCUSSION

Maier, N. R. F. *Problem-solving Discussion and Conferences: Leadership Methods and Skills*. New York: McGraw-Hill, 1963.

Nelson, Oliver W., and Dominic A. LaRusso. *Oral Communication in the Secondary School Classroom*, pp. 93–121. Englewood Cliffs, N. J.: Prentice-Hall, 1970.

RESOURCE PEOPLE

Wheater, Stanley B. "Team Teaching in a Course in Speaking and Writing." *Speech Teacher* 15 (1966): 242–247.

Wiseman, Gordon, and Larry Barker. "Peer Group Instruction: What is it?" *Speech Teacher* 15 (1966): 220–223.

Yeomans, G. Allan, and Henry C. Lindsey. "Telelectures." *Speech Teacher* 18 (1969): 65–67.

AUDIOVISUAL AIDS

GENERAL

Brown, James W., et al., eds. *AV Instruction Media and Methods*, 3d ed. New York: McGraw-Hill, 1969.

Minor, Ed, and Harvy R. Frye. *Techniques for Producing Visual Instructional Media*. New York: McGraw-Hill, 1970.

Training Methodology. Part 4: Audiovisual Theory, Aids, and Equipment. An Annotated Bibliography. Washington, D. C.: U. S. Health Services and Mental Health Administration, May, 1969. Available from Superintendent of Documents, U. S. Government Printing Office, Washington, D. C. 20402 (0–334–248 75¢).

Weisgerber, Robert A., ed. *Instructional Process and Media Innovation*. New York: Rand McNally, 1968.

AUDIO TAPE RECORDER

"Instructional Uses of Recorders: A Symposium." *Speech Teacher* 16 (1967): 209–224.
    Dallinger, Carl A. "Purposes and Uses of Recorders."
    North, Stafford. "Increasing Teaching Resources Through Tapes."
    Scheib, M. E. "Extending the Perimeter of the Classroom."
    Kenner, Freda, "Using the Recording in Teaching Speech in High School."
    Niles, Doris. "Recorder Projects for High School Speech Classes."
    Dickson, Phoebe L. "Using the Tape Recorder in the Elementary School."

Mulac, Anthony John. *An Experimental Study of the Relative Pedagogical Effectiveness of Videotape and Audiotape Playback of Student Speeches for Self-analysis in a Basic Speech Course: Final Report*. Ypsilanti: Eastern Michigan University, 1968.

VIDEO TAPE RECORDER

Bradley, Bert E. "An Experimental Study of the Effectiveness of the Video-Recorder in Teaching a Basic Speech Course." *Speech Teacher* 19 (1970): 161–167.

Deihl, E. Roderick; Myles P. Breen; and Charles U. Larson. "The Effects of Teacher Comment and Television Video Tape Playback on the Frequency of Nonfluency in Beginning Speech Students." *Speech Teacher* 19 (1970): 185–189.

Dieker, Richard J.; Loren Crane; and Charles T. Brown. "Repeated Self-Viewings on Closed-Circuit Television as it Affects Changes in the Self-concept and Personality Needs of Student Speakers." *Speech Teacher* 20 (1971): 131–142.

"Instructional Uses of Videotape: A Symposium." *Speech Teacher* 17 (1968): 101–122.
  Nelson, Harold E. "Videotaping the Speech Course."
  Becker, Samuel L.; John Waite Bowers; and Bruce E. Gronbeck. "Videotape in Teaching Discussion."
  Gibson, James W. "Using Videotape in the Training of Teachers."
  Ochs, Donovan J. "Videotape in Teaching Advanced Public Speaking."
  Reynolds, R. V. E. "Videotape in Teaching Speech in a Small College."
  Hirschfeld, Adeline Gittlen. "Videotape Recording for Self-analysis in the Speech Classroom."
  Pennybacker, John H. "Evaluating Videotape Recorders."

Lynch, Helen C. *Handbook for Classroom Videotape Recording.* Available upon request from Southeastern Educational Corporation, Inc., 3450 International Boulevard, Atlanta, Georgia 30300.

McCroskey, James C., and William B. Lashbrook. "The Effect of Various Methods of Employing Video-taped Television Playback in a Course in Public Speaking." *Speech Teacher* 19 (1970): 199–205.

McVay, Donald R. *Videotaped Instruction for the Teaching of Skills.* Seattle: Shoreline Community College, 1969.

Stewart, David C. "A Teacher's Guide to Telecourse Production." *Speech Teacher* 4 (1955): 270–276.

Toward a Significant Difference: Final Report of the National Project for the Improvement of Televised Instruction, 1965–1968. Washington, D. C.: National Association of Educational Broadcasters, 1969.

FILM

Index to 16-mm. Educational Films, 2d ed. Los Angeles: University of Southern California, National Information Center for Educational Media, 1969. Available from R. R. Bowker Co., 1180 Avenue of Americas, New York, N. Y. 10036.

Index to 8-mm. Motion Cartridges, 2d ed. Los Angeles: University of Southern California, National Information Center for Educational Media, 1969. Available from R. R. Bowker Co., 1180 Avenue of Americas, New York, N. Y. 10036.

Index to 35-mm. Educational Filmstrips. Los Angeles: University of Southern California, National Information Center for Educational Media, 1970. Available from R. R. Bowker Co., 1180 Avenue of Americas, New York, N. Y. 10036.

Jacoby, Beatrice. "Why Do You Use Films?" *Speech Teacher* 2 (1953): 119–121.

Lawndes, Douglas. *Film Making in Schools*. New York: Watson-Guptill, 1968.

Olympic Film Service, 161 West 22 St., New York, N. Y. 10000 will provide free the following three one-page guides to help you use films effectively: "How to Order Films for Preview and Rental," How to Conduct a Film Showing," and "How to Stimulate Lively Film Discussion." The company asks that requests be made on school or organization letterheads and that a stamped, self-addressed envelope be enclosed.

Whitehill, Buell, Jr., and Joe M. Ball. "A Report on the Young America Films Designed for Use in the Teaching of Speech." *Speech Teacher*, 2 (1953): 122–123.

OVERHEAD PROJECTOR

Index to Overhead Transparencies, 2d ed. Los Angeles: University of Southern California, National Information Center for Educational Media, 1969. Available from R. R. Bowker Co., 1180 Avenue of Americas, New York, N. Y. 10036.

Technifax Education Division, Holyoke, Mass. 01040, will provide free on request, "A Teacher's Guide to Overhead Projection."

PROGRAMMED INSTRUCTION

Amato, Philip P. "Programmed Instruction: Its Potential Utility in Speech." *Speech Teacher* 12 (1964): 190–196.

King, Thomas. "Programmed Textbooks in Communications." *Journal of Communication* 17 (1967): 55–62.

Schramm, Wilbur. *Programmed Instruction Today and Tomorrow.* New York: Fund for the Advancement of Education, 1962.

Tolch, Charles John. "Methods of Programming Teaching Machines for Speech." *Speech Teacher* 11 (1962): 233–238.

SIMULATIONS AND GAMES

Harry, Lindy. *Using Simulation Games in the Classroom, Report Number 44.* Baltimore: Johns Hopkins University, Center for the Study of Social Organization of Schools, 1969.

Instructional Uses of Simulation: A Selected Bibliography, 2d ed. Monmouth: Teaching Research, Oregon State System of Higher Education, 1967.

Tucker, Raymond K. "Computer Simulations and Simulation Games: Their Place in the Speech Curriculum." *Speech Teacher* 17 (1968): 128–133.

COMPUTER-ASSISTED INSTRUCTION

Contemporary Education 40 (April, 1969). Available for $1.00 from School of Education, Indiana State University, 217 North Sixth St., Terre Haute, Ind. 47809. This issue concentrates on the computer's role in education; it contains eight articles on computer-assisted instruction.

Reid, J. Christopher. "Learning with Computers." *Speech Teacher* 17 (1968): 259.

MEDIATED SELF-INSTRUCTION

A Handbook for Developing Individualized Instruction in Continuation Education. Fresno, Calif.: Fresno County Schools, 1970.

Postlethwait, S. N. et al. *The Audio-Tutorial Approach to Learning Through Independent Study and Integrated Experiences.* Minneapolis: Burgess, 1969.

SELECTED SOURCES ON INSTRUCTIONAL SKILLS
(INCLUDING REFERENCES)

Allen, Dwight, and Kevin Ryan. *Microteaching*. Reading, Mass.: Addison-Wesley, 1969.

Becker, Albert. "The Speech Characteristics of Superior and Inferior High School Teachers, as Revealed by Student Reaction." Ph.D. dissertation, Northwestern University, 1949.

Bloom, B. S., ed. *Taxonomy of Educational Objectives, Handbook I: Cognitive Domain*. New York: David McKay, 1956.

Borg, W. R., et al. *The Minicourse: A Microteaching Approach to Teacher Education*. Beverly Hills, Calif.: Macmillan Educational Services, 1970.

Canfield, James K., et al. "A Principles of Learning Approach to Analysis of Student Teachers' Verbal Teaching Behavior." Unpublished Ed.D. dissertation. New York: Teachers College, Columbia University, 1965.

Clegg, Ambrose A., Jr., et al. "Teacher Strategies of Questioning for Eliciting Selected Cognitive Student Responses." Paper presented at the AERA annual meeting, Los Angeles, February, 1969.

Ecroyd, Donald H. *Speech in the Classroom*. Englewood Cliffs, N. J.: Prentice-Hall, 1960.

Fessenden, Seth A., et. al. *Speech for the Creative Teacher*. Dubuque, Iowa: Wm. C. Brown, 1968.

Flanders, Ned A. *Analyzing Teaching Behavior*. Reading, Mass.: Addison-Wesley, 1970.

Gall, Meredith D. "The Use of Questions in Teaching." *Review of Educational Research* 40 (1970): 707–721.

Houston, V. M. "Improving the Quality of Classroom Questions and Questioning." *Educational Administration and Supervision* 24 (1938): 17–28.

Nelson, Oliver W., and Dominic A. LaRusso. *Oral Communication in the Secondary School Classroom*. Englewood Cliffs, N. J. Prentice-Hall, 1970.

Phillips, Gerald M., et al. *The Development of Oral Communication in the Classroom*. Indianapolis: Bobbs-Merrill, 1970.

Robinson, Karl F., and Albert B. Becker. *Effective Speech for the Teacher*. New York: McGraw-Hill, 1970.

Sanders, Norris M. *Classroom Questions: What Kinds?* New York: Harper & Row, 1966.

Stevens, R. "The Question as a Measure of Efficiency in Instruction: A Critical Study of Classroom Practice." *Teachers College Contributions to Education* 48 (1912).

FIVE

LESSON PLANNING

Every day of our lives we are presented with problems. How can I get a date for Saturday night? How can I get an A on the next test? What make and model of automobile should I buy? We can react to these problems either systematically or unsystematically. The unsystematic problem solver might go to a fortune teller; ask a friend to make the decision for him; avoid the problem, even refusing to admit that it exists; let the problem intensify until he is forced to act by outside pressures; trust in luck to guide him; or employ the method of trial and error. On the other hand, the systematic problem solver mentally or otherwise defines his problem, analyzes it from many angles, decides upon a solution, follows through, and evaluates as a guide to future action. Solutions reached by the systematic problem solver are preferable to solutions reached by the unsystematic problem solver because they are more flexible and more reliable. They are more flexible because the individual re-examines them in light of new facts and situations; they are more reliable because he bases them on a careful study of the relevant evidence. The purpose of this chapter is to apply the skills of systematic problem solving to the problem of planning and developing learning experiences.

OBJECTIVES

1. Specify a rationale for resource units, teaching units, and daily lesson plans.
2. Specify the five major divisions (and subdivisions) of resource units, teaching units, and daily lesson plans.
3. Describe a method for developing resource units, teaching units, and daily lesson plans.

RESOURCE UNITS

One of the most effective approaches to such planning in recent years has been the use of resource units. While there is no set definition of a resource unit and no single accepted form for producing one, Klohr's (1950, pp. 74–77) investigation reveals a number of common elements in effective resource units:

1. A wealth of suggested learning experiences
2. A survey of possible ways to evaluate the suggested learning experiences
3. A carefully selected bibliography and list of teaching aids
4. A stimulating presentation of the scope of the problem area with which the unit deals
5. A formulation of the philosophy underlying the resource unit and a statement of the specific objectives
6. Suggestions for the use of the resource unit

The following outline contains all these elements in a form convenient for the speech communication classroom:

1. *Rationale.* Outline here the reasons why you believe this unit is important in terms of the prospective students, the community, and the larger social environment.

2. *Objectives.* State here both the general and behavioral objectives you wish students to achieve by the end of the unit.

3. *Subject-matter outline.* In outline fashion, detail the knowledge which students will need to acquire in order to achieve the objectives of the unit.

4. *Instructional strategies.* List under the following three headings various ways of structuring the teaching-learning environment to achieve the objectives of the unit.
   a. *Initiation:* strategies that introduce students to the unit and arouse their interest in it
   b. *Development:* strategies that focus directly on achievement of the objectives
   c. *Culmination:* strategies that clarify and summarize the objectives of the unit

5. *Evaluation.* Explain under the following three headings how you intend to assess the success of students in achieving the objectives of the unit.
   a. *Student-student.* Students evaluate themselves and others on achievement of the objectives.
   b. *Teacher-student.* Teacher evaluates student performance of objectives; teacher and students assess the unit.
   c. *Teacher-teacher.* Teacher evaluates how well he did as a teacher in light of his stated objectives.

A resource unit is a catalogue of potential objectives, subject-matter content, strategies, and evaluation procedures which the teacher of speech communication can choose to use; it presents him with a list of options. In any given teaching-learning situation, he chooses those elements which are most appropriate.

Resource units are not something which are developed overnight and used from then on. They are developmental projects which should grow as you grow. In order to keep your resource units current, you might consider using loose-leaf binders when developing them. New elements you read about, hear about, or devise can then be added conveniently.

The following resource unit, "Interviewing for Information," is presented to illustrate the utility of resource units for teachers of speech communication. It is intended to be illustrative and not exhaustive; you will understand why when you finish reading it.[1]

I. *Rationale*

Regardless of its specific purpose, form, or context, the interview is essentially a method of collecting information. The purpose for which the information is sought varies with both the seeker and the respondent: the physician seeks from his patient information on which to base a diagnosis; the personnel officer seeks from job applicants information about their qualifications; the lawyer seeks from his clients and witnesses information that may serve as legal evidence; the journalist seeks information to retail to his readers or to lead him to further sources; the market researcher seeks from consumers information that will help to design or market a product; the social scientist seeks from a wide variety of respondents information by means of which he can explore a problem or test a hypothesis; and everyone, in the course of daily life, seeks information as a basis for short- and long-range actions—or even for its own sake.

The nature of the information sought varies even more widely. It may consist of a description of events—a narrative account of "what happened" in a situation in which the respondent was a participant or a witness; it may involve behavior—past, present, or intended; attitudes—conscious and unconscious; moral values—overt and covert; habits—of recreation, purchasing, or ethical choice; modes of perception; or feelings—habitual or stemming from a specific event.

The information may be given freely, or with the greatest reluctance; it may be given accurately, or with conscious or unconscious distortion. It may take the form of a single word, a number or a response to one of a series of alternatives; or it may have to be sifted out from a flood of response material given by a respondent who either is doing his best to cooperate with the interviewer and to understand his questions, or is doing his best to mislead. The information may be elicited in a casual, extemporaneous, two-minute conversation; in the course of an hour of intimate discussion; or in a series of interviews extending over many months (Richardson, Dohrenwend, and Klein).

[1]The ideas in this unit are based on the authors' experience in teaching an undergraduate interviewing course at Purdue. Much of what is included they first learned from W. Charles Redding and Charles J. Stewart. Full source references appear in section IV-B-1.

Because the interview is important to students, the community, and the larger social environment, and because the necessary skills need to be learned and can be learned, it is worthwhile to devote a unit of instruction to appreciating, understanding, and improving the process of communication in the interview.

II. *Objectives*
   A. *General.* Three broad objectives underlie the unit:
      1. *Knowledge.* Because knowledge of interviewing theory is basic to improvement in interviewing skills, considerable time is devoted to cognitive knowledge concerned with three factors:
         a. Awareness of the function of interviewing in society
         b. Comprehension of basic principles of interviewing
         c. Comprehension of the special application of these principles in fulfilling various interviewing purposes
      2. *Attitude.* To a large extent, the success or failure of man's attempt to communicate in the interview situation depends on the attitudes with which the interviewer and interviewee approach the communication process. The unit is thus concerned with
         a. The attitude a student holds concerning the nature and importance of effective communication in the interviewing situation
         b. The manner in which a student perceives himself and his relationships with others in the interviewing situation
      3. *Ability.* Because interviewing is a basic unit in speech communication, it is important that a student gain reasonable proficiency as a communicator in actual interview situations. This involves the following:
         a. The ability to evaluate the behavior of both himself and others in the interview situation
         b. The ability to perform both the interviewer and interviewee roles in an interview situation
   B. *Specific.* Twenty-five specific objectives are basic to the unit:
      1. Defining the interview
      2. Distinguishing the interview from other forms of communication
      3. Classifying interviews as to type
      4. Listing unique characteristics of interview speaking
      5. Listing ways in which the content of an interview is different from the content of other kinds of communication
      6. Listing psychological factors which are important in the interview
      7. Specifying the roles of the partners in various types of interviews

8. Recognizing situations which require the establishment of rapport, orientation, and motivation in the opening of the interview
9. Classifying inhibitors and facilitators of communication as to type
10. Eliciting responses in an interview that satisfy the criteria for good responses
11. Classifying questions as to type
12. Recognizing situations that require a closed question
13. Asking filter questions
14. Recognizing situations that require the inverted funnel pattern of questions for developing a topic
15. Devising an interview schedule that exemplifies Gallup's "quintamensional design"
16. Classifying the overall style of the interview as to type
17. Evaluating the choice of wording in a question
18. Establishing common ground with the interviewee
19. Writing an interview guide
20. Providing feedback to the interviewee
21. Asking questions that elicit reliable and valid information
22. Providing encouragement and support for the interviewee
23. Preparing adequately for the interview situation
24. Providing transitions in the interview
25. Dealing with inadequate responses to questions

III. *Subject-Matter Outline*
  A. Nature of the Interview
    1. Definitions
      a. "A conversation directed to a definite purpose other than satisfaction in the conversation itself" (Bingham, Moore, and Gustadt, 1959, p. 3).
      b. A specialized pattern of verbal interaction—initiated for a specific purpose, and focused on some specific content area, with a subsequent elimination of extraneous material" (Kahn and Cannell, 1957, p. 16).
      c. "A form of oral communication involving two parties, at least one of whom has a preconceived and serious purpose, and both of whom speak and listen from time to time" (Goyer, Redding, and Rickey, 1968, p. 6).
    2. The interview as communication
      a. Relationship of the interview to other forms of communication —social conversation, intimate interaction, interrogation or examination, debate, fight, discussion, public speech, etc.

    b. Unique characteristics of interview communication
      1) Purposes of interview are more varied, more complex, more specialized than in other types of oral communication.
        a) Information getting (polls, surveys)
        b) Information giving (job orientation, instruction)
        c) Persuasive (sales, everyday efforts to induce belief or action)
        d) Problem solving (essentially a two-man discussion, inquiry)
        e) Specialized personnel interviews (job application, complaints, reprimands, termination)
      2) Mode of participation—changing from moment to moment, involving intimate interaction and adaptation, alternating speaking and listening.
      3) Content is different from that in other kinds of communication.
        a) Emphasis on all kinds of questions.
        b) Language is less formal.
        c) Logical digression may be necessary at times.
        d) Precise, detailed, and documented factual evidence is crucial because you may be challenged at any time.
      4) Psychological factors are important.
        a) Motivations (rewards and penalties) are likely to be more immediate, obvious, direct—adapted to the specific individual.
        b) Social and economic status factors are very important in the interview (boss to employee, professor to student, parent to child). Many barriers to "upward" communication.
        c) Crucial to preserve ego of interviewee.
          (1) Make it easy for him to save face.
          (2) Avoid making categorical demands or assertions from which it is difficult to retreat.
          (3) Generally unwise to use direct attack upon an interviewee's position, especially a real or implied attack upon his integrity or intelligence.
          (4) Avoid imposing a decision.
      5) There is no possibility of a majority.
  3. Values and limitations of the interview as compared to other data-gathering methods
B. Basic principles of interviewing

1. Roles of the partners in an interview (Goyer, Redding, and Rickey, 1968, pp. 8–9)
   a. Psychological burden of proof
   b. Power of decision
   c. Burden of proof
2. Parts of interview
   a. Opening (when one is necessary, it serves three functions: rapport, orientation, motivation.)
   b. Body
   c. Close
3. The goal of interviewing: maximal information with optimal, rather than maximal, interpersonal relations. This means minimizing the inhibitors and maximizing the facilitators of communication (Gorden, 1969).
   a. Inhibitors
      1) Competing demands for time
      2) Ego threat
      3) Etiquette
      4) Trauma
      5) Forgetting
      6) Chronological confusion
      7) Inferential confusion
      8) Unconscious behavior
   b. Facilitators
      1) Fulfilling expectations
      2) Recognition
      3) Altruistic appeals
      4) Sympathetic understanding
      5) New experience
      6) Catharsis
      7) The need for meaning
      8) Extrinsic rewards
4. General suggestions from various sources
   a. Preparing for the interview
      1) Decide what is to be accomplished.
      2) Know the interviewee.
      3) Make appointment.
      4) Provide for privacy.
      5) Practice taking the interviewee's point of view (empathy).
      6) Know your own personality.
   b. Interviewing

       1) Help the interviewee feel at ease and ready to communicate.
       2) Listen for latent and manifest meaning.
       3) Allow enough time.
       4) Maintain control of the interview.
       5) At the close, watch for additional information or leads in the casual remarks of the interviewee.
C. Basic principles of the informational interview
  1. Giving and getting information
    a. Ways in which information is forfeited
    b. Barriers to sharing information
    c. How to prevent forfeiting of information
  2. Preparing for the information-gathering interview (a summary of seven suggestions in Bingham, Gustad, and Moore, 1959, Chapter 3)
    a. Formulate your problem. (What information do you want?)
    b. Know your field of interest. (Who? Why? When? Where? How?)
    c. Choose interviewee(s) with care.
       1) Knowledge of the subject
       2) Willingness to give information
       3) Ability to give information accurately
    d. Prepare a carefully organized interview guide or schedule.
  3. Formulation of questions
    a. Criteria for good responses (Richardson et al., 1965, Chapter 5)
       1) Satisfactory respondent responses
       2) Validity
       3) Relevance
       4) Specificity and clarity
       5) Coverage
       6) Depth
    b. Methods of achieving good responses
       1) Treatment of the respondents must be considered (Payne, 1951, Chapter 7; Richardson et al., 1965; Chapter 3).
       2) Characteristics of a single question
          a) Openness versus closedness
            (1) Closed (identification, selection, yes–no)
            (2) Open
          b) Antecedents
            (1) One of the last few questions
            (2) Preceding response
            (3) Earlier response

        (4) Breaks with previous response
    c) Question-antecedent relationship
        (1) Silent probe
        (2) Encouragement
        (3) Immediate elaboration
        (4) Immediate clarification
        (5) Retrospective clarification
        (6) Retrospective elaboration
        (7) Echo
        (8) Summary
        (9) Confrontation
       (10) Repetition
       (11) Mutation
    d) Expectations and premises (leading question)
        (1) Weak–strong
        (2) Informed–uninformed
    e) Content or subject matter
        (1) Broad–narrow
        (2) Objective, subjective, indeterminate
        (3) True–false
    f) Vocabulary used in wording the question
        (1) Denotation–connotation
        (2) Level of difficulty
    g) Specific-use questions
        (1) Sleeper
        (2) Cheater
        (3) Intensity
        (4) Filter
3) General patterns of questions for developing a topic
    a) Funnel versus inverted funnel (Kahn and Cannell, 1957)
    b) George Gallup's "quintamensional design" (Payne, 1951)
4) Arranging topics and subtopics within an interview
5) Overall style of the interview
    a) Richardson et al., 1965, Chapter 2
        (1) Standardized
            (a) Nonschedule
            (b) Schedule
        (2) Nonstandardized
    b) Directive versus nondirective (Hard to say whether
       an interview is one or the other)
6) Other factors in the question-answer process (Richardson
   et al., 1965, Chapter 10)

a) The pace
b) The pace from neutral to threatening topics
c) The general tempo
d) Modifying the pace of the interview
e) Transitions
f) The choice of language and level of discourse
g) The loaded question
(1) Prestige
(2) Stereotypes
(3) Proposed legal changes
(4) Biased wording
(5) Personalization of the question
h) The sequence of topics
i) Accent and inflection
j) Interviewee-interviewer communication through observation

IV. *Instructional strategies*
A. Initiation
1. Use memory paragraphs to generate a discussion of (1) ways in which information is forfeited, (2) barriers to sharing information, and (3) how the forfeiting of information can be prevented. In this exercise, three to five students leave the room. Copies of the story are distributed to all but one student. The story is read to the student who has not seen it. This student then relays what he has heard to one of the students called in from the hall. This student relates what he has heard to the next student, and so on. Variations might include allowing the listener to take notes, allowing the listener to ask questions, or having the story repeated.
2. Administer a standardized listening test, and discuss the implications of the results for interviewing.
a. Brown-Carlsen Test of Listening Comprehension
b. "The Dow Test," *Speech Monographs* 20 (1953): 120
c. Sequential Tests of Educational Programs (STEP): Listening. Cooperative Tests Division, Educational Testing Services, 20 Nassau Street, Princeton, New Jersey 08540
3. Conduct a poll to discover how much time students think they spend each day in what could be classified as interviewing.
4. Ask students to keep a diary describing the interview situations they encounter and participate in an analysis of it.

5. Hand out a brief transcription of a sample interview and have the class participate in an analysis of it.

B. Development

1. Assign students portions of the following reading material:
    a. Bingham, Walter V.; Bruce V. Moore; and John W. Gustad. *How to Interview.* 4th rev. ed. New York: Harper & Row, 1959.
    b. Gorden, Raymond L. *Interviewing: Strategy, Techniques, and Tactics.* Homewood, Ill.: Irwin-Dorsey, 1969.
    c. Goyer, Robert S.; W. Charles Redding; and John T. Rickey. *Interviewing Principles and Techniques.* Dubuque, Ia.: Wm. C. Brown, 1968.
    d. Kahn, Robert L., and Charles R. Cannell. *The Dynamics of Interviewing.* New York: John Wiley & Sons, 1957.
    e. Keltner, John W. *Interpersonal Speech-Communication: Elements and Structures.* Belmont, Calif.: Wadsworth, 1970, pp. 260–285.
    f. Payne, Stanley L. *The Art of Asking Questions.* Princeton: Princeton University Press, 1951.
    g. Richardson, Stephen A.; Barbara S. Dohrenwend; and David Klein. *Interviewing: Its Forms and Functions.* New York: Basic Books, 1965.

2. List some stigma words (such as liar, slut, Communist, nigger, bastard, etc.) halo words (such as honest, sincere, Christian, American, democratic, etc.), and some neutral words (such as man, horse, house, paper, chair, etc.) on the board and have students indicate for each of them (1) strong positive reaction, (2) mild positive reaction, (3) no reaction, (4) mild negative reaction, or (5) strong negative reaction. Discuss the implications for interviewing.

3. Provide your students with a list of twenty or so current public personalities or publications and have them rate them in terms of: (1) haven't heard of, (2) credible source, (3) mildly credible source, (4) neutral source, (5) mildly uncredible source, (6) uncredible source. Discuss the implications of this exercise for interviewing.

4. Hand out a written sample interview and have students hand in a written analysis of it.

5. Have students conduct the opening one or two minutes of an interview with you playing the role of the interviewee.

6. Hand out a written sample interview and have students classify the questions as to type.

7. Play an audio or video tape recording of a model interview in class and have your students discuss it.
8. Have students engage in an out-of-class interview to discover the interview practices and interview training of an individual who has had considerable interviewing experience.
9. Have students interview strangers to find out their opinions on controversial topics such as cheating and drugs.
10. Use a case study to test interviewing skill in obtaining information. The instructions to the student might read:
    a. The test of one's skill is the amount, relevance, and accuracy of information he elicits from the interviewee.
    b. An interviewee will be given a case and will familiarize himself with the case so that he knows all the information contained in it. He may use notes on the case while engaging in the interview.
    c. So that the emphasis in this activity is placed on skills entirely (or nearly so) within the interviewer, the interviewee will be requested to give accurate answers. The interviewee, however, is not to supply information beyond that which is specifically elicited by the questioning of the interviewer. The interviewee is to be an honest but reluctant respondent.
    d. The skills to be demonstrated by the interviewer are:
        1) Devising a questioning strategy likely to cover the case
        2) Being sensitive to cues leading to unsuspected areas of data
        3) Making correct inferences
        4) Checking or verifying conclusions and interpretations
        5) Keeping generally alert, flexible, yet organized
    e. To enhance the learning opportunity of students in your class, assign four interviewers to the same interviewee. The class will be able to observe the different strategies, the different mistakes made, and the variance or lack of variance in the eliciting of information. Interviewers assigned to the same case will be assigned times to report to the classroom to conduct their interviews so that the interviewer does not hear preceding interviews on the case.
C. Culmination
    1. Review and summarize the materials covered. Ask students if they believe they have been able to use efficient and effective interviewing techniques in other classes and situations.
    2. Have students write a unit project which (1) acquaints them with some of the theory and research relevant to the interview

process, (2) gives them an opportunity to examine a problem related to the interview in some depth, and (3) allows them to develop skill in researching a selected problem.

3. Use another form of the standardized test given at the beginning of the unit and compare the results.
4. Have students make an audio or video tape recording of a model interview.
5. Give a test on the subject matter of the interviewing unit.

V. Evaluation
   A. Student-student
      1. Have students orally or in writing evaluate their performances during the interviewing unit.
      2. Use peer group evaluation.
   B. Teacher-student
      1. Teacher evaluates pupil performance, based on:
         a. Performance in interviewing exercises (use evaluation forms)
         b. Quizzes on subject matter
         c. Unit project
      2. Teacher and students evaluate unit.
         a. What were our problems at the outset?
         b. How successfully have we answered them?
         c. What new questions have arisen?
         d. Have we managed to state them clearly and find means of answering them effectively?
         e. Where do we go from here? What new doors are now open?
   C. Teacher-teacher
      1. Did the students learn as much as I had hoped for cognitively, affectively, skills-wise?
      2. Which methods proved most effective and most ineffective? Why?
      3. What can I do to improve this unit?

TEACHING UNITS

Once the teacher of speech communication has developed a resource unit, the development of a *teaching unit* is a relatively easy task. The teaching unit is prepared specifically for one class and thus includes only the objectives, subject-matter content, strategies, and evaluation procedures which seem necessary, appropriate, and feasible *for that class.* Such decisions are based on an assessment of student capabilities (see Chapter 3). The teacher of speech communication, then, in preparing a teaching unit, merely checks appropriate sections in the resource unit for use in the teaching unit. Oftentimes, however, a brief outline of the teaching unit is a convenient and useful way of reminding the teacher of his overall plans for the unit.

The teaching unit presented below was prepared by a special committee of the Secondary School Interest Group of the Speech Communication Association (Speech Association of America, 1959, pp. 109–113). Obviously, it was not developed for a particular group of students. When examining it, you should keep in mind that your teaching unit will have to be developed in terms of what you consider necessary, appropriate, and feasible for your particular class.

Time: Three weeks

I. *Introduction:* The following unit is intended to provide an introduction to basic discussion philosophy and techniques for the average secondary school student. It is not intended to provide an experience in every form of discussion or opportunity for mastery of any one form. It is rather the sort of starting point which is essential in any basic course.

II. *Objectives*

A. General

To provide the student with a laboratory for gaining familiarity with the basic concepts of good group interaction based on effective oral communication.

B. Specific

1. The development of sensitivity on the part of the student with respect to personal interaction in a group discussion.

2. The development of the student's ability to:

a. Prepare for effective group discussion.

b. Recognize various types of group discussion.

c. Participate as an effective member of a discussion group.

d. Exercise leadership as a member or chairman of a group discussion.

e. Participate in problem-solving on a democratic basis.

f. Speak in a direct and conversational manner.

g. Evaluate the group discussion presented.

III. *Approach:* A suggested approach might well be the establishment by the class, perhaps as a result of a teacher-guided informal discussion, of an accurate definition of a group discussion. Such a definition should establish the concept of a discussion group as the traditional "two or more persons, listening and speaking intermittently, thinking interactively, and working cooperatively on a common subject or problem."

The complementary nature of discussion and debate, one as cooperative investigation, the other as persuasion or advocacy, will probably need to be established. Logical considerations aside, this process will probably be necessary in order to correct previously formed student impressions of discussion as a type of informal debate activity consisting of a panel of individuals divided into "pros" and "cons." Other erroneous impressions of the nature of discussion may be present in the class as a result of such radio and television programs as "Twenty Questions" or other quiz panels, "Face the Nation" and "America's Town Meeting of the Air," all of which are referred to as "discussions" at times by their moderators and, alas, in some texts.

IV. *Organization and content*
   A. The definition of group discussion
      1. Restatement of the (approach) concept of "two or more persons, etc."
         a. Contrasted with informal conversation
         b. Contrasted with set platform speaking
         c. Contrasted with debating
   B. The nature of group discussion and the forms it commonly takes
      1. Investigative and opinion-sharing groups working cooperatively
         a. To pool information (as in a committee reporting on existing conditions)
         b. To consider and modify the opinions of the group members (as in a group meeting to share intelligence on a subject rather than to take action)
      2. Problem-solving group discussion
         a. To recommend a policy to be adopted (as in the work of a committee charged with the task of making recommendations on a problem to the full group)
         b. To fix action (as in a case conference such as a student government judicial group might have)
      3. Most common types of group discussion
         a. The committee or panel
         b. The round-table group
         c. The symposium
         d. The forum as a method of audience participation in any group discussion
   C. Preparing to participate in group discussion

1. Selecting the topic (criteria)
   a. Is it of general and current interest to the group?
   b. Are research materials available on the topic?
   c. Can it be profitably discussed within the time alloted to the group?
2. Phrasing the topic (criteria)
   a. Can it be phrased as a question?
   b. Can a "yes" or "no" answer be avoided by the phrasing of the question?
   c. Have ambiguous or loaded terms been eliminated from the question?
   d. If the question proceeds from a basic assumption (for example: What can be done to make fraternities improve their membership selection policies?) do the members of the discussion group accept that assumption? (In the above example, one basic assumption would be that there is a need for improvement.)
3. Participating in planning and research
   a. The pre-research planning meeting
      (1) Selection of chairman, or leader, or fixing of leadership rotation
      (2) Division of labor on areas of research, if called for by the nature of the topic.
   b. Reading and observing for use as a panel member
   c. The post-research planning meeting
      (1) For purposes of establishing group agenda
      (2) But *not* for rehearsing the discussion
D. Participating in group discussion
   1. Gaining familiarity with the "reflective thought process."
      a. Methods of defining and locating a subject or problem
      b. Methods of analyzing the causes of a problem
      c. Establishing criteria for solution
      d. Posing possible solutions
      e. Weighing and testing solutions
      f. Choosing the best solution, and fixing responsibility for action when necessary.
   2. Attitudes and skills to be developed by each student
      a. A desire to help other members of the group form ideas
      b. A willingness to admit his own errors and to credit the contributions of others
      c. A willingness to answer the questions of others directly
      d. The ability to present his own contributions directly,

conversationally, concisely, and in a friendly spirit
- e. The ability to stick to the subject
- f. Consideration for the rights of the other group members to their fair share of discussion time
- g. The ability to use facts and other information in an objective manner
- h. The ability to participate in critical examination of contributions made by himself and others
- i. The ability to exercise leadership in the group whenever necessary
- j. The willingness to follow the leadership of the group moderator or chairman
- k. The willingness to change his opinion when such a change is justified
- l. In a problem-solving discussion, the desire to work toward a consensus or a solution which is acceptable to as many of the group members as possible.
- E. Leading a group discussion: Special techniques for the chairman or moderator to develop
  - 1. The ability to keep the group on the track of the discussion
    - a. Use of leading questions
    - b. Use of frequent and concise summaries
  - 2. The ability to keep the group moving toward a consensus or solution in problem-solving discussion
    - a. Assisting the group to allocate its time spent in discussing a single point.
    - b. Skill in using transition statements
    - c. Skill in resolving disagreements or conflicts in the group without being dictatorial or loss of fairness or objectivity of an impartial leader
  - 3. The ability to present the final summary or report of the opinions or recommendations for action accepted by the group in an accurate, impartial, concise, and effective manner.

V. *Pupil experiences and activities*
  - A. Start with group discussion as an informal opinion sharing experience on common topics of interest to teen-agers (such as "Interesting Problems in Double Dating," "Part-time Jobs," etc.)
    - 1. Concentrate attention of the group on development of those items listed under D-2 and E-1, 2 and 3 of the Organization and Content section of this unit.

2. In the post-discussion evaluation, lead the class to a consideration of the possible reorganization of the discussion to fit the more formal problem-solving reflective thought sequence.

3. Discuss with the class the difference in approach between such informal, impromptu discussions and the following experiences which are based on research by the group members.

B. The second group discussion experience should utilize planning sessions, agenda based on the reflective thought sequence, and organization of work with some depth of research on similar topics. In this case, however, some role-playing may be added for variety. For example: The group might be instructed to consider itself a special committee of the student council, or some other youth organization, appointed to solve a typical school problem such as "What Can We Suggest to Improve Student Support of Council-Sponsored Social Events?" etc.

1. Care should be taken to encourage the students to select problem areas which actually exist in the school, and yet which have not been worn threadbare by previous discussion.

2. A premium should be put on such research activities as the interviewing of those in positions of authority, both students and faculty, and the use of library resource materials which are usually available.

3. The planning of a forum period, and the rules for conducting such a session, should be included in the preparation for this experience. Such a feature usually adds more class participation in terms of listener involvement of non-panel members.

4. Post-discussion evaluation should include the criteria established for the first group experience but be expanded to cover the other items included in the Organization and Content section of this unit. (No material was included relative to the forum procedure, since this is an optional subject governed by the availability of course time. Almost any text dealing with discussion and/or parliamentary procedure is an adequate source of suggestions for forum procedure if the instructor is unfamiliar with the techniques.)

5. An experience in serving as a chairman or leader can be provided for each panel member if rotation of the leadership function is established on a time basis (for example, 5–10 minutes per experience). It is, of course, prefer-

able to have sufficient group discussion experiences available to permit each pupil a full-length opportunity to serve as discussion leader or chairman. If six weeks are alloted for group discussion, this is feasible.

C. The third group discussion experience should be a formal problem-solving panel which emphasizes mastery of the reflective thought pattern of organization on a topic which is considerably more complex than that used for the first and second experiences. Topics related to current national or international events, or those with a direct relationship to advanced work in social studies are quite usable for this project. At this point, material can be utilized from those sources used by students involved in interscholastic competitive speech activities. Usually the local or state speech league will assist those instructors whose schools do not participate in these activities to become familiar with the available materials.

1. Care will need to be taken in the phrasing of these topics so that they do not encompass too great an area for the time available for discussion.

2. Mastery of the procedure of outlining the leader and group member outlines will need special emphasis in this experience.

D. There is a host of other types of pupil experiences which can be used provided enough time is available for learning discussion in the basic speech course. Much depends on the ingenuity of the instructor in devising new experiences. Some instructors have found it profitable to utilize mock situations such as the deliberation in a jury room, labor-management controversy, community conferences, a simulated television or radio program, or the semi-dramatization of historical fiction (such as the meeting of a king's council to determine policy) as vehicles for the experience of group discussion. Others have combined discussion with parliamentary procedure (by use of the committee technique) or as an introduction to a unit in debate. We have suggested only a simple, beginning pattern of experiences which should be usable in any basic speech course, but is not intended to exclude other experiences which the instructor may wish to provide.

VI. *Evaluation and testing*

A. Rather than setting forth any dictum regarding specific testing devices or procedures, we would suggest the following broad principles respecting evaluation and testing:

1. Whenever possible, the class as a whole should be motivated to devote some time to the establishment of procedures and criteria for the evaluation of group discussion. The criteria are, of course, suggested by the Organization and Content section of this unit.
2. Evaluation of the discussion performance by the class rather than the instructor usually leads to better attention on the part of the class which is not immediately involved in the group discussion.
3. Evaluation forms which utilize a continuous scale with some brief space for note-taking provide for easiest interpretation and relative economy in terms of audience distractions from the group discussion.
4. The usual objective testing devices used in some other secondary school courses are not as valuable for judging growth in speech skills as the devices indicated above.
5. Careful note-taking by the instructor, providing objectivity is retained, will provide a better record of growth than mathematical computations resulting in grades.
6. In terms of a final pencil and paper test, there are two types of questions which offer good indications of mastery of the theory of group discussion organization; the following are sample questions:
   a. "Recall your last experience as a member or leader of a group discussion. Write an outline of the pattern of that discussion *but* improve the handling of the topic by utilizing the constructive criticism which your group received in the evaluation period and by means of the evaluation forms."
   b. "Below is a problem-solving panel discussion topic. Show what a well-organized leader's outline might be if the subject were to be discussed with little advance notice." Topic: What Can We Do to Improve School Spirit at High School?

DAILY LESSON PLANS

Having prepared a resource unit and a teaching unit, the final step is the preparation of *daily lesson plans*. The daily lesson plan (1) lists the instructional objectives for a particular day, (2) outlines the subject matter,

(3) lists the strategies for achieving the objectives, and (4) suggests a method of appraising whether or not the objectives were met.

The following lesson plan is based on the earlier resource unit "Interviewing for Information."

NAME: Charles Miles   UNIT: Interviewing for Information

DATE: October 31, 1972   GRADE LEVEL: 10th & 11th

HOURS: 8:45–9:45

I. *Objectives.* The general goal for the day is to allow students an opportunity to experience the kinds of things that happen when information is passed from person to person. Hopefully, the students will become more aware of the difficulties involved in giving and getting information in the interview setting. By the end of the hour, each student should be able to do the following:

   A. Describe, orally or in writing, the three ways in which information is forfeited.
   B. Specify, orally or in writing, a minimum of five reasons why deletions, changes, and additions occur.
   C. Specify, orally or in writing, a minimum of nine ways by which deletions, changes, and additions can be minimized.

II. *Subject-matter outline* (Form R.S.G. 1065, CRC, Purdue)

   A. Information is forfeited when:
      1. Omissions—deletions—losses occur
      2. Changes—distortions are made (e.g., making "qualified" statements into definite ones)
      3. Additions are made
   B. Information is forfeited because of:
      1. Physical distance between parties
      2. Individual physical restrictions or inabilities
      3. Role differences (social, economic, etc.) between parties
      4. Specific techniques and media employed
      5. Attitudes, habits of thinking, assumptions
         a. Bases for organizing ideas: abstractions and generalization
         b. Listening only to words
         c. Resisting new ideas
   C. The forfeiting of information can be prevented by:
      1. Taking notes
      2. Previewing the information
      3. Being systematic in giving details
      4. Employing verbal emphasis and attention factors

  5. Asking questions—encouraging "feedback"
  6. Using more than one medium of presentation
  7. Reducing the number of levels (persons) filtering the information
  8. Summarizing frequently
  9. Being sensitive to the other fellow's viewpoint and experience

III. *Instructional strategies*

Use memory paragraphs to generate a discussion of (1) ways in which information is forfeited, (2) barriers to sharing information, and (3) how the forfeiting of information can be prevented. In this exercise, three to five students leave the room. Copies of a story are distributed to all but one student. The story is read to the student who has not seen it. This student then relays what he has heard to one of the students called in from the hall. This student relates what he has heard to the next student, and so on. Variations might include allowing the listener to take notes, allowing the listener to ask questions, or having the story repeated.

IV. *Evaluation*

A. Informally assess how well the objectives were met by having students respond orally at the end of the hour to questions such as:
  1. What were our problems at the outset?
  2. How successfully have we answered them?
  3. What new questions have arisen?
  4. Have we managed to state them clearly and to find means of answering them effectively?
  5. Where do we go from here? What new doors are now open?
B. Ask yourself the following questions:
  1. Did the students learn as much as I had hoped for?
  2. Which methods proved most effective? Ineffective? Why?
  3. What can I do to improve this lesson?

SUMMARY

Chapter 2 was devoted to the selection, writing, and use of behavioral objectives. Chapter 3 suggested that in order for instructional objectives to be effective, they often need to be modified to meet the student's entering behavior. Chapter 4 focused on various instructional strategies and instructional skills which the teacher can use to help students achieve specified instructional objectives. This chapter sought to integrate the material in Chapters 2, 3, and 4 into a plan of action for the speech communication teacher through the use of resource units, teaching units, and daily lesson plans. In the next chapter (the last one in this unit) the focus is on three interacting variables that play a major role in the speech communication classroom at the secondary level: discipline, achievement, and attitude.

REFERENCES

"Advice for the Beginning Teacher of Speech: A Symposium." *Speech Teacher* 18 (1969): 259–275.
    Kenner, Freda. "Motivating the Students."
    Metcalf, Marguerite Pearce. "Discipline."
    Mitchell, Wanda B. "Planning the Course."
    Collins, Betty May. "The Use of Audiovisual Aids."
    Weirich, Dorothy Q. "Participating in Community Affairs."

Balcer, Charles L., and Hugh F. Seabury. *Teaching Speech in Today's Secondary Schools*, pp. 221–240. New York: Holt, Rinehart, and Winston, 1965.

Buys, William E., et al. "Speech Communication in the High School Curriculum." *Speech Teacher* 17 (1968): 297–317.

Clark, Richard W., and Oliver W. Nelson. "Standards for Appraising and Building High School Speech Programs." *Speech Teacher* 18 (1969): 181–186.

Cortright, Henrietta H.; Doris S. Niles; and Dorothy Q. Weirich. "Criteria to Evaluate Speech I in the Senior High School." *Speech Teacher* 17 (1968): 217–224.

Klohr, Paul R. "The Resource Unit in Curriculum Reorganization," *National Association of Secondary School Principals Bulletin* 34 (1950): 74–77.

Mitchell, Anne G., and Clinton W. Bradford. "Teaching a Unit on Television in High School." *Speech Teacher* 16 (1967): 200–204.

Robinson, Karl F., and E. J. Kerikas. *Teaching Speech: Methods and Materials.* New York: David McKay, 1963.

Speech Association of America. "Fundamentals of Speech: A Basic Course for High Schools." *Speech Teacher* 8 (1959): 109–113.

Teague, Oran. "Course Planning." In *Speech Methods and Resources: A Textbook for the Teacher of Speech,* edited by Waldo W. Braden, pp. 75–101. New York: Harper & Row, 1961.

SIX

THE DISCIPLINE–ACHIEVEMENT–
MENTAL HEALTH PARADIGM

Many variables operate in the instructional process to determine the outcome of teaching and learning efforts. Among the most important variables with which a teacher ought to be concerned are discipline, achievement, and classroom mental health or attitudes. The best designed course, the clearest, most relevant instructional objectives, and the most valid and reliable measurement instruments may be of little consequence if discipline is lacking or if the students' attitudes toward learning are negative. The teacher who neglects the activity of the student as he attempts to learn and overlooks the attitudes he is forming toward learning fails to influence one of the most salient elements in the learning process. Discipline, achievement, and attitudes—all three are important components of the learning process. Studies the authors have conducted for the past three years in Indiana secondary schools indicate that most of the problems identified by student teachers fall into one of these three categories. Therefore, this chapter focuses on these three factors—factors which operate forcefully in the speech communication classroom in the secondary school.

This chapter relates directly to three parts of the COSEF teaching-learning model—capabilities, objectives, and instructional strategies and skills. If capabilities and objectives are not equivalent, achievement may not result; and if the instructional strategy is wrong, or if elements in the classroom learning situation are negative (dislike of teacher, rejection by

1. Explain the interactive relationships among discipline, achievement, and attitudes.
2. Identify poor disciplinary strategies and effective ones.
3. Identify eight characteristics or principles of effective discipline.
4. Identify and explain the principles suggested for improving achievement.
5. Identify, explain, and differentiate the most common debilitating classroom attitudes.

peers, etc.), then problems in attitudes, achievement, and discipline may result.

AN INTERACTIVE RELATIONSHIP

The student is a learning organism interacting with his environment. He is one system in the learning process. Included in the process are numerous variables that interact with each other to produce favorable or unfavorable results. Such a relationship exists between discipline, achievement, and classroom attitudes. The specific relationship is that good discipline is conducive to achievement and that achievement promotes wholesome attitudes and mental health. In a circular manner, positive attitudes and good classroom mental health operate to produce more achievement and better self-discipline. Thus a positive, spiraling, interactive force can be set in operation so that the positive effects of these three variables combine to produce successful learning outcomes, to make teaching rewarding.

Conversely, the interaction of the three variables may create a downward spiral or negative influence on the learning process. Experienced teachers can cite countless examples of students who could have done well in school if they had developed different attitudes and if they had disciplined themselves to put forth the effort to learn. There are also students who because of low ability, poor instruction, unfair and prejudiced treatment in previous classrooms, a history of failure, or cultural and social deprivation have not achieved in school and have come to believe they cannot achieve. Such students often become discipline problems in the classroom either as troublemakers or as isolates. In addition, some students enter school with negative attitudes toward teachers, school, study, and learning; and some students develop such attitudes as a result of school experiences. Regardless of how such attitudes are acquired, they can cause problems in discipline and achievement.

Attitudes, discipline, achievement—these are three factors the effective teacher cannot ignore. To be an effective manager of a learning system, he must develop skills in analyzing discipline, achievement, and attitudes of the class as a whole as well as of each individual student. The successful teacher learns to influence these factors so that learning is enhanced.

DISCIPLINE

Following are six short essays written by student teachers from two universities. The essays describe high school classrooms in which the students did their student teaching. The descriptions underscore the relationship between discipline and learning.

Example No. 1   I have learned many things about mental health and attitudes in the classroom during my student teaching. On my first day I could see that the kids were operating out of fear and hatred of the teacher. The kids could say very little without being "jumped on," and most would not cooperate with the teacher. One bad thing was the fact that he would talk about the kids even when they could hear him. He would say things such as "They are just a bunch of jerks; I could take those three boys and add their I.Q.'s and not get a hundred; they will never be any good to society. He will be a burden all his life; he's just wasting his time and our time." These types of statements surely affected the attitudes of the students. These kids are down and out anyway, and then their instructor throws the KO punch by branding them no good. Why should they try? And they didn't. There is little anyone can do for these kids now as their minds are already set against education.

Example No. 2   The students were always talking among themselves and usually not about the topic they were to discuss. There was a great deal of kidding the teacher, and he seemed to take this. There seemed to be a "pal" relationship rather than a student-teacher relationship. He seemed afraid to crack down on them. When the classroom became unbearably noisy and he called them down, they merely laughed it off. This classroom seemed more like a three-ring circus than a place where learning could take place. The class's attitude seemed to be one of "We can get away with almost anything," and the teacher's attitude seemed to be, "They are my friends, and I dare not discipline them lest I irritate them."

Example No. 3   The discipline in this class could be termed "loose" since the students did as they pleased. The room was noisy. When the teacher was talking, so were the students—but on a different topic. Paul and John were constantly trying to gain the class's attention—Paul by making funny comments, and John by bragging about how much he drinks and smokes as well as about the number of dirty jokes he knows. In one instance, Paul volunteered his services at the blackboard for the teacher. While the teacher was lecturing, Paul made funny faces and hopped around like he had bugs in his pants. The class roared with laughter causing Paul to continue until the teacher ordered him to sit down. Although he sat down, he did so in such a manner as to make the class giggle. Paul was then told to stand in the corner where he made the class laugh by wiggling his ears. Finally, he was sent from the room. Then the class watched him as he looked through the small window of the closed door. The teacher ignored him and told the class to read the next chapter in the text.

Example No. 4   Most of the pupils in the class I observed were below-average students. The attitude of the majority of the students was, "I don't care" or "I hate this class." The students made little effort to participate in class. Some were withdrawn and others disruptive and noisy. The teacher had stopped trying to get any response from them. One day, when a short quiz was given over a chapter they were to have read, some of the students refused to take the quiz. Others made a feeble effort to answer some questions. Many of the students seemed to be convinced that they were poor students and, therefore, didn't need to try to do well on a quiz. Most of them had given up on themselves in school. They found the class to be a bore and a horror. I could sympathize with their feelings because I saw plainly that little about the class was relevant to their lives.

There were some students who withdrew rather than express themselves. They acted as if they wanted to become invisible, to be ignored. One skinny little girl hardly looked up from her desk top during the hour. She would sit almost the entire hour every day slumped over, staring at her desk top. I never heard her say one word during my stay at the school.

Another student, a boy, sat isolated at the back of the room, huddled against a file cabinet. He often fell asleep and did not awaken until the bell rang signaling the end of the class period.

Another boy was quick to take offense at any kind of reprimand. He seemed to feel that the teacher was against him and that the teacher "picked on him." He made comments such as, "The whole class is talking. Why do I have to be sent out?" or, "How come I can't go to the library? Everybody else is."

In summary, I found the atmosphere of this class terribly depressing. I always felt emotionally exhausted at the end of the hour, whether I was observing or teaching.

Example No. 5   Discipline is hardly a second thought to Mrs. ———— in this class. Although the class is extremely extroverted and quite free, they exercise a great deal of self-control. They know how to accept the responsibility of self-discipline. Self-control is not the only characteristic of this class. Organized activity comprises at least 90 percent of every class period. The students are interested, motivated, involved, and committed. Discipline seems to take care of itself. Mrs. ———— has provided for these students something to interest and motivate them, and the students, appreciating this, maintain their own self-discipline. This is not to say that the situation is ideal every day. Occasionally, someone will step out of line, but then he needs only a gentle reminder, which is what he gets—a firm, but gentle reminder.

How does Mrs. ———— achieve this discipline? Obviously, she puts certain principles into practice. She is sensitive to the student's level of ability and his respective level of achievement. She does not allow a student to sluff off, nor does she expect a student to achieve more than he is capable of achieving. Also, I noticed that she begins with an amount of work which guarantees success and gradually increases the challenge to the students with progressively more difficult activities and objectives. Also, the assignments are clear, simple, and important.

The good mental health of the class is, I feel, a direct result of good discipline and the achievement realized by the students. The self-control and commitment to participation in relevant, organized learning activities in the class are rewarding and reinforcing to the students. They know they can achieve, and they are given an abundance of opportunities to prove it to themselves.

Example No. 6 The discipline used in Mrs. ⸻'s classes was not the formal, strict type usually associated with older women teachers. There was an amazing freedom. Students didn't raise their hands for permission to speak, but there were no "smart remarks" or disruptions in the class either. Each student had so much love and respect for Mrs. ⸻ that he or she behaved well. Mrs. ⸻ told me that she had never had to kick a student out of class.

If someone was not working up to his potential, she would politely take him into the conference room and tell him that she was disappointed.

The students respected her, and she respected each of them. She was able to get everyone involved in her classes. No person was less important or less liked than any other person.

These examples reveal clearly the important relationship between discipline and learning. Discipline is important since no group of people can work together without some degree of order. Good discipline is a way of achieving teamwork toward common goals, and without it, football teams, industrial organizations, and governments cannot function effectively. The same requirement is necessary in order for learning to occur in a speech communication classroom. Students do not learn without purposeful application to the instructional tasks, and teachers cannot teach without the attention and interest of students. The student has to be *willfully involved in what is to be learned* if he is to learn efficiently. Non-participation, tugs-of-war between teacher and student, emotional and intellectual resistance—these relationships are antithetical to good discipline, and such relationships impair achievement. It is not surprising that problems of mental health are associated with undisciplined atmospheres. Good discipline aids achievement; and, equally important, it affects how students feel about themselves, others, and the speech classroom.

Some people view discipline as anathema to good teaching. They believe students should be understood rather than disciplined. Probably those teachers holding such a view have an old-fashioned idea of what discipline is. Perhaps they see discipline in terms of a paddle and the woodshed. In this text, however, discipline is viewed as ordered, motivated *learning*. *Deviancy* is the term used here for overt misbehavior. Deviancy is one type of discipline problem. It occurs when a student behaves in a way that is prohibited by the teacher. Deviancy constitutes a violation of an implicit or explicit set of rules enforced by the teacher. A deviant is any student who breaks one of the understood rules. Deviancies may range from whispering to striking another student, depending on the implicit or explicit modes of behavior established in the classroom.

When overt misbehavior (deviancy) occurs, the teacher may take some action to put an end to it. These actions are referred to herein as *control techniques*, which may be punitive or nonpunitive, verbal or nonverbal, and persuasive or authoritarian. The classmates of the deviant who observe the deviancy and control techniques are called *witnesses*. What is important to note is that this text does not equate all discipline problems with overt misbehavior but reserves the term "deviancy" for that particular type of discipline problem. "Discipline" is a much broader term than deviancy.

Interest, motivation, order—these are the ingredients of discipline. But how does a teacher elicit such behavior from students in the speech class?

POOR DISCIPLINARY STRATEGIES

Based upon observations of both beginning and experienced teachers in more than 120 classrooms which the authors of this text have visited during the past three years, those teachers who were having trouble with discipline—who were having trouble getting students to be interested, motivated, and orderly in their learning efforts—seemed to be using one of two strategies. The two strategies are opposite, and both appear to be unrewarding.

One strategy could be described as a "tempting the students" or "appeasing the students" strategy. Apparently, such teachers believe that if they are liked by the students and do what the students want them to do, the students will respond by being well disciplined. Such teachers, if they are inexperienced, may try to be "one of the kids" and follow the policy of giving the students a lot of freedom. What often happens is that the teacher abandons his leadership position and loses the ability to manage the learning system. Students, who are not trained in the management of learning systems and do not understand the factors involved, assume the decision-making responsibility. Of course, such "jumping through the hoop" by the teachers fails to produce good discipline and wholesome classroom attitudes on the part of the students. As a strategy, it is psychologically and socio-logically unsound, for the roles and relationships that emerge are contradictory to the classroom learning situation.

The other equally ill-fated strategy is the "cram it down their throats" approach. Such classrooms are characterized by deathly quietness, rigid rules, and an atmosphere of fear and hostility. The result of such a strategy can be seen in the negative, hostile attitudes and poor achievement records of students.

If these are the strategies used by many teachers who have discipline problems in their classrooms, what are the strategies used by teachers who manage the discipline variable effectively?

EFFECTIVE DISCIPLINARY STRATEGIES

To manage the discipline element successfully, good teachers apparently apply three general principles. These principles exemplify the philosophy underlying the teacher education program advocated in this book—namely, that what goes on in the classroom is *process* and that such a process or system can be *rationally* described and influenced. The three general principles are: (1) that discipline problems have many causes and therefore require a variety of coping strategies, that it is necessary to have available a number of options or choices rather than to rely on a single, absolute "answer" to all discipline problems; (2) that discipline problems should be analyzed, diagnosed, and predicted; and that coping strategies should be rationally devised and implemented rather than created emotionally and on the spur of the moment to meet emergency situations; (3) that solutions or coping strategies for discipline problems often utilize achievement and attitude-forming events over a long period of time. Let us consider these principles in greater detail.

First Principle: Variety of Coping Strategies   The first principle, that discipline problems result from various causes and therefore call for various solutions, is apparent to most experienced teachers. Either type of discipline problem—the overt, aggressive, disruptive behavior problems or the withdrawn, quiet, nonparticipative problem—can be caused by influences of the group, by factors within the student himself, by factors in the learning system, or by combinations of these factors.

For example, it is a recognized fact that the particular makeup of a group can have a strong influence upon behavior, attitudes, and achievement in the group. Experienced teachers know this from their observations of the different classes they have taught or the different types of schools in which they have taught. The positive or negative influence of the group upon its individual members is recognized as operating in all groups including elementary classrooms, secondary classrooms, college classrooms, and business and industrial groups. A classroom of students from upper- and upper-middle-class families is different from a classroom composed of students from lower-class families; a given proportion of certain types of students in a class can be expected to produce certain influences on learning outcomes and on discipline.

This cause of discipline problems, the influence of the group, is of special significance to the speech teacher since speech classes sometimes fall into one of two extremes: failure-oriented students or success-oriented students. For example, debate classes, drama classes, advanced speech classes, radio and television classes, and other elective classes in speech are often taken by superior students. Achievement, discipline, and attitudes are usually excellent in such classes. On the other hand, in some secondary schools the general speech course is viewed as a dumping ground for problem students and those with low grade-point averages who are failure-oriented. A speech class composed entirely of this kind of student or of a significant number of this kind of student presents special problems in discipline, achievement, and attitudes.

Other discipline problems may be caused by different factors. For some students, the cause lies in themselves and in the experiences they have had in school, rather than in the influence of the group. Such students may be withdrawn and nonparticipative in the learning situation, or they may be overt troublemakers. The important point is that the person who is not interested, not motivated, and who is resisting the procedure that has been devised for learning may be that way for a number of reasons or combinations of reasons; and the successful teacher will recognize that fact and will avoid handling all students and all classes with one absolute, easy-answer approach.

Second and Third Principles: Rational, Long-range Approach The second and third principles of effective discipline are long-range, and they are based on logical analysis and rational understanding rather than on emotional response or habit. A successful teacher knows each of his students and tailors individual programs as necessary. Such a teacher predicts likely trouble situations for certain students and thinks about and devises possible coping strategies *before* the problem occurs rather than falling blindly into an emergency situation. Similarly, such a teacher predicts student-teacher interaction situations and student study situations that might offer opportunities for initiating change in attitudes, awareness of achievement, or perceptions of interpersonal relations. In short, effective teachers view the learning situation as amenable to rational understanding and control, and they view themselves as professional persons who are ever engaged in attempting to understand students and themselves in the teaching-learning situation.

Besides these three general principles for improving discipline, there are some specific characteristics of good discipline.

SPECIFIC CHARACTERISTICS OF GOOD DISCIPLINE

One characteristic of an effective disciplining act is that it fits the offense. If it is either too harsh or too lenient, it is meaningless to the student and ineffective in encouraging self-discipline. Too often, teachers engage in "trigger discipline"—discipline that is administered impulsively or too quickly. Often such discipline is too harsh for the act it seeks to correct. Students are sometimes moving toward self-discipline and need to be reinforced and waited out. When there is evidence that the student is beginning to move toward compliance with instructional and learning procedures, a teacher may do well to not "jump the gun" with quick, harsh punishment.

A second characteristic of effective discipline is that it is not limited to the negative but is largely positive, based on reinforcement and reward of desired attitudes and behavior. As a corrective device, a disciplining act should point toward positive alternatives and expectancies available to the student. If the teacher *must* point out what is wrong, he should at least give *positive suggestions as to what is right*. Negative discipline (no's, stop's, and don'ts) leads ultimately to punitive action, and—although punishment has its place at times—when it is overused it stops the student in his tracks and allows him no freedom to work out his own attitudes and self-discipline. On the other hand, positively directed discipline, based on reward and reinforcement, specifies what is acceptable and allows the student to make choices for which he will be rewarded.

A third characteristic of effective discipline is that the specific problem is not generalized to the entire student. Often teachers who have difficulty with a student generalize the discipline problem to the student's personality, intelligence, social desirability, etc. They see the student as "dumb," "hard-headed," and "no good." Such attitudes are communicated by the teacher to the student and result in a teacher-student relationship that is not conducive to learning. Teachers can settle too early on a student's shortcomings and overgeneralize to his whole personality rather than keeping within the confines of the discipline problem at hand. Self-defeating overgeneralizing occurs when a teacher takes students' mischief too seriously and acts on the basis that the slightest deviation calls for immediate and complete correction.

A fourth characteristic of effective discipline is that it does not mix education with corrective measures. For example, it is unfortunate that students are sometimes made to study as a form of punishment. Such a procedure negates both the studying and the punishment, and becomes self-defeating. When a student is kept after school and made to study as a penalty for misbehavior, studying is associated with punishment. The success of teaching and learning rests on the assumption that study and teaching-learning strategies *will not be viewed as punishment!*

A fifth characteristic of good discipline is that it does not rely on a plethora of minute corrections but has a limited number of goals toward which the strategy for improving the student's self-discipline is aimed. Some teachers become lost in trivialities. They fill each hour with complaints, pleas, and reprimands; they gripe and ridicule students for a hundred reasons. It is always possible for the teacher to pick out minutiae to hold up for ridicule, but such criticism has little corrective effect, and probably confuses and angers the student. Teachers do well to consider the frequency and importance of disciplinary comments.

Another characteristic of good discipline is that it is consistent. Nothing can undermine the influence of the teacher so much as inconsistent, wishy-washy policies in the classroom. Whether they be instructional policies or disciplinary policies, they must be followed consistently and purposefully if integrity and trust are to be developed.

A seventh characteristic of good discipline is that it is based on reward rather than fear. "Breaking students down," "getting the truth out of them," and "getting them to confess" involve the use of fear, which is a poor disciplinarian. Threats and coercion do not foster self-discipline. If students behaved only out of fear, we would be poor teachers indeed. But when a teacher knows where each student and the class stand in relation to an ideal standard of self-discipline, then he can reinforce progress toward that ideal. The teacher who develops such a skill will find teaching rewarding.

Finally, teachers who cope successfully with discipline problems put into practice the principle that first impressions and first contacts are the most lasting. The first meeting of the class and the subsequent early meetings are of extreme importance because during these first meetings expectancies and relationships are established that will be difficult to change. Successful teachers make their first contacts with students as effective as possible. Many student teachers and beginning teachers are so concerned with being friendly that they overdo it and unintentionally communicate an unspoken message that they can be taken advantage of. Moreover, their behavior— i.e., their reasoning, explaining, cajoling, and giving in to students on items of conduct or learning procedures—sometimes communicates a go-ahead for the students to take over. Unfortunately, first impressions and initial policies and practices are difficult to change. The teacher who starts too loose and finds that he needs to tighten the reins is often in for a difficult time.

These are general principles regarding discipline that effective teachers seem to use. However, deviancy and experimental research findings on control techniques must also be considered.

CONTROL TECHNIQUES:
FINDINGS OF EXPERIMENTAL AND DESCRIPTIVE RESEARCH

The following identification and summary of the findings of experimental and descriptive research has been provided by Gnagey (1965). He lists the findings in the following concise form:

Control techniques to *strengthen self-control*
1. Signaling with finger on the lips, frowning, or shaking the head
2. Moving nearer the noisy student
3. Using humor to indicate that a minor deviancy is or has occurred
4. Diverting attention from deviancy to the planned learning activity
5. Ignoring the minor deviancy for a moment when the teacher believes it will cease by itself

Control techniques to *reduce frustration*
1. "Hurdle help" may be used, i.e., the teacher may spend time with the individual student, the deviant, to help him overcome a learning problem he could not overcome on his own
2. Restructuring a learning activity which appears to be frustrating the entire class and causing deviant behavior
3. Removing temptations to deviancy
4. Establishing routines
5. Using physical restraint (in rare instances)
6. Previewing deviancy-causing situations

Control techniques that *appeal to understanding and reason*
1. "Reason with power" refers to the technique of appealing to the students' understanding by pointing out an inherent harm that will come to them naturally (not from the teacher or the administration, but from nature) as a result of the deviancy
2. "Power with cushion" refers to calling attention to the fact that the class must return to proper behavior while at the same time stating that the teacher understands why they are excited or why the deviancy is occurring
3. "Postmortem" is the discussing with the class a deviancy of yesterday

General findings related to deviant behavior and control techniques

1. Control techniques have a ripple effect, i.e., when a teacher deals with the deviancy of one student, he is dealing with the entire class by proxy. The effects of a control technique spread out from the deviant in concentric wavelets of influence on the witnesses.
2. Highly emotional threats, as control techniques, produce much distracting behavior—disruption among witnesses—and tend to increase, rather than lower, the later number of deviancies by witnesses. Moreover, such control techniques appear to lower the students' estimation of the teacher's helpfulness, likeability, and fairness.
3. Clarity with regard to the desired behavior in which the deviant is to engage, as well as which deviant behavior is to cease, more effectively halts the occurring deviancy while decreasing deviancy generally through the ripple effect. In other words, rather than say, "Hey! Stop that!" it is better to say, "John, stop tapping your desk and get busy on your speech outline."
4. Firmness (not excessive roughness or threats) is effective in increasing the conformance of both the deviant and the witnesses. A serious, businesslike tone of voice, or walking nearer the deviant, or any other communication that indicates clearly that the teacher means it, is preferable to bland suggestions or pleas for conformance. The "I wish" and "Will you please" phrases do not always have good effects.
5. The "focus on the task" technique means that, rather than contingent teacher approval, task completion should be the aim of requests for conforming behavior.

Findings related to the ripple effect of control techniques

1. Witnesses who see a deviant submit to a teacher's control technique rate the teacher as "more capable of handling kids" than when the deviant responds in a defiant manner.
2. Research findings indicate that more learning occurs when deviants submit than when they respond defiantly to control techniques.
3. The general feelings of the witnesses tend to parallel those acted out by the deviant.
4. The influence of the deviant on witnesses is greater if his classmates hold him in high regard. This finding suggests that class leaders should be identified and control techniques should be developed that will cause these leaders to desist from deviancy.

Findings related to the effects of punishment[1]

1. Punishment may suppress deviant behavior, but it does not erase the bad habit. Substitute teachers dread teaching a class that has been controlled almost exclusively by fear of punishment because, in the absence of the dispenser of punishment, deviant behaviors reappear.
2. When punishment is necessary to eliminate a major and serious deviancy, it should be followed by a correct alternative behavior which is performed by the student and reinforced.
3. There appear to be harmful side effects from punishment. Studies indicate strongly that organisms learn to fear the people and objects that are close to them when they are punished. Repeated severe punishment may cause students to learn to react with fear to the teacher, the classroom, the text, the speaking situation, and school in general. This reaction may be generalized to other teachers and other classes. Thus, punishment can be a very costly method for suppressing deviant behavior.

ACHIEVEMENT

Achievement is facilitated by good discipline, and good discipline is facilitated by achievement. Conversely, poor discipline often is related to failure or lack of achievement. Sometimes the most rewarding approach for developing self-discipline is to concentrate on achievement.

Failure in a success-oriented culture is hard to take, and yet students are failing in school at an alarming rate. Nearly 40 percent of those who begin high school—and one in three of those who begin college—drop out before they finish. Many other students fail in fact, if not in recorded grades. They are graduated from the secondary school only because teachers give them a passing grade and push them out of their classes, whether they know anything or not. One suspects that if valid and reliable tests were given at

[1]There is a difference between withholding gratification and inflicting punishment. To withhold privileges from a student differs qualitatively from being purposely embarrassed in front of his peers. Punishment refers to inflicting pain or discomfort on a student. Punishment is retributive. When fear of experiencing pain, discomfort, or unpleasantness becomes the major reason for avoiding a deviancy, the control technique may be termed punishment.

the conclusion of courses to determine whether or not students could be promoted to the next course, many classrooms would bulge with students who could not pass the tests. Many of these students have been turned off by school because they have not achieved, a condition stemming from and resulting in poor classroom attitudes and discipline problems.

Why do students fail to achieve? In many instances it is because they are fearful, bored, confused, or are provided with no productive way to achieve.

Early in school students learn that one must not fail, and they develop an anxiety in this regard. They are afraid of disappointing the many anxious adults around them, whose hopes and expectations hang over their heads like a cloud.

Students are bored because the tasks they are assigned in the classroom are trivial, dull, irrelevant, and demand little of their intelligence and capabilities. They are confused because much of what they read or hear is shallow and makes little sense. Sometimes it contradicts other things they have been told, and it is seldom related to the model of reality they carry with them. In short, poor teaching or poor management of the learning system produces failure, and effective teaching facilitates achievement.

What are the characteristics of effective teaching? The teaching-learning model on which this book is based identifies some of these; however, in this chapter further specific suggestions for fostering achievement are given.

Perhaps the first task for the teacher who has a poorly disciplined nonachiever is to discover what level of achievement can be expected from him in relation to his ability. Chapter 3 was devoted entirely to this objective. Both the student whose achievement is far below his ability and the student whose achievement goals are far above his ability are likely to develop bad attitudes and poor discipline. The most desirable goal in terms of achievement and ability is that the student's level of achievement be equal to his ability. Some students need to be challenged with more meaningful material and more sophisticated learning objectives, and others need to be presented with educational tasks of a much lower level.

A second suggestion for fostering achievement is to begin with small amounts of work and with objectives that the student can complete satisfactorily, and then to reinforce his success. It is necessary to insist that the work be completed; otherwise, no opportunity for using positive reinforcement exists. Once the student is achieving in this modest way, keep presenting work to establish a pattern of successful completion. Thus a success pattern of self-discipline and achievement can be formed. Each student is continually forming habits in the classroom that contribute either to achievement or failure with respect to his work. As a teacher you can help him develop a success pattern in your classroom.

A third suggestion for aiding achievement is to clarify and make efficient the stimulus for learning. There are several methods you can use to help simplify the learning achievement. For one thing, avoid confronting the student with indistinguishable masses of information. Rather, *plan* and *organize* lessons or instructional strategies and objectives so that what is to be learned and how it is to be learned are clear and manageable. Some students lack selective power. They are too easily diverted to thoughts of tonight's party or the ball game this Friday. They are not open to the learning stimulus. Therefore, the effective teacher establishes set, makes the stimulus presentation attractive and powerful, and keeps the material organized and vivid. Preparation is important. Get the student's attention and present what is to be learned clearly and efficiently.

A fourth suggestion is to screen out interference by preguessing distractions and eliminating them. When students are not attending to the matter at hand, they are doing something else. Milling about, walking around, talking to their neighbors at will—all these work against effective study and learning. Freedom in the classroom has gone too far when students spend a large part of their time in nonproductive activity. Some classrooms become social groups rather than learning groups, and little achievement results. Such distractions, even if created by a few students, can militate against achievement by the rest of the students. Whatever the type of distraction, be it mental wandering or physical activity in the classroom, if it can be controlled or screened out, achievement will be aided.

If clear goals, expectations, and orderly teaching and learning procedures are established; if fear and boredom are replaced with curiosity and interest; if achievement expectancies are matched with abilities; if the student sees what is to be learned as worthwhile and important so that he establishes a pattern of self-discipline and success; and if the learning environment is kept clear, efficient, and free of distractions, then achievement will result. Furthermore, the interactive effect upon discipline and classroom attitudes will be positive.

CLASSROOM ATTITUDES

Among the important variables in the learning system are the attitudes and feelings of the learner. Unwholesome and negative attitudes can affect achievement and discipline adversely; thus the effective teacher is concerned with classroom attitudes.

Classroom attitudes are the emotional and social adjustment of the student to instruction and learning in the classroom situation. They denote how the student feels about himself and his relationship to other students, the teacher, and things outside himself. It would be possible to write an entire book on emotional, social, and attitudinal blocks to effective learning; however, only a few of the most common types of problems are presented in this chapter as examples. In many instances, the discovery and awareness of the problem on the part of the teacher will bring him new understanding, which will influence instructional strategies as well as the interpersonal relationships between him and students. Chapters 8 and 9 deal specifically with ways to acquire information about the behavior, feelings, and relationships existing in the speech communication classroom.

One unfortunate attitude in the classroom is that school is not to be taken seriously, that actually one does not have to work or learn anything. Rather, school is a fascinating game of pretending to learn, and one might just as well recognize that fact and play the game according to those rules. Besides, there is not much that is worth learning. Such an attitude is likely to be held by the class as a whole except for the unusual, highly motivated, learning-oriented students.

The blame for the development of such a debilitating attitude can be placed for the most part on the teacher and on previous teachers who have not managed the learning system well. They, too, may take school so lightly and place so little importance on it that they take the easy way out and do not actually teach. They may assume that because learning tasks and materials are presented, learning occurs. Perhaps, because of oversize classes and pressing schedules, the teacher does not take the time to specify instructional objectives, to accurately measure day by day and unit by unit what the student has learned, and to feedback to the student his progress so that he will be aware of learning and thus be reinforced for his appropriate learning behavior. Instead, there are endless, meaningless activities.

Students observe such looseness, and because they lack the maturity to see the ineffectiveness of such classroom procedure, they believe they are simply putting something over on the teacher by not learning. The rule for playing the game is to pretend you are learning, do what you are forced to do, get away with as much as you can, and have as good a time in this activity hour as you can. Such attitudes constitute poor classroom mental health, and if they are not modified, they give rise to social and emotional problems. Looseness in the expectations expressed to students and in instructional strategies eventuates in poor achievement, poor attitudes, and discipline problems. Students are skillful in avoiding responsibility, and they look upon such maneuverings as fun. The effective teacher understands that wholesome attitudes toward learning are important, and he manages the entire learning system in order to foster appropriate attitudes.

Another debilitating attitude is fear. Some teachers rely on fear to motivate students to study and learn, although it is generally agreed that fear is not a wholesome attitude for learning. For some students in the secondary school speech classroom, fear is a block to learning cognitive material, and it is a major block to learning effective communication behavior. Anxiety levels can be raised to such a state that learning is impossible. One way to reduce tension is to be aware of it. The teacher must learn to set limits on the amount of tension under which a particular student, or the class in general, is placed. If he does not, the students will set their own limits by not paying attention, by playing around, or by withdrawing from the learning procedure in other ways. Instructional objectives must be within the limits of the student's abilities, and the student needs to believe he can reach them—that he can learn—rather than fear that he will be wrong, that he will fail again. Students ought to have the freedom and right to "fail," to repeat, to go back through the strategy, to request further explanation, or to be rerouted through new strategies.

Closely related to fear is the attitude "I am dumb, I am a failure." Many students do "die at an early age." Kozol (1967) has recorded accurately that some students develop self-concepts that are unfavorable almost to the point of self-contempt and self-hatred. Not infrequently, such students are advised to enroll in speech and are found in the speech communication classroom. For many of these students, their history in school is one of failure, incompetence, and worthlessness as recorded in the formal and informal judgments of peers and teachers. It is little wonder that such students often drop out of school.

The teacher who finds a student with such attitudes in the speech class must be aware of those attitudes, understand them, and devise strategies for best coping with the situation. Few persons start off stupid. Babies, except for the most grossly retarded, demonstrate an amazing ability and desire to learn. They learn an immense amount in the first three to four years. What happens to this positive and wholesome attitude toward learning and intellectual growth? In some students it is destroyed by the education process. It can be destroyed by making students afraid—afraid of not pleasing, of making mistakes, of failing, of being wrong. These students become afraid to gamble, to experiment, to try the difficult. The resulting deterioration in self-concept constitutes a major force that operates to inhibit learning.

In few classes is the instructional strategy more involved with the total person than in the speech class. When one engages in interpersonal communication or speaks before an audience, he puts almost his whole self on display. Listeners, consciously and unconsciously, form attitudes and evaluate the speaker; and the awareness of this—and of the consequences—strike fear into the hearts of many novice communicators. Social fear and speech anxiety in the communication situation are opposites to confidence and poise. Many students enter the speech class with a relatively high degree of anxiety in regard to giving a public speech and participating in inter-personal communication situations. The effective speech teacher is able to capitalize on successes, to focus concern on the development and acquisition of speech-making skills, and to reinforce learning efforts so that speech anxiety decreases. The goal is *not* to emphasize concern with speech anxiety. Students should be rewarded and reinforced for meeting the instructional objectives that have been specified.

Whether or not the typical speech class can solve all students' speech anxiety problems is highly questionable (Brooks and Platz, 1968, pp. 44–49; Giffin and Gilham 1968, pp. 70–73). Even though students learn to feel secure in the speech class while engaging in communication activities, they often discover that the newly found confidence does not transfer in a one-to-one manner to communication situations outside the classroom. Probably more experience in diverse communication situations and environments is needed to reduce speech anxiety across situations; and perhaps, for some students, special theraputic sessions are necessary to significantly modify deeply rooted social fears (Griffin, 1968). The point is that putting oneself on display in communication activities can be an acute, fear-producing event for some students in the speech class, and it is possible for an insensitive teacher to increase the anxiety rather than decrease it. As far as possible, however, the effective teacher devises strategies to remove pressure and to enable the student to increase his ability to live and cope with speech anxiety.

These are only selected examples of mental health problems in the class-room. There are other social, emotional, and attitudinal problems that a given student or class may have. The effective teacher is aware of the role that social relationships, emotional feelings, and attitudes can play in the learning situation. He uses metacommunication and systematic observation to assess the situation in his classroom; and he devises means of coping with the discipline, mental health, and achievement factors in the learning system.

SUMMARY

This chapter has focused on an often neglected area—the effect of discipline, achievement, and attitudes on learning—which the teacher ought to include in his instructional planning. The main point is that these three factors are *interactive;* one can probably deal most effectively with any one of the three by concentrating on *all* three. Careful study of the particular student or class may indicate where the spiral can best be broken and where influence should be exerted to begin motion in another direction.

It has been suggested in this chapter that good discipline is not solely a matter of punishment. Instead it involves establishing clear educational and behavioral objectives, informing the student what the objectives are, and telling him how he can attain them. The chapter has emphasized the development of a structure or system conducive to learning, achieving, and wholesome attitudes. Good discipline is systematic, ordered learning, which promotes achievement and social and emotional growth. Good discipline in a classroom fosters the development of self-discipline generally; and self-discipline contributes to self-assurance and positive attitudes—in short, wholesome mental health.

Emphasis has been placed on the fact that teachers should be more analytical and *more deliberate* in their dealings with the average student and the problem student. Where problems in conduct, achievement, or mental health exist, teachers who are willing to try considered, new approaches are more likely to solve them. Students who cannot concentrate, who will not study, who play all the time, who will not cooperate, who are withdrawn, or who continually cause trouble do so for various reasons. No one thing is wrong with all of them. The effective teacher views teaching-learning as a process and looks for salient factors in the system which are amenable to influence. Such an approach helps make teaching successful and rewarding.

Good discipline is essential to accomplishment and mental health. Mental health is enhanced by the student's forming a realistic good opinion of himself, which he does by successfully meeting reasonable expectations commensurate with his abilities, expectations which he perceives as relevant and important to his living.

REFERENCES

Brooks, William D., and Sara J. Platz. "The Effect of Speech Training upon Self-concept as a Communicator." *Speech Teacher* 27 (1968): 44–49.

Giffin, Kim, and Shirley Masterson Gilham. "Relationships Between Speech Anxiety and Motivation." *Speech Monographs* 38 (1971): 70–73.

Gnagey, William J. *Controlling Classroom Misbehavior.* No. 32 in the *What Research Says to the Teacher* series. Washington, D. C.: National Education Association, 1965.

Kozol, Jonathan. *Death at an Early Age.* Boston: Houghton Mifflin, 1967.

PART TWO   **THE INSTRUCTIONAL PROCESS:**
                    EVALUATION AND FEEDBACK

Chapter 1 developed the idea that teaching-learning is a complex process that requires a systems approach. Two important elements in that approach, evaluation and feedback, are the remaining two variables in the COSEF model and the focus of Part Two. Chapters 7 and 8 discuss two interrelated aspects of evaluation. Chapter 7 is a general discussion of evaluating, grading, and reporting speech communication performances, while Chapter 8 provides in-depth treatment of testing and evaluating student knowledge and skills by means of teacher-made tests. Many topics mentioned in Chapter 7 are developed more thoroughly in Chapter 8. Chapters 9 and 10 develop two approaches to monitoring teacher-student behavior in the speech communication classroom. Chapter 9 describes metacommunication as a tool which the speech communication teacher can use to foster learning, and Chapter 10 describes systematic observation as a useful method of monitoring behavior in the classroom.

SEVEN

EVALUATING, GRADING,
AND REPORTING
SPEECH PERFORMANCES

EVALUATING

Probably nothing has frustrated beginning teachers of speech communication more than the necessity of evaluating speech communication performances of students. While there is an abundance of theoretical literature on the subject, little evidence exists that one approach is more effective than another in achieving the major goal of such evaluation—the improvement of students' communicative ability. Consequently, although this text makes specific suggestions on the evaluation of speech communication performances, each teacher must *test* the effectiveness of any approach he decides to use.

Because the test of any evaluative approach is the improvement of students' communicative ability, the first problem facing the evaluator is formulating the standards for evaluation in terms which students understand. This requires, as emphasized in Chapter 2, that a teacher state his objectives in behavioral terms.

Once the teacher has defined behaviorally the skills which he wishes his students to acquire, the question becomes one of deciding how best to help students achieve them. The teacher has three major types of evaluation to choose from: teacher evaluation, peer evaluation, and self-evaluation. All three types can take either an oral or written form and be handled in a variety of ways. Written evaluations may be recorded on blank sheets of paper, on checklists, or on rating scales. Oral evaluation may occur at various

OBJECTIVES

1. Describe a rationale for evaluating speech communication performances.
2. List three major types of evaluation and specify potential instructional uses for each.
3. Describe a rationale for grading.
4. Specify a method of making grading meaningful.
5. Describe two methods of reporting grades.
6. List eight guidelines for parent-teacher conferences.

times during the class period (immediately following a student's performance, after several students' performances, during the last ten to fifteen minutes of the class period), or in a private, personal conference outside the classroom setting. Since there is no empirical basis for choosing one form of evaluation over the other, the wise instructor of speech communication will try a variety of approaches to determine which one best increases student communicative ability. Below are a number of specific guidelines for using various types of evaluation.

TEACHER EVALUATION

If evaluation is to be meaningful and useful, it is important that students understand the rationale for it. As stated earlier, the purpose of evaluation is to improve student communicative ability. Evaluation is not a destructive, tearing-down process. When communicating this fact to students, consider using the word "evaluation" rather than "criticism." To many people the word "criticism" implies a destructive process.

Use a variety of approaches. When engaging in evaluation, don't rely on just one method of oral evaluation or one method of written evaluation. Use writtten evaluations to reinforce and supplement oral evaluations. Vary the use of blank sheets of paper, checklists, and rating scales. For one assignment conduct the oral evaluations immediately following each student's performance; for the next assignment conduct them during the last ten to fifteen minutes of the class. Remember that there is no one method of evaluation that will always work best to increase student communicative ability.

Concentrate evaluation on a limited number of important areas.   Avoid the tendency to overemphasize minor, easily detectable aspects of communication performance. While it may be easier for you to comment on aspects of delivery such as eye contact and posture, it will probably benefit the student more if you concentrate on such areas as content, organization, and language. Students will judge what you consider important by what you select to evaluate.

Allow adequate time for evaluation.   If you are rushed, you will tend to overemphasize minor, easily detectable points; you will be unable to focus on the important aspects of communication performances. Evaluation can make its maximum contribution toward improving student communicative ability only if you allow yourself adequate time.

Individualize your evaluation.   Students are individuals and respond differently to different approaches. While one student may respond well to sarcasm, another may tearfully leave the room. It is therefore important that you study the student you are evaluating and adapt your evaluation to him. Avoid repeating the same advice to everyone.

When using oral evaluation, focus on the positive.   In evaluating any speech communication performance, it is possible for you to locate something that was done well. By pointing to the positive you can aid both the class and the individual student involved. Suggestions for individual improvement can be handled best through written evaluation. In following this guideline, however, be aware of the student's ability to recognize the shallow, obvious, or manufactured compliment. It is an embarrassment to the student in question and an insult to the intelligence of the class as a whole.

When engaging in oral evaluation, strive to be a model of the effective communicator.   Nothing is more counterproductive than a teacher who exhibits the precise behavior he is seeking to help the student modify.

Avoid prescriptions.   As a general rule, you should be more concerned with raising questions and issues about the communication performance than with supplying prescriptions. Prescriptions frequently hinder comunication effectiveness rather than aid it.

Develop a language that is precise and unambiguous.   Nothing is more frustrating for the student than being unable to decipher what the evaluator is saying. Constantly be on the alert for feedback about the messages you are sending.

As frequently as feasible, have private conferences with your students.
Many of the aims of evaluation can best be achieved in a private, one-to-one setting.

PEER EVALUATION

Training is necessary.   An essential prerequisite to peer evaluation is that students be taught criteria by which to evaluate the communication of their peers. Without such training, peer evaluation not only is unproductive but can actually be counterproductive to the goals of evaluation.

Use a variety of approaches.   Some of the possibilities that the authors have found useful are:

1. During the last ten to fifteen minutes of the class period, moderate (or appoint a student to do so) a discussion of the student performances that day.
2. Select a panel of evaluators to discuss communication performances during the latter part of the class period.
3. Assign specific persons to evaluate specific aspects of the communication performances such as content, organization, and language.
4. Appoint one student evaluator for each student performer in advance of a communication performance.
5. Ask students who are not performing to evaluate those who are, using a blank sheet of paper or rating form. The evaluations may or may not be signed and may or may not be seen by the teacher.
6. Assign evaluators to focus on the audience during the communication performance for overt signs of interest, concern, agreement, etc.

SELF-EVALUATION

Training is necessary.   As with peer evaluation, in self-evaluation it is important that the student first learn criteria by which to evaluate his performance. Without this training period, self-evaluation can be very destructive.

Use several different approaches.   Some useful approaches when using the self-evaluation method are:

1. Ask the student to write down his reaction to his communication performance. Some questions he might ask himself are: What went well? What would I now do differently? What reactions of others did I observe?
2. Schedule personal conferences with each student and ask him to assess his strengths and weaknesses as a communicator.
3. Video-tape or audio-tape the student's communication performance and allow him to view and evaluate it.

GRADING

In a society that places increasing emphasis on educational progress, grades have become the basis for crucial decisions about the educational and occupational destiny of the student. As DeCecco (1968, pp. 646–647) points out: The student uses grades to appraise his own educational accomplishments, to select major and minor areas of study, and to decide whether to terminate or to continue his formal education. Teachers and counselors use grades to assess past accomplishments, to assess present ability, and to help the student make educational and vocational plans for the future. Parents use marks to determine which of their children they should send to college and to estimate the probability of success any one child might have in advanced study and particular vocations. School and college administrators use grades as the basis for admission to advanced study and as indications of the student's progress after admission. And employers use grades in selecting the applicant most likely to perform best the service they require. Thus, despite the rather obvious limitations of validity, reliability, and interpretation, reforms advocating the elimination or change of the grading system have had only temporary appeal. It is almost certain, therefore, that you will be required to grade your students.

A grade should be based on the student's achievement of the instructional objectives—it should indicate how well he achieved the terminal performances described in the objectives. Unfortunately, not all teachers use achievement of objectives as the exclusive basis for grading. Many base grades on such factors as the student's attitude, amount of effort, or how much he has progressed—even though the achievement falls short of that required by the instructional objective. This is unfortunate because such grades are based on highly subjective judgments and are ambiguous. They provide no real basis for making important educational decisions.

One approach that you can use to ensure that grades are meaningful has been proposed by Travers (1950, p. 58). He suggests that the grade of A means that all major and minor goals are achieved; B, that all major goals were achieved but *some* minor ones were not; C, that all major goals were achieved but *many* minor ones were not; D, that a few major goals were achieved but that the student is not prepared for advanced work; and E or F, that none of the major goals was achieved. Oliver (1960, pp. 9–10) reports a rough attempt at Pennsylvania State University to operationalize the criteria for the grading of a public speech:

I. Normally, an "average" speech (C) should meet the following standards:
   A. Conform to type assigned (expository, persuasive, etc.)
   B. Conform reasonably to the time limit
   C. Exhibit sound organization; a clear purpose supported adequately by main ideas that are easily identified
   D. Fulfill any special requirements of the assignment such as: to use three illustrations, or statistics, or authority
   E. Be intellectually sound in developing a topic of worth and adequate and dependable evidence
   F. Exhibit reasonable directness and communicativeness in delivery
   G. Be correct grammatically and in pronunciation and articulation
   H. Be ready for presentation on date assigned

II. The "better than average" speech (B) should meet the foregoing tests and also:
   A. Contain elements of vividness and special interest in style
   B. Be sure of more than average stimulative quality in challenging the audience to think or in arousing depth of response
   C. Demonstrate skill in winning understanding of unusually difficult concepts or process; or in winning agreement from

   auditors initially inclined to disagree with the speaker's purpose
   D. Establish rapport of a high order through style and delivery which achieve a genuinely communicative circular response.

III. The "superior" speech (A) not only meets the foregoing standards but also:
   A. Constitutes a genuinely individual contribution by the speaker to the thinking of the audience
   B. Achieves a variety and flexibility of mood and manner suited to the multiple differentiation of thinking and feeling demanded by the subject matter and by the speaker-audience relations
   C. Achieves a demonstrable progression from the initial uncertainty [of knowledge or belief] held by the audience toward the subject and, by orderly processes, toward a final resolution of the uncertainty in a conclusion that evolves naturally from the materials used by the speaker
   D. Illustrates skillful mastery of internal transactions and of emphasis in presentation of the speaker's ideas

IV. Speeches which must be classified as "below average" (D or F) are deficient in some or several of the factors required of the "C" speech.

REPORTING

The most widespread method of reporting grades is the report card. On it the teacher is usually required to record grades and also to mark check lists of such items as effort, conduct, homework, and social development. Schools often use parent-teacher conferences to supplement the report card. In these conferences the teacher can provide fuller descriptions of the student's scholastic and social development, and parents have an opportunity to ask questions. In addition, there is an opportunity for parents and teacher to plan together what they might do to assist the student's educational development. Fessenden et al. (1968, p. 278) make a number of useful suggestions for the successful conduct of such a conference:

   1. Try to put the other person at ease. Most parents feel uncertain and sometimes "inwardly disturbed" at the prospect of a conference with teacher. Above all, do not be condescending. Seek

a common level, a level of mutual respect, that will encourage frank response and a feeling of confidence.

2. Maintain, insofar as possible, a positive approach. In discussing a pupil's achievement, for example, stress first those aspects of the child's behavior that are commendable. What does he do well? What worthy interests is he developing? This constructive method or approach in "drawing the total picture" of pupil behavior pays dividends in terms of amicable relations and cooperative response.

3. Negative aspects are not to be ignored, but they are to be placed in perspective. They can often be brought to the fore by questions about out-of-school attitudes or about the parent's own assessment of the child's needs rather than by blunt statements that are likely to produce argument and hostility.

4. Be cautious in rendering "final" judgments. You accomplish nothing by being dogmatic, by telling the parents "what has to be done." The same principle applies here that applies in pupil counseling conferences. Listen more than you talk. Try to draw out by appropriate questions the parent's own ideas. Often, the solution or the action which you would like to suggest will automatically evolve without urging or dictation from you.

5. Guide the conference as skillfully as possible to prevent too much digression. There may be a temptation to "get off the track" and talk about dozens of interesting but doubtfully relevant experiences. Only as such experiences contribute to a better understanding of environmental influences and possible causative factors is the conference objective being served.

6. Keep note-taking to a minimum. Writing things down has an inhibitory effect on the free flow of ideas. Some parents become unduly suspicious, and the conference (in their minds) begins to resemble an inquisition rather than a friendly discussion.

7. Avoid being argumentative. Debate simply emphasizes differences. It is much more important to find points of agreement and establish grounds for common understanding.

8. Be terminal. Find a tactful way to bring the conference to a conclusion after an appropriate length of time. In most cases, fifteen to twenty minutes will suffice to accomplish what can be accomplished in an initial session. If in your opinion, a follow-up conference would be desirable, it should be arranged by mutual agreement—with some explanation of the reasons for "keeping in touch."

SUMMARY

This chapter has focused on evaluating, grading, and reporting speech communication performances in the classroom setting. It was suggested that the goal of evaluation—improving students' speech communicative ability—can best be achieved by testing a variety of approaches to evaluation. Next, since grades play such an important role in our society, it was argued that the speech communication teacher needs to make sure that they are meaningful by basing them solely on the achievement of instructional objectives. Finally, two methods of reporting grades—the report card and parent-teacher conferences—were discussed. In the next chapter we turn to a consideration of teacher-made tests—their role, construction, and use.

REFERENCES

Baker, Eldon E. "Aligning Speech Evaluation and Behavioral Objectives." *Speech Teacher* 16 (1967): 158–160.

Balcer, Charles L., and Hugh F. Seabury. *Teaching Speech in Today's Secondary Schools*, pp. 241–268. New York: Holt, Rinehart and Winston, 1965.

Barker, Larry L. "The Relationship between Sociometric Choice and Speech Evaluation." *Speech Teacher* 18 (1969): 204–207.

Bostrom, Robert N. "The Problem of Grading," *Speech Teacher* 17 (1968): 287–292.

Braden, Waldo W. "Teaching Through Criticism." In *Speech Methods and Resources: A Textbook for the Teacher of Speech*, edited by Waldo W. Braden, pp. 398–410. New York: Harper & Row, 1961.

DeCecco, John P. *The Psychology of Learning and Instruction: Educational Psychology*, pp. 646–653. Englewood Cliffs, N. J.: Prentice-Hall, 1968.

Dedmon, Donald N. "Criticizing Student Speeches: Philosophy and Principles." *Central States Speech Journal* 17 (1967): 276–284.

Fessenden, Seth A., et al. *Speech for the Creative Teacher*, pp. 275–282. Dubuque, Iowa: Wm. C. Brown, 1968.

Gruner, Charles R. "Behavioral Objectives for the Grading of Classroom Speeches." *Speech Teacher* 17 (1968): 207–209.

Holtzman, Paul D. "Speech Criticism and Evaluation Communication." *Speech Teacher* 9 (1960): 1–7.

Montgomery, Keith E. "How to Criticize Student Speeches." *Speech Teacher* 6 (1957): 200–204.

Oliver, Robert T. "The Eternal (and Infernal) Problem of Grades." *Speech Teacher* 9 (1960): 9–10.

Travers, R. M. W. *How to Make Achievement Tests.* New York: Odyssey Press, 1950.

White, Eugene F. "A Rationale for Grades." *Speech Teacher* 16 (1967): 247–252.

EIGHT

TEACHER–MADE TESTS

Military organizations, industrial organizations, and the professions have come to accept testing and evaluation as a way of life. Positions are offered and promotions granted on the basis of tests and evaluations. Of course, testing and evaluation are even more integral to education. So important are testing and evaluation to learning that when evaluation is inaccurate or absent, the effects upon the entire instructional system and upon learning outcomes are disastrous.

For this reason, evaluation is included as a major component of the teaching-learning process and as such is represented in the model of the instructional system presented in this text. The assessment of student achievement in the speech communication class is a major responsibility of the teacher. It is ironic that some speech teachers stress audience contact, the circular response, and the importance of feedback, and then provide no objective, valid feedback in terms of assessment of speech communication performance and knowledge. It is important that constructive, valid evaluation be *fed back* to the student so that he knows *what* and *how* to improve.

It is not adequate for teachers to guess at learning outcomes or to

1. Define and differentiate test, measurement, and evaluation.
2. Explain the five functions of teacher-made tests.
3. Identify and explain the types of educational tests.
4. Identify the characteristics of a good test.
5. Identify and explain the most commonly used procedures for determining test validity and reliability.
6. Compare and contrast objective and essay tests.
7. Explain the function of a test blueprint.
8. State the eight general principles for constructing teacher-made objective tests.
9. State the guidelines for writing multiple-choice test items, true-false test items, and short-answer or completion test items.
10. State the guidelines for writing essay test items.
11. State the guidelines for scoring objective tests and essay tests.
12. Identify and explain the factors to be used for evaluating teacher-made tests.
13. Construct an objective test or an essay test, and evaluate it from student-response data according to the principles identified in this chapter.

intuitively judge a student's achievement. Yet many speech teachers either must rely solely on such intuitive processes because they have had no specific training in testing and evaluation, or they must proceed about the business of testing and evaluating students in indefensible and grossly unfair ways. It is not surprising that students often view tests as puzzles the teacher devises to fool them instead of as integral aids to the objectives of the course. Testing and evaluating are important skills which the speech communication teacher cannot afford to ignore.

DEFINITIONS

Three terms must be defined and differentiated: "test," "measurement," and "evaluation." In a test a person is presented with a set of constructed stimuli to which he responds: a numeral or set of numerals is assigned to the responses so that inferences can be made about his possession of what- ever the test measures. In short, a test is a type of measurement instrument.

Not all measurement instruments are tests, however, since some require no conscious response to a stimulus. For example, one can determine the length of a pencil by a measurement instrument, a ruler. Similarly, weight scales are measurement instruments, but they are not tests. Tests, rulers, and scales are measurement instruments having at least one thing in common— the assignment of numerals to objects according to rules, which is the definition of measurement.

The rules for assigning numerals to objects or events are the guides, methods, and explanations that tell one how to assign the numerals. Bad rules result in invalid measurement; good rules, in sound measurement. Some things are easy to measure because the rules for assigning numerals are easy to establish and follow. Measuring sex, for example, is relatively easy most of the time since several fairly clear, simple criteria can be stipulated and applied. The same is true for color, height, and weight. Unfortunately, many important human characteristics in speech communication are more difficult to measure because it is harder to establish clear rules.

The third term that needs to be defined is "evaluation." This word is sometimes carelessly used interchangeably with the words "test" or "measurement." Evaluation, however, is *not* the equivalent of measurement because measurement has no *valuing aspect* (goodness or badness), while evaluation *is* concerned with making a judgment in terms of goodness or badness. Evaluation is a judgment process. It is the position of the authors that the best judgments rest upon objective data. Such data are, for the most part, provided by measurement procedures and specifically by tests. Chapter 7 was concerned with the evaluation of speech communication performance and presented various measurement and evaluation procedures (other than tests). The focus of this chapter, however, is on tests— specifically, teacher-made tests.

THE FUNCTIONS OF TESTS

Tests are directly related to all the major factors in the teaching-learning system. It is through tests, for the most part, that comprehensive assessment of learning capabilities is carried out at the beginning of the school year. Tests are used to establish the level at which instruction should begin. During the semester or throughout the year, tests can be used as a part of the instructional strategy, both as a learning vehicle and as a means of reinforcement. In addition, a primary function of tests is to measure the achievement of instructional objectives; thus tests are related directly to the instructional objectives component of the teaching-learning process. Another part of the instructional model to which tests are directly related is feedback.

Not every test can serve equally well all five functions just identified. If the test is to function primarily as an instructional test or a learning strategy, then ideally it should be an easy test designed to reinforce those important points which the student is to learn. When tests have this purpose, test scores are not usually weighed heavily as a factor in the assignment of marks or grades.

Most classroom tests serve primarily to measure student achievement of instructional objectives, which is the focus of this chapter. Such tests, given throughout the course as well as at the end of the course, are of primary importance in evaluating the student's achievement and the instructional system the teacher has devised. Just as explicit objectives guide and direct the planning of instructional strategies, so valid and reliable tests of students' achievement of the objectives enable one to monitor and evaluate the instructional system that has been used. The practice of testing only at the end of the course to determine whether a student has failed or passed is a gross form of controlling the instructional process. Continuous monitoring and testing by the teacher are postulated as aiding learning, for they are a significant part of the feedback function in learning.

Before discussing types of teacher-made tests for speech and how to construct and evaluate good tests, let us look at the various kinds of tests in general.

METHODS OF CLASSIFYING TESTS

Tests may be classified in several ways: in terms of the type of learning they measure—cognitive, affective, or psychomotor; and as verbal or nonverbal; written or oral; objective or subjective; speed tests or power tests; tests administered to individuals or to groups; standardized or nonstandardized. Figure 1 illustrates several of these criteria.

STANDARDIZED TESTS

Standardized tests are tests that have been given to a fairly large and representative sample of the target population and for which a *standard* or *norm* has been determined. For example, a given student's score on the

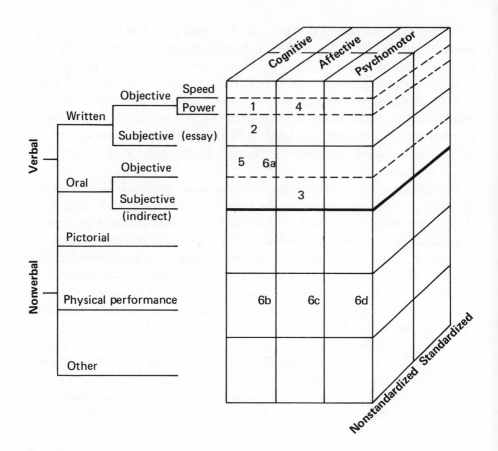

FIGURE 1 *Schema for classifying tests*

test can be compared to the national norm, or the scores of an entire class can be compared to established regional or national norms. For the most part, standardized tests are made available commercially by various publishing companies or educational organizations and institutions. The major producers of them are Educational Testing Service of Princeton, New Jersey; Psychological Corporation of New York City; Science Research Associates of Chicago; California Test Bureau of Los Angeles; and Harcourt Brace Jovanovich. Examples of standardized tests sometimes used in speech communication are the *Brown-Carlson Listening Test*, the *STEP Listening Test*, and the *Watson-Glaser Test of Critical Thinking*.

In the speech communication class in the secondary school, most tests are teacher-made (nonstandardized), written, objective, power tests of cognitive learnings. In Figure 1, the number 1 identifies that type of test in the classification grid. Some teachers give essay tests to measure cognitive learning (2). When a teacher gives the Brown-Carlson Listening Test, he is giving a standardized, objective, speed test, which is located on the back side of the box in Figure 1.

Tests that teachers compose for use in the classroom are nonstandardized tests. This chapter is concerned with nonstandardized, teacher-made tests.

TYPES OF TEACHER-MADE TESTS

Speech communication uses essentially three types of tests: written, oral, and performance. Chapter 7 was concerned with performance tests. This chapter focuses on written and oral tests with the major emphasis on written ones.

WRITTEN TESTS

These tests are classifiable as subjective or objective. Objective tests include such items as true-false, multiple-choice, matching, completion, and short-answer. The subjective test is the essay test. It requires the examinee to write a paragraph or a longer passage, and it demands subjective judgment regarding quality and completeness when it is scored.

Three of the five types of objective test items (multiple-choice, true-false, and matching) are *recognition* items, while the other two types (short-answer and completion) are *recall* test items.

ORAL TESTS

Probably one of the earliest methods of testing, or determining how well students have learned, is the oral quiz. It originally was called recitation because students were often required to memorize data, and their learning was tested by their reciting orally what they had memorized. The memorization of facts as an objective of education has fallen into ill repute; thus while the oral test continues to be used, it is not in the "stand up and recite" format.

The oral test has several weaknesses, and it should not be used as the sole method of appraising achievement. One serious weakness is that the test must be given privately to one student at a time if the *same test* is given to all students in the class. Such a procedure is too costly in time to warrant its frequent use. In addition, even if the same test is given to the entire group the sampling of the abilities of any one student cannot be very comprehensive. For example, in a class of twenty-five students it would be difficult to ask each student more than three or four questions during an hour examination. It would be virtually impossible, therefore, to measure the extent of any one student's learning. Moreover, since students are not usually asked the same questions, *no valid comparisons of achievement can be made*, although some teachers write scores in their gradebooks which are precisely that—comparative measures.

A second disadvantage of the oral test is that no tangible evidence and permanent response data are available for reexamination. The entire scoring and evaluating process must take place immediately after the response to each question is made. Such judgment can easily be affected by the psychological and physical states of the teacher.

The position the authors take is that the oral test is better used as an instructional strategy to reinforce learning and as a practice or repetition factor in learning. It has serious shortcomings as a measurement instrument.

CHARACTERISTICS OF A GOOD TEST

A good test, one used to measure pupil achievement, must be valid, reliable, and usable. Without all three of these essential qualities a testing instrument is useless. Validity is the extent to which a test measures what the teacher wishes to measure. Reliability is the accuracy of a test. Usability is the ease with which a test can be used: how easy it is to administer, to score, to interpret; how appropriate it is for the type of learning being measured, and how economical it is in terms of time, money, and materials required.

VALIDITY

When a person uses a tape measure to determine the length of a board, he has high confidence that what the tape measures is in fact length and not color or weight. Long experience with the manufactured tape measure has confirmed its validity as an instrument for measuring length. All he need do is observe the marks and record the numerals at each mark. However, when a speech teacher composes a multiplie-choice test to measure achievement in the speech communication class, it is not a directly observable phenomenon that he will be observing but pencil marks on an answer sheet. He counts the number of pencil marks made in the predetermined right places and records the number of right answers as the person's score. The score itself is not achievement in speech communication; it is a sample of behavior that he believes is related to achievement, and on the basis of that relationship he makes inferences in regard to achievement. Validity is not self-evident as it is in measuring with a steel tape. It is necessary to find some way of establishing the extent to which the written questions and the responses to those questions actually correspond to the trait being measured. There are three types of evidence used to determine the validity of a test: content validity, criterion validity, and construct validity. Content validity is the type used most of the time for classroom, teacher-made tests and is the only type explained in this chapter.

To establish content validity, the teacher matches the content of the test against the *content of the course*. He carefully identifies from the instructional objectives the knowledge and skills that were taught. If the objectives and what was taught are represented in the test, the test is valid. Content validity is achieved during the preparation of the test, i.e., when the teacher selects the *content*. Thus a valid test tests what has been taught; the test content and classroom instruction are closely related. If a test covers only two areas when five were taught, it is not a valid test of the achievement resulting from the course. Or if a test measures only the recall or recognition of facts when higher-type learnings such as application and problem solving were stressed in the objectives and instruction, the test is not a valid one. The best way to assure content validity in a teacher-made test is to use a test grid or blueprint. Too often students' complaints are true—complaints that tests are unfair, include the trivial, do not cover what was taught, and cover only one area ignoring other major areas in the unit or course. When teachers construct tests with no plan to guide their selection of items, the result is usually an invalid test.

RELIABILITY

Reliability is concerned not with what the test measures but with how accurately it measures. It is possible for a test to be reliable but not valid. It is not possible, however, for a test to be valid but unreliable. The test must be reliable to be valid.

There are four ways to determine the reliability of a test: the test-retest method, the alternate forms method, the split-half method, and the Kuder-Richardson method. Since it is time-consuming and difficult to prepare two equivalent forms of a test, and since it is impractical to give all teacher-made tests twice to obtain retest data, only the split-half and Kuder-Richardson methods of determining reliability are recommended for classroom tests. When the split-half method is used, the single test is divided so that half of the test comprises one set of scores and the other half comprises a second set of scores. Every other item (e.g., the odd-numbered items) is used to form one-half of the test, with the remaining items (e.g., the even-numbered items) forming the other half of the test. Correlation coefficients are figured to indicate the reliability of the test. Probably the easiest method of determining reliability is the *Kuder-Richardson test of reliability*. The formula for deriving the reliability coefficient is:

$$r_{11} = \frac{n}{n-1} \quad 1 - \left[\frac{Mt\left(1 - \frac{Mt}{n}\right)}{st^2} \right]$$

where r_{11} is the estimate of reliability
n is the number of items in the test
st is the standard deviation of the test
Mt is the mean score of the group

Within limits, lengthening a test increases reliability, provided that the items added are of equal quality to those in the original test. Of course, a three-hour test is too long because boredom and fatigue tend to reduce reliability, but a ten- or fifteen-item test is too short to be reliable. Some teachers make a practice of giving short daily quizzes, such as a ten-item, true-false quiz. Such short quizzes are completely unreliable as measuring devices unless the scores on four or five of them are accumulated to give one score. It is suggested that generally objective tests have no fewer than forty to fifty items.

USABILITY

The third characteristic of a good test is that it is usable or practical. A teacher-made test has to meet certain requirements in terms of economy. It must be within the limitations of the time available for testing in a course, the money available, and the materials available. The test must be easy to administer to a class and easily understood by the students. It needs a good format and clear, full instructions. Finally, the test should be appropriate for the type of learning that is measured.

COMPARISONS OF OBJECTIVE AND ESSAY TESTS

Objective tests can be compared to essay tests in terms of the three characteristics of good tests. Regarding reliability, many studies have demonstrated that objective tests are likely to have higher reliability than essay tests. If the test items are of the quality that will provide a spread in scores and also of sufficient number, the objective test is usually quite reliable. If several different persons score the test or if the test is scored at different times by the same person, the scores will be the same. On the other hand—in the case of subjective tests—when different persons score the same essay test, they arrive at different scores; or when the same person scores the same essay test at different times, the scores are often different each time. An overwhelming amount of the research on essay tests shows that they are unreliable. P. L. Dressel (1958, pp. 136–153) used a table to indicate how ten student essays were scored by forty-seven graders. Eight of the ten papers received all five of the possible scores—i.e., some graders assigned the paper an A grade, some assigned it an F grade—and the other two papers each received four of the five possible scores from the graders. Whether the student received an A, B, C, D, or F on the paper *depended entirely on who happened to grade the paper.*

Pidgeon and Yates (1957, pp. 32–47) did a study of the scoring of essay tests. They summarized their conclusions by stating that the results of the experiments showed that even in ideal conditions, which cannot in practice be achieved, tests of this kind do not reach the level of reliability maintained by objective tests. The Educational Testing Service (1961) reported a study in which three hundred essays were scored by fifty-three graders. One hundred (33 percent) of the essays were given all the possible scores (i.e., one to nine on a nine-point scale), and 60 percent of the essays received seven or eight of the possible nine scores. Clearly, objective tests hold an advantage over essay tests with regard to reliability.

Regarding validity, both types of tests, objective and essay, have certain advantages. Lindvall (1961, p. 55) states that essay tests are quite valid for measuring ability to express oneself in writing, ability to organize ideas, and ability to demonstrate a broad understanding of the material learned (i.e., ability to synthesize). On the other hand, as Remmers, Gage, and Rummel (1965, p. 214) point out, the objective test has greater validity because, having fifty to one hundred items, it can draw upon a wider range of pupil achievement and can more nearly sample all the content areas at all levels of learning than can the essay test. Thus the objective test is a more valid test of all that was taught. Essay tests often force students, when preparing for such tests, to guess which of several areas will be covered by three or four essay questions. Another reason the essay test is less valid than the objective test is that it tests skills and abilities unrelated to the stated objectives of the course. For example, as pointed out above, the essay test measures phenomena such as writing ability and vocabulary—skills that may aid or harm one in demonstrating his achievement of the objectives supposedly being measured.

Regarding the third characteristic of good tests, usability, the objective test is more easily scored than the essay test, and clear-cut directions are more easily given.

From these comparisons of essay and objective tests, it may appear that the authors believe that essay tests should not be used. The position taken in this text is rather that *essay tests should not be used when an objective test can do the job*. However, there are two situations in which the essay test seems especially appropriate. First, it is useful when the purpose of the teacher-made test is to measure the higher-order learnings: analysis, synthesis, and creativity. It should not be used to measure the lower levels of learning: *recall* or *recognition* of factual data, principles, or theories. For these levels objective tests are much more efficient. However, *objective tests are not limited to recall or recognition testing*. They are quite capable of measuring intellectual skills, problem solving, application, and even analysis, synthesis, evaluation, and criticism when constructed by a skillful test-maker.

The second situation in which the essay test may profitably be used involves motivation. Lindvall (1961, p. 55), Remmers, Gage, and Rummel (1965, p. 215), and Green (1963, p. 5) value the use of the essay test when the purpose of testing includes motivating the student to seek a broad understanding of the material. Table 1 identifies briefly the strengths and weaknesses of the various types of teacher-made tests.

CONSTRUCTING THE CLASSROOM TEST

As stressed previously, the quality of a teacher-made test is primarily a product of the construction of the test. Good tests are not thrown together haphazardly; they are not created by chance or intuition. They result from the application of relevant principles of test making, just as a good speech by a student is the product of the application of relevant principles of speech making. A teacher is not a competent manager of a learning system until he learns the concepts and principles for making a reliable, valid, and usable classroom test.

GUIDELINES FOR CONSTRUCTING THE OBJECTIVE TEST

1. Do not include essay questions.
2. Use a table of specifications (a test blueprint) to assure that you write items for each objective and for each content area at the various levels

TABLE 1. *Strengths and weaknesses of teacher-made tests*

Type of test	Strengths	Weaknesses
Objective	1. Gives extensive test sample 2. Can be made highly reliable 3. Can be graded objectively 4. Can be graded quickly 5. Can be subjected to item analysis 6. Can measure almost all levels or types of learning 7. Prevents bluffing	1. Can overemphasize rote learning 2. Encourages guessing
Essay	1. Especially applicable for testing writing, organizing, and creative abilities 2. Promotes proper type of study	1. Gives limited test sample 2. Has low reliability 3. Is difficult to grade 4. Favors verbally inclined students 5. Encourages bluffing
Oral	1. Gives extensive measurement if given to individual 2. Is useful as instructional strategy 3. Improves test rapport for students who fear written tests	1. Gives severely limited test sample of each person when given in group situation 2. Is time-consuming if given individually 3. Is not subject to refinement 4. Gives poor comparative evaluation of pupils

of learning. Table 2 illustrates in abbreviated form such a table of specifications.

3. Make the test long enough (at least forty items) to be valid and reliable but short enough to be usable. The average high school pupil can complete two typical multiple-choice items or three typical true-false items per minute.

4. The test should be a power test with items of all difficulty levels between

TABLE 2   *Specifications for a test on a unit or course called "Fundamentals of Speech Communication"*

Content Areas

Levels of instructional objectives	Nature of communication	Interpersonal communication: Dyadic	Interpersonal communication: Small group	Speaker-audience communication: Message	Speaker-audience communication: Speaker	Speaker-audience communication: Audience	Mass communication	Number of items
1. Recognizes terms and vocabulary	2	2	2	2	2	2	2	14
2. Identifies specific facts	2	3	3	2	2	2	2	16
3. Identifies principles, concepts, generalizations, and theories	4	4	4	4	4	4	4	28
4. Applies principles, generalizations, and theories to problem situations	6	6	6	6	6	6	6	42
Number of items	14	15	15	14	14	14	14	100

low and high. The first items should be simple enough so that most or all students can answer them correctly.

5. A good test includes one or two types of items (no more), and all the items of one type should be included in one section.

6. The test format and test items should be clean, clear, concise, attractively arranged, and free of grammatical and spelling errors.

7. Test directions should be clear and explicit.

8. Test items should be written in accordance with the rules or principles of good item writing.

WRITING MULTIPLE-CHOICE ITEMS

Writing good multiple-choice test items, like writing other kinds of objective test items, is a difficult task calling for considerable ingenuity and creative ability. Rules or guidelines in themselves do not guarantee good multiple-choice items. An item can be well written in that it follows the rules and still test a trivial idea. Nevertheless, if all teachers would observe certain principles of writing multiple-choice items, there would be a significant improvement in the quality of classroom tests.

Multiple-choice items have four components: stem, options, distractors, and key. The stem is a statement that gives the directions or presents the problem. The options include all the responses or answers that are provided. The distractors are the incorrect options. And the key is the correct option.

The following principles or guidelines should be observed in writing multiple-choice items:

1. The item must be as clearly and concisely written as possible. Verbosity has no place in a test measuring knowledge and skills of speech. The item must be long enough, however, to indicate clearly what is expected. Ambiguous items destroy the reliability and validity of a test.

2. All multiple-choice items should have the same number of options; either four or five-option items should be used.

3. All options for a particular item should be of approximately the same length so that the key is not identifiable by being noticeably different in length from the distractors.

4. The item must have a correct or best answer on which experts would agree.

5. A pattern of answers should be avoided. Place the key in different positions so that each option—a, b, c, and d—is randomly but proportionately used as the keyed answer.

6. Negatively stated items should be avoided. If such an item must be used, the "not" should be underlined.

7. All options should be plausible so that each one is selected as a correct response by some members of the class taking the test. The only exception is the use of two to four very easy items at the beginning of the test.

8. Each item should be an independent problem which gives no clues to the answers of other items in the test.

9. When the stem is a statement, the options should come at or near the end of the statement.

10. Any qualifying words that have to be repeated in each option should be placed in the stem.

11. Avoid using specific determiners, i.e., cues or giveaways of the answer. Notice the cue in the following item:

Man is an:
   a. bird
   b. animal
   c. reptile
   d. plant

The article "an" gives away the answer.

WRITING TRUE-FALSE ITEMS

True-false items are widely used in teacher-made tests because they are easy to prepare. The true-false test has some serious weaknesses, however. For one thing, it is easy to write bad items. Second, the use of true-false items is limited to measuring knowledge of facts, and it can test only facts that are unequivocally true or false. The result is that many items strain to cast debatable matter into a format of universal truth or deal with unequivocable facts that are trivial. A third weakness is that the true-false test is subject to guessing and chance; any pupil has a 50 percent chance of getting a true-false item right by guessing. If the teacher plans to use true-false items, however, the following guidelines can be helpful in writing good items.

1. The item must be unequivocably true or false.
2. Avoid the use of determiners such as "all," "never," "no," and "always" (such broad generalizations are likely to be false), as well as determiners such as "usually," "sometimes," and "maybe" (such qualified statements are likely to be true).
3. Avoid the use of negative statements.
4. Keep true-false statements approximately equal in length. There is a tendency for true statements to be longer than false ones.
5. Make certain that the element that makes the statement true or false is an important part of the statement rather than a minor clause inserted in the sentence to trick the student.
6. Use simple sentences rather than complex ones.

WRITING SHORT-ANSWER AND COMPLETION ITEMS

Restricted response items may be in the form of questions (short-answer items) or statements with blanks to fill in (completion). For either type, the answer is a word, number, date, list of words, or at most a sentence or two. The following guidelines should be observed when writing restricted response items:

1. In a completion item, the blank should be placed near the end of the statement.
2. Only significant words should be omitted in completion items.
3. Too many blanks should not appear in a completion statement. Over-mutilation of an item reduces the task of the student to a guessing game. Use only one or two blanks.
4. Ideas or sentences should not be quoted exactly from the textbook. Using textbook statements encourages learning by rote.
5. Blanks in all completion items should be uniform in length.

WRITING MATCHING ITEMS

Matching items are useful for measuring recognition and recall of factual knowledge. The following rules should be observed when writing them:

1. Only homogeneous premises and homogeneous responses should be used in a single matching set.

2. Relatively short lists of responses should be used, preferably no fewer than five and no more than ten.

3. Premises should be in the left-hand column and responses in the right-hand column. One of the lists of items, preferably the responses, should consist of single words, numbers, short phrases, or other material that can be examined quickly.

4. Answer blanks should precede the premises.

5. Response options should be arranged alphabetically or chronologically.

6. Directions should clearly indicate the basis for matching.

7. All the responses and premises for a matching set should be kept on the same page.

8. The number of responses should be larger than the number of premises, or a single response may be used to answer more than one premise.

GUIDELINES FOR CONSTRUCTING THE ESSAY TEST

Essay tests, as earlier pointed out, are especially applicable for measuring broad understandings, creativity, original thinking, and verbal expression. Instruction aimed at imparting Gestalt concepts of "wholeness" and insight into complex concepts and theories is more adaptable to essay testing. The strengths of the essay test, as well as its emphasis on freedom of expression and depth and scope of knowledge, must be balanced against its greatest weakness, low reliability. Only the essay test which overcomes this weakness can be a true measure of teaching-learning outcomes. The following guidelines should be observed:

1. The use of essay tests must be restricted to those topics which cannot be measured satisfactorily by objective tests.

2. Essay items must be sufficiently directive to make clear the desired behavior. The questions must be carefully defined and restricted so that the score that a student gets is a measure of how well he can do a specified task, not a measure of how well he can figure out what the task is that he is supposed to do. The student should not have to guess at what is wanted, nor should the graders have to guess at what has been provided in the response of the student. The type of answer desired can be identified in the question, the kind of organization indicated, and the extent of comprehensiveness described.

3. The written directions for the test should be explicit. They should include the point value for each question and should specify when factors such as spelling, grammar, and handwriting are to be considered in the scoring.

4. There should be no optional questions on an essay test. The use of optional questions destroys the ability to compare students' scores. Hence all students should be required to answer the same questions.

5. Open-book essay tests should be avoided when the purpose of the test is to measure learning. Open-book tests may be beneficial as an instructional technique but are not useful as measurement instruments.

6. Essay questions should begin with such phrases or words as "compare," "contrast," "give examples of," "present arguments for and against," "explain how," "explain why," "criticize," "differentiate," and "illustrate." The use of such words, combined with novel material or novel organization, requires the student to select, organize, and apply his knowledge. Essay questions should not begin with such words as "discuss," "what," "who," or "list" since these words lead to tasks requiring only the recall of information. Essay tests should measure the higher cognitive skills.

SCORING OBJECTIVE TESTS

In objective tests in which the student supplies the response (completion and short-answer), if spelling, sentence structure, or grammatical errors are to be considered in the scoring, *each of these factors must be given a separate score.* As Thorndike and Hagen (1969, pp. 85–86) state:

> If more than one distinct quality is to be appraised, make separate evaluations of each. In an essay in a subject matter field . . . the teacher is generally trying to appraise the achievement of objectives that are directly and explicitly related to the content area, such as knowledge of facts, principles, and theories of the content area. . . . He may also wish to appraise the development of generalized skills of writing such as logical organization, English usage, and spelling. These two dimensions are quite different and should be rated separately and reported to the student separately.

A second rule is that each blank or response on objective tests should be scored as one point when it is correct and as zero when it is incorrect. Partial credit should not be given for a response, nor should some responses count more than other responses. If the teacher believes a single item is worth more than other items, he should write additional items.

Third, a scoring key which lists all acceptable answers should be prepared for completion and short-answer items. If other answers that are also correct are discovered or given by students, they must be added to the scoring key, and any previously scored papers rescored.

A fourth consideration when scoring objective tests is whether to use a correction for guessing. There are considerable differences among students in their willingness to guess on an objective test, and these differences introduce variation in the test scores which is not related to the real achievement of the students. For that reason some teachers use a correction formula to offset the effect of guessing. The formula for correcting for guessing is:

$$\text{Corrected score} = R - \frac{W}{n-1}$$

where R is the number of items answered correctly
W is the number of items answered incorrectly
n is the number of options for each item

Since there are two options in true-false items, the corrected score for each student is the number of items he answers correctly minus the number of items he answers incorrectly. For a four-option, multiple-choice test, the corrected score is determined by dividing the number of items answered incorrectly by three and then subtracting that quotient from the number of items answered correctly. Correction for guessing should be used in scoring true-false tests since such tests will be more dependable as a result. Many authorities believe that multiple-choice tests containing four or five options for each item gain little from correcting for guessing. A score that is the number of right answers is quite satisfactory.

SCORING ESSAY TESTS

The main problem in scoring essay tests is the need to maintain consistent standards for all scoring regardless of who does the scoring. There are two basic methods of scoring essays: the holistic and the analytical. In the holistic approach, the scorer attempts to get a general impression of the quality of the essay and records this impression on a scale. In the analytical approach, the scorer has before him a set of criteria by which he evaluates the essay. Several authorities (Remmers, Gage, and Rummel, 1965, p. 229; Green, 1963, p. 67; and Lindvall, 1961, p. 57) suggest that the analytical method is the better one.

When the holistic method is used, a set of standard sample essays are often provided to help define the scoring scale. The standard sample essays are judged to be clearly below average, average, and above average. Each student essay is then read and placed in one of the three categories. The essays may be further sorted into six or seven categories, with each category representing a point on the scale.

When the analytical method is used, the following guidelines are useful:

1. Construct a grading key which includes the major aspects the student should include in his answer.

2. Do not permit irrelevant characteristics to influence the evaluation and scoring. Do not allow neatness or lack of neatness in handwriting to influence the score. If the test is to be valid, the score must reflect the pupil's achievement of the specified objectives. Gosling (1966, p. 386), Scannell and Marshall (1966, p. 125), and Marshall (1967, p. 375) have clearly shown that the score a student receives on an essay test can be influenced by his skill in written expression, his spelling, his conformity to rules of grammar, and the quality of his handwriting. As Thorndike and Hagen (1969, p. 54) state, "If a student knows nothing, or very little, in a subject matter area but has a high degree of skill in written expression, he can clothe his ideas in words that make a favorable impression on some readers (that is, bluff), and get a high mark even though he really knows little or nothing."

3. Score the essay test, if possible, without knowing the identity of the student who wrote the answer.

4. Read and score a single essay question through all the test papers, and then return to the first paper to read and score the second essay question, following it through all papers. This procedure helps the scorer to keep the standards or outline for a given question clearly in mind and uniform for all papers. Also, the good or poor performance of a student on one essay question is less likely to influence the scorer's judgment on other essay questions.

5. Read and score all papers in one sitting, or at least score each essay item through all papers in one sitting.

EVALUATING OBJECTIVE TESTS

The purpose of evaluating teacher-made tests—test analysis—is to enable the teacher to construct better ones. Also, the individual items can be analyzed—item analysis—to determine their quality and usefulness so that they may be refined for future use. Conscientious teachers who recognize the importance of testing and evaluation in the learning process will want to increase their knowledge and skill in constructing tests.

TEST ANALYSIS

DIFFICULTY

One characteristic of a good objective test is a medium level of difficulty. If the test is to measure achievement, it must not be too difficult or too easy. A classroom, teacher-made test should produce a mean score of about 60 percent of the possible score. A mean score of 75 or 80 percent would indicate that the test is too easy, and a mean score of 45 or 50 percent would indicate that it is too difficult.

DISCRIMINATION

A second characteristic of a good classroom test is that it discriminates between good and poor students. The test must discriminate accurately, i.e., it must identify as good students those who really are good students. The good test is a test on which poor students do poorly and good students (students who have learned and possess the relevant knowledge and skills) do well. Ideally, the test should consist of items that have a discriminating power or discrimination index of .40 or higher.[1] Zero or negative discrimination items should not be used again. Items of low discrimination (.01 to .09) should constitute no more than 15 percent of the items on the test; items of moderate discrimination (.10 to .39) should not exceed 25 percent of the items on the test; and at least 60 percent of the items ought to have a discrimination index of .40 or better.

[1]The procedure for calculating the discrimination power of an item will be explained in the next section dealing with item analysis.

Another indication of the test's ability to measure across a wide range of degrees of achievement is the standard deviation of the scores. Standard deviation is a measure of the variance in the scores produced by the test. Generally, the larger the standard deviation, the better the test. However, a standard deviation equal to one-sixth of the range between the highest possible score and the expected chance score (the expected chance score equals the number of items in the test divided by the number of choices per item) is satisfactory. A standard deviation of less than one-tenth of the available range is considered poor. If a test produces a set of scores with too small a standard deviation, then the test scores deviate very little from the mean and hence deviate little from each other. In other words, differences in learning are not revealed by the test. It does not discriminate.

Standard deviation is calculated by the following formula:

$$s = \sqrt{\frac{\Sigma x^2}{N-1}}$$

where s is the standard deviation
Σx^2 is the sum of squared deviations from the mean of a set of scores
N is the number of scores

The calculation of the standard deviation may be summarized in the following steps:

1. Find the mean.
2. Find the deviation of each score from the mean.
3. Square each deviation.
4. Sum the squared deviations.
5. Divide the sum of the squared deviations by N–1.
6. Extract the square root to find the standard deviation.

RELIABILITY

Finally, if the test is a good one, it will be a reliable measuring instrument. One way to determine the reliability of a classroom test is to use the Kuder-Richardson Formula 20 (KR-20), given previously in this chapter. When the reliability of a test is low, it may be improved by increasing the test length or by increasing the number of items with difficulty indices in the .50 to .60 range.

Finally, the teacher is interested in the standard error of measurement (probable error) when the test is evaluated. Probable error can be calculated from the reliability coefficient and the standard deviation of the test scores by using the formula:

$$Sm = St \sqrt{1 - r_{11}}$$

where Sm is the standard error of measurement
St is the standard deviation of test scores
r_{11} is the reliability coefficient

The standard error of measurement is inversely related to the size of the reliability coefficient—the higher the reliability coefficient, the smaller the probable error in measurement. A good test has a low error in its measurement, i.e., it produces a measure (score) that is as close as possible to the person's true amount of the trait being measured (knowledge, skill, etc.). When that is the case, the teacher can *believe* the measure or score produced; the test is a reliable measuring instrument.

ITEM ANALYSIS

An important aid to the teacher who constructs classroom tests is a pool of tested items. If he has such a pool, he will find it considerably easier to construct a good test. Item pools can be established as tests are given and the items are analyzed to discover which are good items that should be kept, which are potentially good items (revisable), and which are poor items that should be discarded.

Answers to the following questions can be obtained from item analysis: (1) How difficult is the item? (2) Is the item discriminating between good and poor students? and (3) Are all the distractors functioning?

ITEM DIFFICULTY INDEX

The item difficulty index is the proportion of correct answers for the key of an item. The p-value of an item can range from .00 to 1.00. If every student selects the key, the proportion of students getting the question right is 100 percent, and the p-value (item difficulty index) is 1.00. Such an item is an extremely easy one. If every student misses the item, the item difficulty index is .00, and the item is an extremely difficult one. Theoretically and practically, the best recommendation concerning difficulty levels of test items is to use items which range from very difficult to very easy with one-half to two-thirds of the items at the p-value midway between the chance level and 1.00. For example, in a four-choice item there is a probability of .25 of being correct by chance alone. The p-value midway between .25 and 1.00 is .62. Therefore, a fifty-item test composed of four-option, multiple-choice items should have from twenty-five to thirty-five items with difficulty indices about .60; while a true-false test of fifty items should have twenty-five to thirty-five items with difficulty indices about .75.

ITEM DISCRIMINATION INDEX

The discrimination power of an item is its ability to differentiate among students of different abilities. This power can be determined by comparing the number of errors that high-scoring persons (persons who score high on the total test) make on the item with the number of errors that low-scoring persons make on the same item. If the item is missed equally by both groups, it is not a discriminating item. All students in both groups may answer the item correctly; all students in both groups may answer the item incorrectly; half of each group may answer the item correctly; and so on. If the two groups do equally well on the item, the item does not discriminate. If an item is missed by more students in the low group than in the high group, the item discriminates in a positive manner as it should; but if more students in the high group than in the low group answer the item incorrectly, the item penalizes learning or achievement. It is an invalid one because it discriminates negatively.

The most common index of the discriminative power of an item is the correlation between the item and the total test score. A high positive correlation between an item and a total test score indicates that students with high total scores tend to answer the item correctly more often than those with low total scores. A negative correlation means that students with low total test scores give more correct responses than do those with high total test scores. Table 3 is a sample item analysis form with four examples, which will be discussed to further clarify the function and interpretation of item analysis.

TABLE 3   *Item Analysis Form A*

Item No.	Difficulty index (Percentages)				Discrimination index (correlation coefficients)			
	A	B	C	D	A	B	C	D
1	.000	.000	1.000*	.000	.000	.000	.000*	.000
2	.120	.660*	.100	.120	−.260	.414*	−.127	−.114
3	.260*	.060	.160	.520	.098*	−.302	−.291	.254
4	.000	.130	.160	.710*	.000	−.127	−.203	.492

* Key

Item No. 1 in Table 3 is an easy one since the p-value is 1.000. All students selected the correct answer. When 80 percent or more of a group of examinees select the correct answer, an item should be checked closely to see if there are clues or giveaways in it. An item answered correctly by all students does not discriminate (note discrimination index for item No. 1).

Item No. 2 has a difficulty index of .66, a desirable difficulty level. Also, all distractors are working. Of the examinees, 12 percent selected option A, 10 percent chose C, and 12 percent marked D. In terms of difficulty and the functioning of distractors, item No. 2 is an excellent one. The item is also excellent in terms of discrimination since the positive correlation of the keyed option (B) indicates that high scorers on the test tended to select the correct answer more often than did low scorers. The distractors correlate negatively with total test scores—another desirable discrimination characteristic.

Item No. 3 is a difficult item since only 26 percent answered it correctly. All options are working—especially option D, which attracted 52 percent of the students. There are problems with the item that are revealed in the discrimination index, however. Two distractors (B and C) have negative correlations and are satisfactory, but the key (option A) has a correlation of .098 compared to *positive* correlation of .254 for option D. This means that the people with higher total test scores tend to select option D rather than the correct answer, option A. This item should be investigated to determine whether it is keyed incorrectly. It is at least an ambiguous item that will require major revision or perhaps removal from the test.

Item No. 4 discriminates well and is of satisfactory difficulty. Distractor A is not functioning and should be rewritten to make it more attractive.

The correlation coefficients reported in the discrimination index in

TABLE 4 *Item Analysis Form B*

Item: "Everyone's using glory!" is an example of the propaganda technique called:

A. Glittering generality
B. Bandwagon
C. Testimonial
D. Plain folk

Scoring group	Options			
	A	B	C	D
Upper 25%		10		
Middle 50%		18	3	
Lower 25%	2	5	2	4
Totals	2	33	2	4

N = 40

Table 3 require considerable time to compute; therefore, many schools provide IBM or other types of machine-scorable answer cards or answer sheets. When tests are scored by machine, the computer printouts can include item difficulty and discrimination indices. If the teacher does not have access to such service, however, alternative procedures and item analysis forms are available. Table 4 is an alternative item analysis form which utilizes a simpler procedure for determining discrimination indices.

From the raw data on the item analysis card, the teacher can evaluate the difficulty, discrimination, and attractiveness of the distractors of the item. The item in Table 4 is a relatively easy item since thirty-three out of forty students (83 percent) answered correctly. All distractors are functional and the item discriminates well inasmuch as no student in the high-scoring group (upper 25 percent) selected incorrect options; these for the most part were chosen by students in the low-scoring group (lower 25 percent). Although such a method is not as accurate as the one previously described, it is usable by any teacher.

SUMMARY

This chapter has defined and differentiated the terms "test," "measurement," and "evaluation." The functions and value of tests in the instructional process have been identified. A schema for classifying tests was presented.

The characteristics of a good test—validity, reliability, and usability—were discussed in detail, and methods of determining test validity and reliability were presented. A rather thorough discussion of the strengths and weaknesses of objective and essay tests was given, and comparisons of the two types of teacher-made tests were presented. Guidelines for writing various types of test items, as well as for constructing teacher-made tests in general, were offered. Finally, scoring procedures, item analysis, and test analysis and evaluation were discussed. Although this chapter has presented a wide range of topics on teacher-made tests for speech communication in a rather concise form, it is hoped that the skills and understandings covered will be acquired and used to improve the quality of the teaching-learning process.

REFERENCES

Dressel, P. L. *Evaluation in the Basic College.* New York: Harper & Row, 1958.

Educational Testing Service Annual Report 1961–1962. Princeton, N. J.: The Service, 1962.

Ebel, Robert L. *Measuring Educational Achievement.* Englewood Cliffs, N. J.: Prentice-Hall, 1965.

Gosling, G. W. H. *Marking English Compositions,* pp. 22–37. Victoria, Australia: Australian Council for Educational Research, 1966.

Green, John A. *Teacher-made Tests.* New York: Harper & Row, 1963.

Lindvall, C. M. *Testing and Evaluation: An Introduction.* New York: Harcourt, Brace & World, 1961.

Marshall, J. C. "Composition Errors and Essay Examination Grades Reexamined." *American Educational Research Journal* 4 (1967): 375–386.

Pidgeon, D. A., and A. Yates. "Symposium: The Use of Essays in Selection at 11:IV. Experimental Inquiries into the Use of Essay-Type English Papers." *British Journal of Educational Psychology* 27 (1957): 3247.

Remmers, H. H.; N. L. Gage; and J. F. Rummel. *A Practical Introduction to Measurement and Evaluation.* New York: Harper & Row, 1965.

Scannell, D. P., and J. C. Marshall. "The Effect of Selected Composition Errors on Grades Assigned Essay Examinations." *American Educational Research Journal* 3 (1966): 125–130.

Thorndike, Robert L., and Elizabeth Hagen. *Measurement and Evaluation in Psychology and Education.* New York: John Wiley and Sons, 1969.

NINE

METACOMMUNICATION
IN THE CLASSROOM

Most of us find ourselves in a great variety of interpersonal relationships. We listen to some persons and tell others; share our innermost thoughts with some and guard ourselves with others; play with some and work with others. We know people as friends, relatives, professional colleagues, neighbors and mere acquaintances. Some of these relationships are formal, structured, and definitive, others are informal, loose, and ill defined. Some relationships are superficial and of little import in our lives, while others whether of short or long duration involve our deepest feelings and influence us strongly.

Many fields of study now recognize the importance of interpersonal relationships and devote significant time and energy to study and research on this subject, incorporating the findings in training and instructional programs. Areas such as business and organizational administration, family life and child development, and counseling have emphasized the salient role of interpersonal relationships in problem solving, group relations, parent-child relations, and marital relations. Also of great importance is the student-teacher relationship. There is much intellectual intimacy (as well as emotional intimacy) in the teaching-learning situation, and the effective teacher promotes good interactions between his students and himself.

This chapter deals with the *effects* and *meanings* of interpersonal communication events that express and define relationships, attitudes, and

OBJECTIVES

1. Define metacommunication and include an explanation of the modes of transmitting the message.
2. State and explain the five axioms of communication.
3. Present the arguments for the validity of nonverbal communication.
4. Explain how the teacher may use metacommunication to aid the learning process.
5. Explain the relationship of metacommunication to the various parts of the COSEF model.

emotions in the classroom. Such relationships direct and control subsequent interactions and establish the communication environment of the group. For any group—the husband-wife dyad, the United States Senate, or the speech communication class—a complex process is carried on continually by which the rules of behaving and existing for that group are established and enforced. These rules of behaving and existing, which deal with the establishment and maintenance of relationships and attitudes, are for the most part identified and negotiated through *indirect communication.* As we know, communication includes not only direct, verbal, primary messages but also indirect, nonverbal, secondary ones. Secondary messages are those separate from but often imbedded in primary messages. Because communication is not a one-way phenomenon but an interaction process having all these implications as well as others, teachers can ill afford to ignore certain implications for the classroom. In the classroom, as in all other interpersonal systems, the behavior of each person affects and is affected by the behavior of every other person. (The two terms "communication" and "behavior" are used synonymously since the data of both are identical and include words, the nonverbal concomitants of words, body language, and clues inherent in the context in which communication or behavior occurs.

Metacommunication is defined as *communication about communication.*

It is communication about the rules and relationships that govern the behavior or communication of two persons or a group. Watzlawick et al. (1967, pp. 39–40) draw an analogy between communication and metamathematics:

> When mathematicians no longer use mathematics as a tool to compute, but make this tool itself the object of their study—as they do, for instance, when they question the consistency of arithmetic as a system—they use a language that is not part of but about mathematics. . . . When we no longer use communication to communicate but to communicate about communication, as we inevitably must in communication research, then we use conceptualizations that are not part of but about communication. In analogy to metamathematics this is called metacommunication.

Reusch and Bateson (1951, pp. 23–24) have described metacommunication:

> A social situation is established as soon as an exchange of communication takes place. . . . The mutual recognition of having entered into each other's field of perception equals the establishment of a system of communication. *The criteria of mutual awareness of perception are in all cases instances of communication about communication.* If a person "A" raises his voice to attract person "B's" attention, he is thereby making a statement about communication. He may, for example, be saying, "I am communicating with," or he may be saying, "I am not listening to you; *I* am doing the talking"—and so on. Similarly statements which implicitly or explicitly assign roles either to the self or the other, are statements about communication.

Every person needs to learn how to interpret the meaning of messages not only by assessing the content but also by looking for the metacommunication cues. Punctuation, emphasis, assignment of roles and relationships, and the expression of emotion can all be seen as messages about communication. Metacommunication refers to those verbal, nonverbal, aural, visual, gestural, or contextual cues that identify, negotiate, and determine the relationships that govern the interactions of the persons involved, as well as what emotions and feelings are engendered by their interactions. Before giving examples of metacommunication in the speech classroom, and before describing the role of metacommunication analysis as a feedback source as well as a teaching skill, let us look at some tentative axioms of communication which help to clarify the role of metacommunication in the classroom.

TENTATIVE AXIOMS OF COMMUNICATION

The following characteristics of communication in the form of axioms will help you apply metacommunication analysis to teaching. The axioms are adapted from the list of Watzlawick et al. (1967, pp. 48–71).

Axiom No. 1: One cannot not communicate. Behavior has no opposite; there is no such thing as nonbehavior. And since all behavior has message value, it follows that one cannot *not* communicate. Even inactivity and silence have message value and influence others, who cannot avoid responding to these communications. As Watzlawick et al. (1967, p. 49) have pointed out, the mere absence of talking or of taking notice of each other does not mean that there is no communication. The person in the waiting room at the physician's office who avoids eye contact or sits with his eyes closed communicates that he does not want to talk to anybody, and people "get the message" and respond by leaving him alone. This, obviously, is just as much an interchange of communication as is conversation.

Communication may be intentional or unintentional, conscious or unconscious, and successful or unsuccessful, but it cannot *not* be. When persons are in each other's field of awareness, there is no way to avoid communication. Withdrawal, postural immobility, silence, nonsense sounds, or any other form of denial or attempt to not communicate is itself a communication. Any communication defines the sender's view of his relationship with the receiver. Even though the husband hides behind his morning paper so as to not talk with his wife, his behavior communicates something to her. Though the student opens his book to study, as requested by the teacher, his facial expression and the way he opens the book may communicate clearly his "negative compliance" attitude; and he may observe the teacher's response to his behavior to test how much power he has to define their relationship or how much influence his attitude has on her. One thing that neither of them can do is *not* communicate.

Axiom No. 2: There are two levels in any communication: content and relationships. Content refers to the informational aspect of a message. The information may be true or false, valid or invalid, relevant or irrelevant. Messages also contain cues about what to do with the message, what the message imposes in terms of relationships between the communicants, information about the information—in other words, there is a metacommunication aspect along with the primary communication.

For example, two identical primary verbal messages can be sent. Accompanying one of the messages is a metacommunication that says clearly, "This is an order! I am the order-giver, and you are to obey!" In the second instance, a different metacommunication accompanies the primary message indicating clearly, "I am only joking." In each instance there are both a content aspect to the message and a relational or metacommunicational aspect. The ability to metacommunicate appropriately and to interpret metacommunication accurately is the *sine qua non* of all successful communication. It is possible to send messages in which the metacommunication is ambiguous. Whether the ambiguity is accidental or intentional, such messages make successful communication difficult. For example, to write in a letter of recommendation, "I cannot recommend this person too highly" leaves the recipient wondering whether it is a bad recommendation or an exceptionally good one. Similarly the statement "Students who think their teachers are stupid should see the principal" can be understood in two entirely different ways. These examples emphasize the importance of clarity between the two levels: communication and metacommunication.

Axiom No. 3: The nature of a relationship depends on how the communicants punctuate their communicational sequences.   This axiom is concerned with each person's perception of who is the initiator and who is the responding communicator of a given communication sequence or series of messages. Participants in communication, according to Whorf (1956) and Bateson and Jackson (1964), always punctuate a sequence of communicational events. They may punctuate the series in the same manner or differently. Bateson and Jackson explain this axiom as follows (pp. 273–274):

> The stimulus-response psychologist typically confines his attention to sequences of interchange so short that it is possible to label one item of input as "stimulus" and another item as "reinforcement" while labeling what the subject does between these two events as "response." Within the short sequence so excised, it is possible to talk about the "psychology" of the subject. In contrast, the sequences of interchange which we are here discussing are very much longer and therefore have the characteristic that every item in the sequence is simultaneously stimulus, response, and reinforcement. A given item of A's behavior is a stimulus insofar as it is followed by an item contributed by B and that by another item contributed by A. But insofar as A's item is sandwiched between two items contributed by B, it is a response. Similarly, A's item is a reinforcement insofar as it follows an item contributed by B. The ongoing interchanges, then, which we are here discussing, constitute a chain of overlapping triadic links, each of which is comparable to a stimulus-response-reinforcement sequence. We can take

any triad of our interchange and see it as a single trial in a stimulus-response learning experiment.

If we look at the conventional learning experiments from this point of view, we observe at once that repeated trials amount to a differentiation of relationship between the two organisms concerned —the experimenter and his subject. The sequence of trials is so punctuated that it is always the experimenter who seems to provide the "stimuli" and the "reinforcements," while the subject provides the "responses." These words are here deliberately put in quotation marks because the role definitions are in fact only created by the willingness of the organisms to accept the system of punctuation. The "reality" of the role definitions is only of the same order as the reality of a bat on a Rorschach card—a more or less overdetermined creation of the perceptive process. The rat who said, "I have got my experimenter trained. Each time I press the lever he gives me food" was declining to accept the punctuation of the sequence which the experimenter was seeking to impose.

It is still true, however, that in a long sequence of interchange, the organisms concerned—especially if these be people—will in fact punctuate the sequence so that it will appear that one or the other has initiative, dominance, dependency or the like. That is, they will set up between them patterns of interchange (about which they may or may not be in agreement), and these patterns will in fact be rules of contingency regarding the exchange of reinforcement.

The classroom is not exempt from this axiom of communication. There, as in any group, roles are assigned—leader-follower, teacher-student, resource person, etc. Agreement or disagreement in such assignments depends in part on the punctuation of communicational interchanges.

Axiom No. 4: People utilize two types of communication: verbal, to convey and receive information and knowledge; and nonverbal, to establish relationships and reveal emotions and feelings. The term nonverbal communication is sometimes mistakenly limited to bodily movement, i.e., to the behavior known as kinesics. However, the term means much more than just bodily movement. It refers also to posture, gesture, facial expression, voice inflection, rhythm, controlled pitch, and any other behavior of the organism that is not verbal. It includes too the clues that are present in the context of the communication.

Man communicates *verbally* to share information and to transmit knowledge and *nonverbally*, for the most part, to reveal emotions and feelings and to communicate relationships. Thus metacommunication, the communication about the relationship and feeling underlying or imposed by verbal messages, is for the most part nonverbal.

In the vast area of relationships, man relies almost entirely on non-verbal communication. Watzlawick et al. (1967) have stated that when relationship is the central issue of communication, verbal language is almost meaningless. In courtship, love, and combat, nonverbal communication is the effective mode. It is easy to profess one's love, trust, or hope, but it is most meaningful when it is communicated through nonverbal behavior.

One of the implications of this axiom for the speech classroom is that when a teacher wishes to discover relationships, attitudes, feelings, and emotions, he should pay attention to the nonverbal communication (the metacommunication) rather than ask students to reveal these states and relationships verbally. It has been the experience of the authors, as well as of the teachers who have gone through their training program, that in every speech classroom a wealth of information is available to teachers through nonverbal communication from students in regard to attitudes, feelings, and relationships.

A second implication of the axiom is that the teacher communicates feelings, attitudes, and relationships through nonverbal communication. If the teacher really wants to communicate an attitude effectively or to establish a relationship, just talking about the attitude or relationship will probably be unsuccessful—and will definitely be so if his nonverbal communication contradicts the verbal message.

Axiom No. 5: All communicational interchanges are either symmetrical or complimentary.   We have noted previously that messages have two elements—content and relationships—and that every message imposes some kind of relationship. Axiom No. 5 states that the relationships and roles imposed may be accepted by the participants (be complimentary) or they may be rejected (be symmetrical). If both persons want to play the same role (e.g., to be the leader), they have a symmetrical or competitive relationship, a situation in which both reject the metacommunication implication that he is to be the follower. However, if both are willing for A to be the leader and B to be the follower, then a complementary relationship exists. Although the two roles differ, they *fit* with or compliment each other and are not competitive. Either a complementary or a symmetrical relationship results in some degree from all communicational interchanges.

When each person tends to mirror the behavior of the other, the interaction is symmetrical. When the behavior of one differs in the desired manner from the behavior of the other, the interaction is complementary. In the complementary relationship, one partner occupies the superior or primary position and the other partner the inferior or subordinate position. If equated with "good" and "bad," these terms are useless, and attaching these value labels to the positions should be avoided.

These communication axioms are advanced by Watzlawick as tentative, preliminary principles. However, their usefulness in aiding an understanding of the role of metacommunication, in utilizing metacommunication analysis for feedback and as a rewarding teaching skill, has been demonstrated in the authors' training programs.

VALIDITY OF NONVERBAL MESSAGES

Nonverbal messages may be sent consciously or unconsciously. Unconsciously sent nonverbal messages are often of high validity. Watzlawick (1967, pp. 62–63) referring to analogic (nonverbals) and digital (verbal) communication, states:

> Analogic communication has its roots in far more archaic periods of evolution and is, therefore, of much more general validity than the relatively recent, and far more abstract, digital mode of verbal communication. . . . Children, fools, and animals have always been credited with particular intuition regarding the sincerity or insincerity of human attitudes, for it is easy to profess something verbally, but difficult to carry a lie into the realm of the analogic.

The validity of nonverbal messages that express emotions, feelings, and relationships has been demonstrated by Bell (1844), Darwin (1965, Reprinted Edition), Spencer (1855), Eckman and Friesen (1967), and Rousey (1965).

Darwin, in summarizing Bell's research and commenting on his third edition of *Anatomy and Philosophy of Expression* (1844), stated that Bell's service consisted chiefly of showing that an intimate relationship exists between emotions and physical movements, and that one of the most important points is that the muscles around the eyes are involuntarily contracted during violent effort. Darwin (1965, pp. 2–3) continued, "He does not try to explain why different muscles are brought into action under different emotions; why, for instance, the inner ends of the eyebrows are raised, and the corners of the mouth depressed, by a person suffering from grief or anxiety." Similarly, in the same book, *The Expression of the Emotions in Man and Animals,* Darwin's own careful study and report, he points toward a validity of the nonverbal expression of emotions and feelings that is consistent across different individuals, different cultures, and animals as well. Darwin has stated (p. 12), "With mankind some expressions, such as the bristling of the hair under the influence of extreme terror, or the uncovering of the teeth under that of furious rage, can hardly be understood, except on the belief that man once existed in a much lower and animal-like condition." Darwin distinguished (p. 15) conventional expressions or gestures which are culture-bound from movements of the body and face that express emotion and are the same across races of mankind. He said (p. 17), "The same state of mind is expressed throughout the world with remarkable uniformity; and this fact is in itself interesting as evidence of the close similarity in bodily structure and mental disposition of all the races of mankind." In summary, Darwin states (pp. 347–366):

> I have now described, to the best of my ability, the chief expressive actions in man, and in some few of the lower animals. . . . Movements which are serviceable in gratifying some desire, or in relieving some sensation, if often repeated, become so habitual that they are performed, whether or not of any service, whenever the same desire or sensation is felt. . . . I have endeavoured to show in considerable detail that all the chief expressions exhibited by man are the same throughout the world. The movements of expression in the face and body are in themselves of much importance for our welfare. They serve as the first means of communication between the mother and her infant . . . they reveal the thoughts and intentions of others more truly than do words, which may be falsified. . . . There is an intimate relation that exists between almost all emotions and their outward manifestation.

This finding of the validity of nonverbal communication—especially metacommunication (emotions, feelings, relationships)—by Bell, Spencer, Duchene, and Darwin has been verified by various researchers during the past few years, including Ekman (1967), Friesen (1967), Rousey (1965), Hebb (1946), and Labarre (1947). Labarre noted that successful psychiatrists, artists, anthropologists, and teachers rely on the validity of nonverbal communication when he stated (pp. 64–65):

> Dr. A. S. Sullivan, for example, is known to many for his acute understanding of the postural tonuses of his patients. Another psychiatrist, Dr. E. J. Kempf, evidences in the copious illustrations of his "Psychopathology" a highly cultivated sense of the kinesthetic language of tonuses in painting and sculpture, and can undoubtedly discover a great deal about a patient merely by glancing at him. The linguist, Dr. Stanley Newman, has a preternatural skill in recognizing psychiatric syndromes through the individual styles

of tempo, stress, and intonation. The gifted cartoonist, Mr. William Steig, has produced, in *The Lonely Ones,* highly sophisticated and authentic drawings of the postures and tonuses of schizophrenia, depression, mania, paranoia, hysteria, and in fact the whole gamut of psychiatric syndromes. Among anthropologists, Dr. W. H. Sheldon is peculiarly sensitive and alert to the emotional and temperamental significance of constitutional tonuses. I believe that it is by no means entirely an illusion that an experienced teacher can come into a classroom of new students and predict with some accuracy the probable quality of individual scholastic accomplishment—even as judged by other professors—by distinguishing the unreachable, unteachable *Apperceptions masse-less* sprawl of one student, from the edge-of-the-seat starved avidity and intentness of another. Likewise, an experienced lecturer can become acutely aware of the body language of his listeners and respond to it appropriately until the room fairly dances with communication and counter-communication, head-noddings, and the tenseness of listeners soon to be prodded into public speech.

Similarly, Richardson et al. (1965, p. 235) in their textbook on interviewing say, "Because we are trained to focus on verbal communication and generally disregard nonverbal communication, we are probably far less guarded in our nonverbal behavior and may reveal information that we carefully control or censor in speech." Hebb (1946) has stressed how emotions are recognized by animals and men from postural communication, tonuses, and facial expression. Rousey (1965) and Starkweather (1956) have reported on the communication of feelings and emotions through vocal components such as tonal variation and voice quality. Starkweather, in summarizing research on content-free speech as a source of information about emotions and feelings, has pointed out that while the verbal channel carries semantic information, it is the vocal channel that carries affective information; and that if a person is interested primarily in the personality of the speaker or in the affective messages, he should consider the vocal component of speech more important than the verbal component.

Clearly, there is evidence of the validity of unconscious nonverbal communication. However, it appears that adults who have become adept at communicating verbally begin to focus on verbal communication only and tend to ignore the messages that are sent nonverbally which have to do with emotions, attitudes, and interpersonal relationships. Therefore, it is necessary for counselors, interviewers, and others to learn purposefully to attend to nonverbal communication in order to be receptive to it, to learn to interpret it accurately (the nonverbal communication that is culture-bound as well as the nonverbal communication that is culture-free), and to respond appropriately to these messages. The same need exists for teachers.

METACOMMUNICATION AS A FEEDBACK SOURCE

A major component of the COSEF model of instruction is feedback. Feedback to the student is necessary if learning is to occur efficiently, and feedback to the teacher is equally important since the teacher, as a systems manager, is always in a learning situation himself. In fact, the teacher must receive feedback on all the components in the system. If student attitudes, feelings, and interpersonal relationships are salient components in the instructional system, then the teacher must receive feedback on them confirming the efficiency and success of the system. Only through feedback can intelligent adjustments and modifications be made.

Thus it is clear that not only is feedback vitally important in determining how well the student has achieved the instructional objectives, but it is also important in determining the adequacy of the instructional strategies the teacher has used. Student terminal performance furnishes the feedback data on achievement of instructional objectives and also, on the efficiency of some (but not all) instructional strategies. But such data are of limited value for evaluating those instructional strategies dealing with roles, interpersonal relationships, and attitudes. It is in these areas that metacommunication analysis can function as an important source of feedback to the instructor. As Fiedler (1969, p. 40) has pointed out on the basis of his research, the effective leader tends to be "relationship-oriented" while the person who scores low as a leader tends to be "task-oriented." On the basis of research findings already identified in this chapter, it appears that the same principle applies to teachers in the classroom. Thus metacommunication skills are especially important in the analysis of existing relationships as well as in the creation of more productive relationships.

THE TEACHER'S USE OF METACOMMUNICATION TO AID LEARNING

To a certain extent, the effectiveness or ineffectiveness (helpfulness or harmfulness) of a teacher's metacommunication depends on the kind of person he is. Hamachek (1969, p. 343) has stated:

> A good teacher is a good person. Simple and true. A good teacher rather likes life, is reasonably at peace with himself, has a sense of humor, and enjoys other people. If I interpret the research correctly, what it says is that there is no one best better-than-all-others

type of teacher. Nonetheless there are clearly distinguishable "good" and "poor" teachers. Among other things, a good teacher is good because he does not seem to be dominated by a narcissistic self which demands a spotlight, or a neurotic need for power and authority, or a host of anxieties and tremblings which reduce him from the master of his class to its mechanic.

The teacher with wholesome attitudes and feelings communicates them to the students, and a teacher with negative attitudes and feelings communicates those to students. For an individual to alter extensively his metacommunication would probably require considerable soul-searching and effort to change his outlook. As the teacher develops a more accurate concept of himself, however, the possibility of changing his attitudes increases. When teachers "face themselves," they feel more adequate as individuals and function more effectively as teachers. Moreover, in many instances, the teacher can eliminate or reduce selected gross behaviors and metacommunications that have adverse effects on students. The person who desires to improve his teaching effectiveness should therefore be concerned with his use of metacommunication.

There are several specific teacher behaviors, largely controllable, that constitute wholesome metacommunication. One set of behaviors deals with the way the teacher treats students. Teachers are concerned with the attitudes that students have toward them, and Chapter 5 dealt with the interactive effect of student attitudes on discipline and learning. Students need to have a positive attitude toward the teacher, and they establish such an attitude as they observe the behavior of the teacher toward them.

One guiding rule in treatment of students is that the teacher must be fair. Recently, a great deal of research has revealed that the negative effects of treating another person unjustly are salient and long-lasting. Berscheid and Walster (1969, pp. 14–28) have provided an excellent summary of the findings of research on the effects of treating others unjustly. Specific unjust treatments are exploiting the other person, insulting or making fun of him, and making negative evaluations of him. The speech teacher who falls into the habit of doing these things creates negative attitudes in students. The teacher should instead strive to be fair and seek to acquire that reputation. No teacher can afford to make sarcastic or derogatory remarks about students, give nothing but negative evaluations of them, change established rules or in other ways exploit them or be unfair.

Teachers should concentrate on positive rewards to students for appropriate learning and behavior rather than on punishment or negative evaluations for inappropriate behavior. Skinner (1968, pp. 9–29) identifies and analyzes two educational practices that are sources of failure: the absence of control over reinforcement and the overwhelming reliance on aversive or punishing consequences to control learning. He derogates the use of punishment and negative evaluation, arguing that often it is not as effective as positive reinforcement.

A second type of behavior the teacher can exhibit in order to win respect and to demonstrate concern and expertise is to create a supportive climate for learning. Hart's study (1934) showed that students appreciate teachers who are helpful in schoolwork and who clearly explain lessons and assignments. Spaulding (1963) reported that students' self-concepts are higher and more positive when the teacher is learner-supportive. In short, the teacher who *manages the instructional system well* fosters the growth of good attitudes.

A third type of teacher behavior that constitutes wholesome meta-communication is to be human in the fullest sense of the word. Cogan (1958, p. 124), Reed (1962, p. 486), and Heil, Powell, and Fiefer (1960) have found that teachers who are warm, fair, empathetic, and democratic and have a sense of humor seem to be more effective in creating good attitudes in students and in facilitating achievement. Apparently good teachers view teaching primarily as a human process involving human relationships. They are aware of the importance of roles and relationships and give attention to these factors.

A fourth type of teacher metacommunication is the definition of himself the teacher communicates. The teacher's appearance (dress, neatness, hygiene) communicates his social perceptiveness, the image he holds of his role and position, and his identification with various groups. The dynamism, interest, enthusiasm, and sincerity of a person are communicated generally through his countenance, facial expressions, and general behavior. These metacommunications are received by students. Equally important are the metacommunications embedded in the verbal messages of the teacher. The teacher who makes excuses or uses scapegoats for his own unprepared-ness and incompetence metacommunicates his definition of himself as a failure. As Berscheid and Walster (1969, pp. 11–12) say:

> When someone admits to us that everyone is out to get him, and that all his attempts to improve his lot are blocked by a malevolent fate, we become suspicious. We usually reject the possibility that through no fault of his own, the last 270 people he met just happened to be sadists. . . . We automatically assume that people get what they deserve. Since we know that many of the things that happen to people are in some way a consequence of their own actions, our best guess is that the person is probably at least partially responsible for his fate.

The teacher who complains to the students that bad situations are their fault, or that this school and its history are the cause of his poor teaching, defines himself as an inept manager of the instructional system. Regardless of the reasons he offers for his condition, students, like other people, will hold him responsible and will perceive the image he holds of himself. On the other hand, the teacher who sees himself as capable of managing an instructional system that permits students to learn will communicate that self-concept, which will create favorable student attitudes toward him.

A final kind of teacher metacommunication that has an important, wholesome influence on the teaching-learning process is honesty—honesty about himself in terms of his fears, prejudices, motives, and feelings. Some teachers attempt to present themselves to students as gods: all-knowing, all-powerful, always rational, always right, and always loving. Such teachers would never dream of saying, "I haven't the faintest idea," in response to a question they cannot answer, and when they have made a mistake, they will never admit it to the class. Rather, they present a psuedo front which students soon recognize. The real message then comes through, and the dishonesty has a negative effect upon student-teacher relationships. John Holt (1964, p. 172) has described the disastrous consequences of dishonest communication of feeling in the classroom:

> The people who write books that teachers have to read say over and over again that a teacher must love all the children in a class, all of them equally. If by this they mean that a teacher must do the best he can for every child in a class, that he has an equal responsibility for every child's welfare, an equal concern for his problems, they are right. But when they talk of love they don't mean this; they mean feelings, affections, the kind of pleasure and joy that one person can get from the existence and company of another. And this is not something that can be measured out in little spoonsful, everyone getting the same amount.
>
> In a discussion of this in a class of teachers, I once said that I liked some of the kids in my class much more than others and that, without saying which ones I liked best, I had told them so. After all, this is something that children know, whatever we tell them; it is futile to be worried about it. Naturally, these teachers were horrified. "What a terrible thing to say!" one said. "I love all the children very much." Not that there is anything wrong with that, plenty of adults don't like children, and there is no reason why they should. But the trouble is they feel they should, which makes them feel guilty, which makes them feel resentful, which in turn makes them try to work off their guilt with indulgence and their resentment with subtle cruelties—cruelties of a kind that can be seen in many classrooms.

Above all, it makes them put on the phony, syrupy, sickening voice and manner, and the fake smiles, and forced bright laughter that children see so much of in school, and rightly resent and hate.

Although Holt is describing elementary and junior high school incidents and experiences, the same principles and problems apply to the high school and college classrooms.

SUMMARY

Relationships, feelings, and attitudes are important factors in the instructional process. It is through metacommunication that feelings and relationships are made known. The effective teacher recognizes the importance and presence of metacommunication in the classroom and attempts to develop a sensitivity to those messages. He is concerned with interpreting those messages accurately, as well as with his own use of metacommunication to foster learning. This chapter has focused on precisely these points.

REFERENCES

Bateson, Gregory, and Don D. Jackson. "Some Varieties of Pathogenic Organization." In *Disorders of Communication*, edited by David M. Rioch, vol. 42, pp. 270–283. New York: Association for Research in Nervous and Mental Disease, 1964.

Bell, Sir C. *Anatomy and Philosophy of Expression*, 3d ed., 1844.

Berscheid, Ellen, and Elaine H. Walster. *Interpersonal Attraction*. Reading, Mass.: Addison-Wesley, 1969.

Cogan, M. L. "The Behavior of Teachers and the Productive Behavior of Their Pupils." *Journal of Experimental Education* 27 (1958): 89–124.

Darwin, Charles. *The Expression of Emotions in Man and Animals*. Chicago: University of Chicago Press. Reprinted from the Authorized Edition of D. Appleton, New York, 1965.

Ekman, Paul. "Personality, Pathology, Affect and Nonverbal Behavior." Paper read at Western Psychological Association Convention, Honolulu, June 1965.

Ekman, Paul, and Wallace V. Friesen. "Nonverbal Behavior in Psychotherapy Research." In *Research on Psychotherapy*, edited by J. Shlien, vol. 3. Washington, D. C.: American Psychological Association, 1967.

Fiedler, Fred E. "Style or Circumstance: The Leadership Enigma." *Psychology Today* 2 (1969): 38–43.

Hamachek, Don. "Characteristics of Good Teachers and Implications for Teachers Education." *Phi Delta Kappan* 50 (1969): 341–344.

Hart, W. F. *Teachers and Teaching.* New York: Macmillan, 1934.

Hebb, D. O. "Emotion in Man and Animal: An Analysis of the Intuitive Processes of Recognition." *Psychological Review* 53 (1946): 88–106.

Heil, L. M.; M. Powell; and I. Feifer. *Characteristics of Teacher Behavior Related to the Achievement of Children in Several Elementary Grades.* Washington, D. C.: Office of Education, Cooperative Research Branch, 1960.

Jersild, A. T. *When Teachers Face Themselves.* New York: Teachers College, Columbia University, 1955.

Labarre, Weston. "The Cultural Basis of Emotions and Gestures." *Journal of Personality* 16 (1947): 49–68.

Reed, H. B. "Implications for Science Education of Teacher Competence Research." *Science Education* 46 (1962): 473–486.

Richardson, Stephen A.; Barbara S. Dohrenwend; and David Klein. *Interviewing: Its Forms and Functions.* New York: Basic Books, 1965.

Rousey, Clyde L. *Diagnostic Implications of Speech Sounds.* Springfield, Ill.: Charles C. Thomas, 1965.

Ruesch, Jurgen, and Gregory Bateson. *Communication.* New York: W. W. Norton, 1951.

Skinner, B. F. *The Technology of Teaching.* New York: Appleton-Century-Crofts, 1968.

Spaulding, R. "Achievement, Creativity, and Self-concept Correlates of Teacher-Pupil Transactions in Elementary Schools." University of Illinois, U. S. Office of Education Cooperative Research Project No. 1352, 1963.

Spencer, Herbert. *Principles of Psychology.* New York: D. Appleton, 1880.

Starkweather, John A. "Content-Free Speech as a Source of Information About the Speaker." *Journal of Abnormal and Social Psychology* 52 (1956): 394–402.

Watzlawick, Paul; Janet H. Beavin; and Don D. Jackson. *Pragmatics of Human Communication.* New York: W. W. Norton, 1967.

Whorf, Benjamin Lee. "Science and Linguistics." In *Language, Thought, and Reality,* edited by John B. Carroll, pp. 207–218. New York: John Wiley & Sons, 1956.

TEN

SYSTEMATIC OBSERVATION:
A METHOD OF MONITORING
TEACHER-STUDENT BEHAVIOR

At several points in this book the observation has been made that few generalizations regarding strategies of teaching speech communication in the secondary school have solid empirical support. In view of this fact this book seeks to enlarge the number and quality of strategies that future speech communication teachers may consider and *test* in order to acquire a broad range of teaching skills. In this chapter we examine one tool which the teacher can use to study his own teaching: systematic observation.

Medley and Mitzel (1963, p. 253) define systematic observation as a classification system which the teacher uses to abstract and record

> relevant aspects of classroom behaviors as (or within a negligible time limit after) they occur, with a minimum of quantification intervening between the observation of a behavior and the recording of it. Typically behaviors are recorded in the form of tallies, checks, or other marks which code them into predefined categories and yield information about which behaviors occurred, or how often they occurred, during the period of observation.

The teacher who uses systematic observation does the following: first, he states the teaching behavior he intends to observe in terms of the

OBJECTIVES

1. Define systematic observation.
2. List five changes in teacher behavior that occur as a result of learning and using systematic observation.
3. List four reasons why systematic observation produces changes in teacher behavior.
4. Describe the differences between affective, cognitive, and multidimensional systematic observation instruments.
5. List the ten categories of Flanders' "Interaction Analysis."
6. List the seven categories of Galloway's nonverbal category system.
7. List the twenty-two categories of the Reynolds-Abraham-Nelson "Classroom Observational Record."
8. List the four categories of Gallagher and Aschner's classification of questions.
9. List the thirty categories of Amidon's "Expanded Interactional Analysis Categories."
10. Develop a rationale for using more than one systematic observation instrument.
11. Describe differences between sign systems and category systems.

categories of the instrument he is using for analysis; second, he collects a record of (or observes) the specified teaching behavior in the actual classroom by using an observer, films, audio or video tape recordings, or some combination of these; third, he compares proposed strategy with the data collected. This comparison should lead to a consideration of alternative strategies and help the teacher discover why he did or why he did not achieve his teaching objectives.

Flanders makes the following points (Amidon and Hough, 1967, p. 234):

There seemed to be four essential elements of teacher influence in the classrooms in which achievement and attitudes were superior. First, the teacher was capable of providing a range of roles, spontaneously, that varied from fairly active, dominative supervision, on the one hand, to reflective, discriminating support, on the other hand. The teacher was able not only to achieve compliance but to support and encourage student initiative. Second, the teacher was able to control his own spontaneous behavior so that he could assume one role or another at will. Third, he had sufficient understanding of principles of teacher influence to make possible a logical bridge between his diagnosis of the present situation and the various actions he could take. Fourth, he was a sensitive, objective observer who could make valid diagnoses of current conditions. All of these skills, which seemed to characterize the most successful teachers, were superimposed upon a firm grasp of the subject matter being taught.

The use of systematic observation instruments can help one to become a better teacher. Numerous studies indicate that the use of such systems leads to the following changes in teacher behavior: (1) Teachers become more flexible in style and method. (2) They become more accepting and less critical. (3) They actively encourage student-initiated comments. (4) They become more sensitive to pupil attitudes and hence make adjustments which help to avert many discipline problems. (5) They become more encouraging and less restricting. The reason these results occur is that the use of systematic observation instruments provides the beginning teacher with (1) a model—in behavioral terms—of the kind of teaching behavior he may choose to develop, (2) the framework for conceptualizing and developing a variety of teaching roles, (3) feedback concerning progress toward the development of those teaching behaviors he has chosen, and (4) insight into principles of effective teaching *through personal inquiry.*

Presently there are more than one hundred systematic observation systems, and there is no simple way to classify them. They might, for example, be classified by a focus on verbal behavior, nonverbal behavior, or both; a focus on teacher behavior, student behavior, or both; coding done in terms of time, thought, content area, or sequence of behaviors; a focus on affective dimension, cognitive dimension, or a multidimensional one. This chapter will use the last method of classification and examine representative instruments in each of the three areas. Following this, a description will be provided of how the teacher can develop his own instrument to focus on local needs and interests not provided for by established systems.

AFFECTIVE DIMENSION

Affective systems focus on teacher behavior as positive/negative reaction to students, praise, criticism, encouragement, acceptance, and support. The instruments used most often for observing the affective level of classroom interaction have been devised by Flanders (1970) and his colleagues. Flanders' original instrument, "Interaction Analysis," which grew out of earlier attempts to describe the effects of the social-emotional climate on learning in the classroom, focuses on verbal interaction. As diagramed herein, it is organized around two teacher behavior patterns that create contrasting classroom climates: *direct influence,* which consists of such behavior as the teacher's justification of his authority or his use of that authority; and *indirect influence,* which consists of such behavior as praising or encouraging the participation of students. The system is composed of ten categories with appropriate code numbers, the first seven of which are teacher-talk categories and the next two student-talk categories. The first four are classified further as indirect influence, and the next three as direct influence. Student talk is divided into two categories of response to the teacher, direct and self-initiated. The tenth category is used for all noncodable events. Here is the "Interaction Analysis" (Amidon and Flanders, 1967, p. 14):

Teacher talk: Indirect influence
1. *Accepts feeling:* Accepts and clarifies the feeling tone of the students in a nonthreatening manner. Feelings may be positive or negative. Predicting or recalling feelings is included.
2. *Praises or encourages:* Praises or encourages student action or behavior. Jokes that release tension, but not at the expense of another individual; nodding head, or saying "um hm?" or "go on" are included.
3. *Accepts or uses ideas of students:* Clarifying, building, or developing ideas suggested by a student. As teacher brings more of his own ideas into play, shift to Category 5.
4. *Asks questions:* Asking a question about content or procedure with the intent that a student answer.

Teacher talk: Direct influence
5. *Lecturing:* Giving facts or opinions about content or procedures; expressing his own ideas, asking rhetorical questions.
6. *Giving directions:* Directions, commands, or orders with which a student is expected to comply.
7. *Criticizing or justifying authority:* Statements intended to change student behavior from nonacceptable to acceptable pattern; bawling someone out; stating why the teacher is doing what he is doing; extreme self-reference.

Student talk
8. *Student talk—Response:* Talk by student in response to

teacher. Teacher initiates the contact or solicits student statement.

9. *Student talk—Initiation:* Talk by students which they initiate. If "calling on" student is only to indicate who may talk next, observer must decide whether student wanted to talk. If he did, use this category.

Noncodable

10. *Silence or confusion:* Pauses, short periods of silence, and periods of confusion in which communication cannot be understood by the observer.

It should be stressed that *no scale* is implied by these numbers; they merely classify—designate a particular *kind* of communication event. To write these numbers down during observation is to *enumerate,* not to judge a position on a scale.

When the instrument is used, the observer sits in the back of the room and allows himself ten minutes or so to get adjusted to the classroom atmosphere. He then records a code number every three seconds, or whenever a category change occurs, to indicate the appropriate behavior. The numbers are recorded in sequence in a column in ten- to fifteen-minute segments. Since recording procedures preserve information regarding the sequence of events, the code numbers can be recorded in a ten-by-ten matrix, as shown in Figure 1. The category totals may be added in numerous combinations in order to produce a wide variety of interaction ratios. The two most widely used ratios are determined as follows:

$$\frac{I}{D} = \frac{\text{Indirect}}{\text{Direct}} = \frac{\text{Sum totals for Categories 1 to 4}}{\text{Sum totals for Categories 5 to 7}}$$

$$\frac{i}{d} = \frac{\text{indirect}}{\text{direct}} = \frac{\text{Sum totals for Categories 1 to 3}}{\text{Sum totals for Categories 6 and 7}}$$

Once the teacher's verbal behavior has been quantified into an interaction ratio, it is possible to determine the effect of such teacher behavior on achievement and attitude development.

One criticism of Flanders' instrument is that it minimizes the nonverbal dimension of interaction. If, as some social scientists suggest, at least 65 percent of social meaning is nonverbal, this is indeed a serious oversight. In formulating a system for observing nonverbal interaction, Galloway views a teacher's behavior on a continuum which ranges from restricting communication to encouraging communication. Using this concept, he has designed an observational system which provides seven categories for

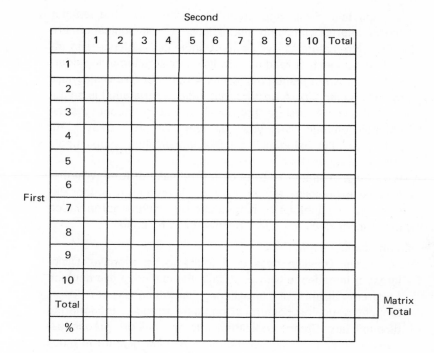

Second

	1	2	3	4	5	6	7	8	9	10	Total
1											
2											
3											
4											
5											
6											
7											
8											
9											
10											
Total											
%											

First

Matrix Total

FIGURE 1 *Sample matrix form*

observing the nonverbal behavior of teachers. Galloway notes that recording in the categories calls for a sensitivity to nuances, inflections, and subtle cues and requires the use of video tapes which can be viewed several times. His system is as follows (1970, pp. 11–12):

Encouraging communication
1. *Enthusiastic support.* Enthusiastic approval, unusual warmth, emotional support, or strong encouragement. A smile or nod to show enjoyment, pleasure, or satisfaction. A pat on the back, a warm greeting of praise, or any act that shows obvious approval. Vocal intonation or inflection or approval and support.
2. *Helping.* A spontaneous reaction to meet a pupil's request, help a pupil, or answer a need. A nurturant act. A look of acceptance and understanding of a problem, implying "I understand," or "I know what you mean," and followed by an appropriate action. An action intended to help. A tender, compassionate, or supportive voice. Or a laugh, a vocalization that breaks the tension.
3. *Receptivity.* Willingness to listen with patience and interest

to pupil talk. By paying attention to the pupil, the teacher shows interest, implying that "lines of communication are open." He maintains eye contact, indicates patience and attention, suggests a readiness to listen or an attempt to understand. A pose or stance of alertness, readiness, or willingness to have public talk. A gesture that indicates the pupil is on the "right track." A gesture that openly or subtly encourages the pupil to continue: "yes, yes" (um-hm), "Go on," "Okay," "All right," or "I'm listening." Such a vocalization supplements and encourages the pupil to continue.

4. *Pro forma.* A matter of form or for the sake of form. Whether a facial expression, action, or vocal language, it neither encourages nor inhibits communication. A routine act in which the teacher does not need to listen or to respond.

Inhibiting communication

5. *Inattentive.* Unwillingness or inability to be attentive. Disinterest or impatience with pupil talk. Avoidance of eye contact. Apparent disinterest, impatience, unwillingness to listen. Slouchy or unalert posture. "Don't care attitude," the ignoring of pupil talk. Stance indicating internal tension, preoccupation, or concern with own thoughts. A hand gesture to block or terminate pupil talk. Impatience, or "I want you to stop talking."

6. *Unresponsive.* Failure to respond when a response would ordinarily be expected. Egocentric behavior, openly ignoring need, insensitive to feeling. An obvious denial of pupil feelings, noncompliance. Threatens, cajoles, condescends. Withdrawing from a request or expressed need of a pupil. Disaffection or unacceptance of feeling. A gesture suggesting tension or nervousness. Obvious interruption and interference.

7. *Disapproval.* Strong disapproval, negative overtones, disparagement, or strong dissatisfaction. Frowning, scowling, threatening glances. Derisive, sarcastic, or disdainful expression that "sneers at" or condemns. Physical attack or aggressiveness—a blow, slap, or pinch. A pointed finger that pokes fun, belittles, or threatens pupils. Vocal tone that is hostile, cross, irritated, or antagonistic. Utterance suggesting unacceptance, disappointment, depreciation, or discouragement.

Galloway and others have gone on to design systematic observation instruments which focus on both verbal and nonverbal behaviors simultaneously. The selected sources listed at the end of this chapter will guide you to them.

COGNITIVE DIMENSION

Cognitive systems focus on the level of abstraction of a statement, logical processes, and the type of logical or linguistic function a particular behavior seems to serve in the classroom. The first example of a cognitive system presented here is the Reynolds-Abraham-Nelson (1971) "Classroom Observational Record." The twenty-two categories of this instrument are adapted primarily from the work of Bellack and Flanders. The instrument and the definitions of its various categories, along with their numerical designators, are as follows:

I. *Structuring Moves:* Any statement which establishes a center of cognitive focus and does not directly elicit a verbal response is defined as a Structuring Move. The instrument defines three categories of Structuring Moves.
   (0) *Reviewing:* Summarizing one or more previous cognitive focuses from reading or class experience.
   (1) *Informing:* Presenting new facts, ideas, opinions, etc., about the content.
   (2) *Directing:* Giving instructions about actions to be carried out.

II. *Soliciting Moves:* Any question which (a) initiates a new transaction by establishing a new center of cognitive focus and/or (b) maintains an existing center of cognitive focus is defined as a Soliciting Move. There are four categories of Soliciting Moves.
   (3) *Recalling:* Calling for specific information about a previous cognitive focus(es) from reading or class experience [e.g., What was the thesis of the speech Bill gave yesterday?].
   (4) *Collecting Data:* Calling for specific information from direct observation of a book, chart, map, etc. [e.g., According to page 23 in your text, what are the steps in Monroe's "Motivated Sequence?"].
   (5) *Processing Data:* Calling for comparisons, grouping, categorizing, labeling, differentiating properties, inferring, developing, and using relationships or hypotheses, etc. [e.g., From the information we have, what conclusions can you draw about the effects of the nature of language on interpersonal communication?].
   (6) *Evaluating or Verifying Principles and/or Conclusions:* Calling for application and testing of hypotheses, conclusions, or principles [e.g., In light of what you just said, how can you explain the effectiveness of speeches which do not contain adequate supporting material?].

III. *Reacting moves:* Any response which (a) accepts or rejects, or

(b) elicits evaluation, clarification, or explanation of an immediately preceding Move is classified as a Reacting Move. There
are eight categories of Reacting Moves.
  (7) *Accepting:* Expressing agreement with a previous Move(s).
  (8) *Rejecting:* Expressing disagreement with a previous
      Move(s).
  (8') *Rejecting Personal Behavior:* Expressing disapproval of
      conduct (e.g., I don't like the way you are behaving; or, Sit
      in your chair and be quiet; or, Why are you making so much
      noise today?).
  (9) *Calling for Clarification:* Asking that a previous Move(s) be
      more fully explained [e.g., Do you mean that establishing
      rapport is always a function to be performed in the opening
      of an interview?].
  (10) *Calling for Evidence or Explanation:* Asking that the ration-
      ale for a previous Move(s) be presented [e.g., Why do you
      say that small-group communication is the most important
      communication activity form?].
  (11) *Calling for the Opinion of Another Person:* Asking that an-
      other individual evaluate a preceding Move(s) [e.g., Do you
      agree with Steven's statement, John?].
  (N) *Answering a Raised Hand:* Calling for a response by name
      only [e.g., John? or by pointing and saying "Yes?", etc.].
  (R) *Repeat:* Repeating a preceding Move(s) [e.g., Q: Do you
      agree with Steven's statement? A. Do I agree with Steven's
      statement?].
IV. *Responding Moves:* Any statement in response to a Soliciting or
    Reacting Move is defined as a Responding Move. There are
    five categories of Responding Moves.
  (3') *Recalling:*
  (4') *Presenting Data:*   (Responses correspond
  (5') *Processing Data:*   to criteria set up in
  (6') *Evaluating or Verifying Data:*   sub-division II, Solicit-
  (K) *I don't know:*   ing Moves.
V. *Non-moves:* Any occurrence which is not categorizable under
   the four preceding subdivisions is categorized as a Non-move.
   There are two categories of Non-moves.
   (12) *Silence:*
   (Z) *Confusion:* Content of discussion not discernible.

The rules for recording the categories are much the same as those in the
Flanders system. The tally sheet consists of two columns: one for

teacher moves, the other for pupil moves. Thus the same designators can be used for both teacher and pupils. A tally recording the appropriate numerical designator is made every three seconds or whenever a change occurs. A check (√) is made in the appropriate column if the speaker, type of move, and cognitive focus continues for another three seconds. A slash (/) is made between two moves when the speaker remains the same but the cognitive focus changes. Immediately after the encoded lesson, the data are ready for analysis. Visual scanning of the tally sheet reveals who did the talking; on what cognitive level(s) the interactions took place; the sequence of questioning levels; the level and duration of responses of pupils to the questioning; and the reactions of the teacher to the pupil responses.

A second example of a cognitive system is Gallagher and Aschner's (1968, pp. 121–123) application of Guilford's four operations of the intellect to an analysis of teacher's questions. You will notice similarity between these four levels and the six levels of Bloom's taxonomy of cognitive objectives.

The first level, consisting of *cognitive-memory operations,* requires the simple reproduction of facts, formulas, or other items of remembered content. The processes required of the student include recognition, rote memory, and selective recall. An example of a question at this level is, Please list the steps necessary for starting and maintaining a problem-solving discussion.

If you were to ask a student "Which functions of the opening of an interview did Bill neglect?" you would have asked a question at the second level—*convergent thinking.* Convergent thinking leads to one expected end result or answer. It is based on the analysis and integration of given or remembered data.

The third level is labeled *divergent thinking.* In divergent thinking there is no definite end result. The student is free to generate independently his own response or to take a new direction or perspective on a given topic. A question to prompt this type of response is, What might Bill have done to establish rapport in the opening of the interview?

The final level, *evaluative thinking,* requires the student to deal with matters of judgment, value, and choice. The question, How do you think Bill did as a discussion leader? is characterized by its judgmental quality and thus would be classified at this final level.

The Gallagher-Aschner system is only one of many systems that focus on the cognitive dimension of classroom communication. Others can be located in the references listed at the end of this chapter.

MULTIDIMENSIONAL

Multidimensional systems attempt to identify classroom factors from both the affective and cognitive dimensions of behavior. A number of such systems have expanded Flanders' ten basic categories in a variety of ways. One of these, Amidon's "Expanded Interactional Analysis Categories," is especially useful (1967, p. 389):

Teacher talk: Indirect influence
   1. *Accepts students' feelings*
      1a. Acknowledges feelings
      1c. Clarifies feelings
      1r. Refers to similar feelings of others
   2. *Praises*
      2w. Without criteria
      2P. With public criteria
      2p. With private criteria
   3. *Accepts students' ideas*
      3a. Acknowledges ideas
      3c. Clarifies ideas
      3s. Summarizes ideas
   4. *Asks questions*
      4f. Factual question
      4c. Convergent question
      4d. Divergent question
      4e. Evaluative question

Teacher talk: Direct influence
   5. *Lectures*
      5f. Factual lecture
      5m. Motivational lecture
      5o. Orientation lecture
      5p. Personal opinions
   6. *Gives directions*
      6c. Cognitive directions
      6m. Managerial directions
   7. *Criticizes*
      7w. Without criteria
      7P. With public criteria
      7p. With private criteria

Student talk
   8. *Student talk—predictable*
      8f. Factual response
      8c. Convergent response

  9. *Student talk—unpredictable*
    9d. Divergent response
    9e. Evaluative response
    9i. Student-initiated talk

No talk
  10. *Silence or confusion**
    10s. Silence
    10c. Confusion

*10 without a subcategory letter indicates:
—a change of speakers in student-to-student interaction
—the beginning and end of a coding sequence in matrix construction

The use of Amidon's expanded system is basically the same as the use of Flanders' ten categories. A code number (and subscript) is recorded every three seconds or whenever a category change occurs. Since recording procedures preserve information regarding the sequence of events, the code numbers can be recorded in a thirty-by-thirty matrix. The category totals may be added in numerous combinations in order to provide a wide variety of interaction ratios. The matrix can then be analyzed to answer questions such as: What kind of teacher behavior generates student-initiated talk? What type of teacher question produces student generalization?

The advantage of the Amidon system, then, is that it abstracts more features of classroom communication and thus allows the teacher to see better the results of his classroom behavior. At the same time, however, many features of classroom communication are not covered by the Amidon system. When you find that this is the case, it will be helpful for you to search the references at the end of this chapter for systems which allow you to observe what you want to observe; or, failing to locate such an instrument, you can devise your own. The next and final section of this chapter explores how to do this.

SELF-DEVISED SYSTEMS

This chapter has introduced you to a number of systematic observation instruments and has pointed out that many others are available. Since there are well over one hundred such systems and all focus on some aspect of behavior in the classroom, you may well ask: Would it not be better to devise a single instrument for the speech communication classroom which incorporates all that is useful from each of the instruments? Surely many of the instruments discussed contain strengths which are not present in other instruments. Can we not combine these individual strengths to create a uniquely powerful instrument which will give us added insight into classroom communication and enable us to make more comprehensive and verifiable predictions concerning classroom behavior than are presently possible?

Although this line of reasoning is intriguing and finds much support, there are theoretical and practical obstacles to carrying out such a plan. First, this point of view assumes that it is possible to select the categories for the "perfect" instrument on the basis of demonstrated empirical utility. The truth of the matter is that the amount of empirical testing of the usefulness of the categories in the various systems is minute compared to the range of problems with which the various instruments deal. More than one thousand skills have been identified. There is evidence that teachers can be trained both to exhibit these skills in the classroom and to elicit specified student behaviors. Yet when Rosenshine (1970) set out to summarize all of the *experimental* studies in which some teachers had been trained to teach a class of students in a specific manner, observational measures had been obtained to verify that teachers had behaved as intended, and end-of-experiment measures (such as achievement scores) had been obtained, he was able to locate only fifteen such studies. His summary of those studies clearly indicates one reason why the "perfect" systematic observation instrument cannot be devised at this time (pp. 19–20):

> In many of our activities in teacher training, we have assumed that certain processes will yield certain products. These processes have included the asking of questions at a higher cognitive level, encouragement of student decision making, providing greater affect in the classroom, and increasing student participation. The products are student achievement in the classroom. Unfortunately, the belief that increased use of these processes will lead to improved produce measures has not, as yet, been supported by the research; training teachers to use these processes has *not* resulted in measurable improvement in student achievement.
>
> ... the major conclusion of this review is that of the hundreds of research studies completed every year, an insignificant number have been experimental studies of the type described above. As long as we lack such research we shall be bound to myths and superstitions which are interesting subject matter for our methods courses, but which have little relevance for the real world.

The first reason, then, why the "perfect" systematic observation system cannot be devised is that there is not as yet an empirical basis for selecting the categories to include. As a result, the teacher will have to do the empirical testing. The second reason is a practical one. When the teacher devises categories to include in a systematic observation instrument, he abstracts important features of classroom communication—features which he considers to be important for the particular classroom situation he wishes to observe. It is necessary for the teacher thus to devise systems with a particular purpose in mind since there is a limitation on the number of categories he can operate with effectively and since the number of possible abstractions is almost limitless. The second obstacle, then, is that a "perfect" instrument that could be used for all conceivable purposes would require so many categories that it would be unmanageable.

Because it is clearly impossible to devise a universal systematic observation system, the teacher of speech communication will not only want to familiarize himself with numerous existing instruments but will also want to devise his own instruments which focus on local needs and interests. He must first decide which behaviors, and which aspects of these behaviors, are to be recorded. The purpose for which the instrument is to be used usually determines which behaviors are to be observed. Oftentimes preliminary informal observation is helpful in identifying promising categories. In addition, an examination of existing category systems will often suggest categories.

After giving some thought to potential categories, the teacher can decide to construct his instrument in one of two ways. With the *sign system*, he lists a number of specific behaviors which may or may not occur during a period of observation. Then during the period of observation he records which of these incidents actually occurred and, in some cases, how frequently each occurred. With a *category system*, on the other hand, the teacher limits observation to one aspect of classroom communication, determines a convenient unit of behavior (time, thought, content area, sequence of behavior, etc.), and constructs a finite set of categories into which every unit observed can be classified.

Both approaches are useful for the teacher of speech communication. Sign systems are normally used when theory provides little guidance on what to look for. It is often a first step in the development of a category system. Since category systems are supposed to be exhaustive of the behavior recorded, they presuppose a fairly thorough understanding of the nature of the behavior. Sign systems can often be helpful in developing this understanding.

To illustrate how you might devise a systematic observation system, let us assume that you want to analyze your behavior in orally criticizing communication performances. Since this is a somewhat limited area and you have a fairly good idea of what is involved, you choose to work with a category system. You decide that one way of abstracting your comments is to classify them as focusing on psychomotor, affective, cognitive, and procedural aspects of the performance. Your behaviors within each of these categories are either positive or negative. The positive or negative behaviors can be engaged in without criteria, with public criteria, or with private criteria. Your systematic observation system, then, would look like this:

Affective
  1a. *Accepts student feeling:* Accepts and clarifies the feeling tone of the student in a nonthreatening manner.
    1a. Accepts without criteria.
    1aP. Accepts with public criteria.
    1ap. Accepts with private criteria.
  1r. *Rejects student feeling:* Discourages, rejects, or ignores student expression of feeling.
    1r. Rejects without criteria.
    1rP. Rejects with public criteria.
    1rp. Rejects with private criteria.

Cognitive
  2a. *Accepts student ideas:* Praises, encourages, clarifies, builds, or develops ideas presented by student.
    2a. Accepts without criteria.
    2aP. Accepts with public criteria.
    2ap. Accepts with private criteria.
  2r. *Rejects student ideas:* Questions or criticizes ideas expressed by student.
    2r. Rejects without criteria.
    2rP. Rejects with public criteria.
    2rp. Rejects with private criteria.

Psychomotor
  3a. *Accepts student skills:* Praises or encourages student's communication skills such as physical and vocal elements of delivery.
    3a. Accepts without criteria.
    3aP. Accepts with public criteria.
    3ap. Accepts with private criteria.
  3r. *Rejects student skills:* Criticizes or questions techniques used; includes suggestions of ways for improvement.
    3r. Rejects without criteria.

3rP. Rejects with public criteria.

3rp. Rejects with private criteria.

Procedural

4s. *Silence or confusion:* Pauses, short periods of silence, and periods of confusion in which communication cannot be understood by the observer.

4p. *Procedural comments:* Comments by teacher indicating how he will proceed; other comments not classified above.

SUMMARY

This chapter has described and illustrated three different categories of systematic observation instruments for monitoring teacher-student behavior in the classroom: affective, cognitive, and multidimensional. It has also developed the argument that since there is evidence that the use of systematic observation instruments can aid you in improving your teaching, you should familiarize yourself with other existing instruments as well as devise your own instruments to focus on local needs and interests.

It will not be enough, however, for you only to familiarize yourself with a number of these instruments. If you expect to use them to improve your teaching, you will need much practice, which you can get in a number of ways. For example, after mastering a particular instrument (be sure to read the selected sources at the end of the chapter), you can use the instrument to describe the teaching occurring in the classes you are enrolled in this term. You can also use the instruments to describe your own teaching behavior by video-taping or audio-taping yourself while engaged in microteaching (see Chapter 4) and then studying your behavior with various systematic observation systems. Although mastering the use of systematic observation requires a great deal of effort, your increased effectiveness as a teacher will make the effort worthwhile.

REFERENCES

Amidon, Edmund J. "Interaction Analysis." In *Methods of Research in Communication,* edited by Philip Emmert and William D. Brooks, pp. 373–425. Boston: Houghton Mifflin, 1970.

Amidon, Edmund J., and Ned A. Flanders. *The Role of the Teacher in the Classroom: A Manual for Understanding and Improving Teacher Classroom Behavior*. Minneapolis: Association for Productive Teaching, 1967. A manual for learning the basic ten categories of Interaction Analysis.

Amidon, Edmund J., and John B. Hough, eds. *Interaction Analysis: Theory, Research, and Application*. Reading, Mass.: Addison-Wesley, 1967.

Amidon, Paul S., and Associates, 5408 Chicago Avenue South, Minneapolis, Minnesota 55417. This is a private firm which produces and distributes a variety of training kits for Interaction Analysis.

Bebb, Aldon M.; Arlene F. Low; and Floyd T. Waterman. "Supervisory Conference as Individualized Teaching." *Association for Student Teaching Bulletin*, No. 28, 1969.

Flanders, Ned A. *Analyzing Teaching Behavior*. Reading, Mass.: Addison-Wesley, 1970. Discusses recent innovations in Interaction Analysis.

Friedrich, Gustav W., and William D. Brooks. "The Use of Systematic Observation Instruments for the Supervision of Teaching." *Speech Teacher* 19 (1970): 283–288.

Gallagher, James J., and Mary Jane Aschner. "A Preliminary Report of Analyses of Classroom Interaction." In *Teaching: Vantage Points for Study*, edited by Ronald R. Hyman, pp. 118–129. Philadelphia: J. B. Lippincott, 1968.

Galloway, Charles M. "Teaching is Communicating: Nonverbal Language in the Classroom." *Association for Student Teaching Bulletin*, No. 29, 1970.

Medley, Donald M., and Harold E. Mitzel. "Measuring Classroom Behavior by Systematic Observation." In *Handbook of Research on Teaching*, edited by N. L. Gage, pp. 247-328. Chicago: Rand McNally, 1963.

Nelson, Lois N., ed. *The Nature of Teaching: A Collection of Readings*. Waltham, Mass.: Blaisdell, 1969.

Reynolds, William W., Jr.; Eugene C. Abraham; and Miles A. Nelson. "The Classroom Observational Record." Paper read at American Educational Research Association Convention, New York, February 1971.

Rosenshine, Barak. "Experimental Classroom Studies of Teacher Training, Teaching Behavior, and Student Achievement." Paper presented at meeting of the National Council for the Social Studies, New York, November 1970.

Sandefur, J. T., and Alex A. Bressler. *Classroom Observation Systems in Preparing School Personnel.* Washington, D. C.: ERIC Clearinghouse on Teacher Education, 1970. An anthology of instruments.

Simon, Anita, and E. Gil Boyer, eds. *Mirrors for Behavior II,* vols. A and B. Philadelphia: Research for Better Schools, 1970. The most complete anthology of instruments to date.

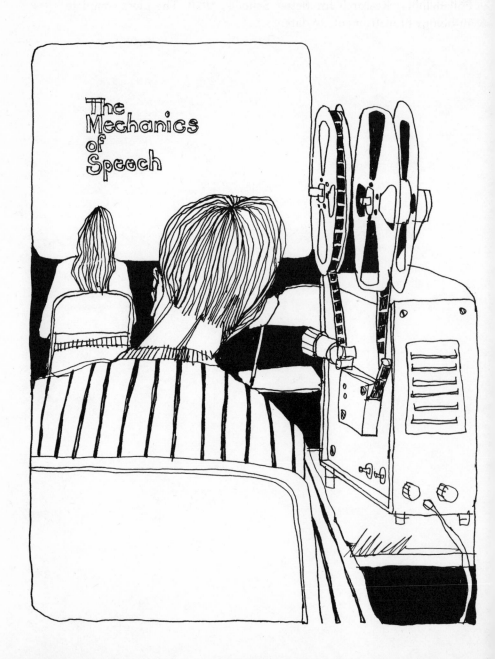

PART THREE

RESOURCE MATERIALS FOR THE SPEECH TEACHER

Part Three of this text has four chapters, each of which is simply a file of resource materials and student assignments for the speech communication teacher. These chapters do not contain complete lessons. They do not contain behavioral objectives, and the assignments described are not linked with specific objectives. These four chapters are to be used simply as a *reference file* rather than as content related directly to the theory of teaching speech communication.

The suggested assignments for students are, of course, instructional strategies, but it is not expected that a speech communication teacher will use all these assignments in a single course. Neither is it expected that all four areas covered—interpersonal communication, public speaking, radio and television, and oral interpretation and theater—will be included in the basic speech communication course. It is the authors' belief, in fact, that radio and television, as well as oral interpretation and theater, should *not* be included in the basic course but are handled more effectively as separate courses. Nevertheless, units in oral interpretation, theater, and radio and television are included in some basic speech courses in secondary schools, and therefore Chapters 13 and 14 have been added to provide resource materials and assignments in these areas. Also, the speech communication teacher who teaches a separate course in radio and television, oral interpretation, or theater is faced with the problem of selecting materials and instructional strategies to enable students to meet specific objectives, and he can select films, books, and learning activities from these catalogs and incorporate them into the lessons he devises for achieving his objectives.

The assignments have various origins. Some have been used in classes in which the authors were students; many have been passed to us by word of mouth from graduate students, members of our staff, and professional colleagues throughout the nation; others have been passed from teacher to teacher on unsigned, undated mimeographed sheets of paper. Credit has been given to the people whose contributions could be identified.

ELEVEN

INTERPERSONAL COMMUNICATION: ASSIGNMENTS AND RESOURCE MATERIALS

Interpersonal communication is communication in which two or more persons are engaged directly with each other in situations in which each can send messages freely and overtly to the other. Interpersonal communication is dialogical, while public communication is usually monological. Interpersonal communication includes forms of dyadic communication and small-group communication, ranging from formal to informal situations and including such specific situations as the employment interview, the social conversation, a conference between subordinate and superior, the committee meeting, and on-the-job communication.

Most of the communication in which people engage daily is interpersonal rather than public. For this reason, speech communication teachers at the secondary level, as well as at the college level, are adding interpersonal communication units to the basic communication course. The inclusion of interpersonal communication objectives, along with public speaking objectives, relates the basic communication course more closely to the day-to-day communication needs of our society. While the sixteen areas for which student assignments are provided in this resource chapter are not *all* the areas in interpersonal communication, they do represent some of the most common ones.

ASSIGNMENT AREAS

Introductory assignments

Receiving information and perception

Using language

Knowing oneself

Values, attitudes and goals

Feedback

Nonverbal communication

Interviewing

Conversation

Small-group communication

Listening

Protest communication

Communication breakdowns

Improving thinking and problem solving

Parliamentary procedure

Family communication

ASSIGNMENTS

INTRODUCTORY ASSIGNMENTS

1. Evaluating yourself as a communicator   Write an evaluation of yourself as a communicator. How effective are you in one-to-many situations (public communication), in one-to-one situations (dyadic communication), and in small groups? What do you consider to be your strengths and weaknesses?

2. Student journal   Keep a record of your communication experiences and periodically assess your development and growth as a communicator.

3. Communication profile   Prepare a descriptive chart of your communication activities during one day. You may construct your own classification system, which may focus on any aspect of communication.

4. Communication activities   Talk with five persons about the amount of time each spends in the various kinds of communication activities.

5. Communication model   Prepare your own communication model or make a diagram of someone else's model and explain it to the class.

RECEIVING INFORMATION AND PERCEPTION

1. Perception and receiving information   Ask the students to listen to their alarm clocks at home and answer the following questions: Does it ring? Or buzz? Or snarl? Or hum? What is its pitch? Do you hear its sound as a vowel? What vowel? Do you hear its sound as a consonant?
 Now think about your best friend. Could you recognize his footsteps? Listen to feet passing in the hall, approaching the room, or walking beside you on a sidewalk. How do they differ?

2. Interpersonal perception   Some students may dismiss the idea that accuracy in perception of others can be developed. Discuss: How do children develop accuracy in understanding the motives of others? If you went to Mexico or France, would you not expect your "reading" of the cues given off to increase over time? Can you likewise improve your understanding of people in your own culture? (This might be a time to discuss T-groups and sensitivity training.)

3. Aural information   Have the students close their eyes and listen for a number of seconds. Then ask them to list every different sound they heard during that time.

4. Recall   Read aloud rapidly the names of different objects, including three or four different categories. Ask one team to remember only the toys, another team only the tools, etc.

5. Focusing   Read a short selection, asking students to count the number of times they hear a particular word, such as "the" or "a."

6. Following directions   Play games that involve cutting and folding paper, drawing, or writing according to oral directions.

7. Following directions   Using prepared worksheets, have students follow directions such as: "Put an X on . . . ," "Cross out . . . ," "Underline . . . ," etc.

8. Following directions Have students listen to and repeat directions to a traveler.

9. Discrimination Record short sequences of drum beats, bell sounds, or piano tones at various pitch or volume levels. As each group of sounds is played, ask students to note which sounds in the sequence are loudest and softest, highest and lowest, longest and shortest.

10. Sound identification Play sound-effects recordings, and ask students to identify the sounds. Tap a rhythm pattern with a pencil, and have students repeat it.

11. Recall Read aloud a series of numbers or letters with one-, two-, or three-second pauses after each. Following each sequence of three, four, five, or six, ask students to write all the numbers or letters they can remember.

Read polysyllabic words. Ask students to note the number of syllables in each word and to repeat the syllables. This can be done with English words, nonsense words, or words of a foreign language.

12. Recall Read telephone or ZIP code numbers aloud and ask students to write them.

13. Using Context Read a sentence containing an unfamiliar word or one in which a familiar word is used in an unfamiliar manner. Then ask students to discuss the clues provided by the context and the meaning that they indicate.

14. Using context Read aloud sentences in which certain words are omitted. Ask students to listen to the sentences and then fill in suitable words.

15. Using context Build sentences by having each student add one or two words. One goal would be to create a run-on sentence that tells a complete story. Another version would be to limit the number of conjunctions in each sentence and to charge one point against each student who ends a sentence.

16. Using context Read the beginnings of sentences and allow students to supply the ends to show that they understand the function of word signals.

17. Distinguishing relevant and irrelevant information Read a paragraph aloud in which one sentence does not belong. Ask students to identify the sentence that does not fit the topic.

18. Distinguishing relevant and irrelevant information Read sentences which contain one word which is poorly chosen, perhaps an inappropriate adjective, noun, or verb. Ask students to spot the word which does not belong and to substitute a better word.

19. Distinguishing relevant and irrelevant information After stating the purpose of an account or description, read the selection, sentence by sentence, and ask the students to accept or reject each sentence on the basis of its relevance to the purpose.

20. Sensory images A number of sentences, each containing an appeal to one or more of the five senses, are read aloud. Students are asked to write or check the sense appealed to. For example, "The thick smoke filled the room and caused me to run, choking, to the cabin door." The students should check sight and smell.

21. Sensory images Read to the students short stories, essays, or poems that are high in sensory impact. The first reading should be for appreciation only. During a second reading, ask students to analyze the words or phrases chosen to produce a particular sensory appeal.

22. Identifying common sounds Divide students into two teams and have each team prepare a tape recording of various common sounds. The tapes will be played for the class and students asked to identify the sounds, their source, and their function, purpose, or meaning.

23. Perception Plan an incident in class involving two persons or more. Following the "spontaneous" incident, ask the two participants to leave the room. Then ask each student to write down what happened and to describe fully the persons involved. The reports can then be compared and discussed.

24. Judging another's viewpoint Have students list one person they know fairly well and describe how they believe he sees his world and how his picture of the world differs from theirs.

25. Perception and the generation gap Have students talk with someone "over forty" about his perception of the high school generation and about their perception of his generation, and then write a report showing why a generation gap exists.

USING LANGUAGE

1. Signal response   Ask students to list a number of words to which they have a signal response and then list the reason why.

2. Language   Have each student select four words and see how he can change their meaning by changing context. Some examples:

> It is a *fast* car.
> The colors are *fast* and will not run.
> The flag is *fast* to the pole.

3. Language   Ask students to write samples of an abstraction ladder.

4. Using language   Have students read this sentence to themselves— "The Dean said that the freshman who came in yesterday decided to go home"—and then do the following:

a. Read as a statement of fact.

b. Read as if asking for information or confirmation (change of pitch).

c. Read to emphasize *who* made the statement—the dean, not his secretary (intensity).

d. Read as if it is pleasant news (thank goodness he's gone), then, sadly, as if somone failed to help him (pitch and quality).

e. Read as if tossing it over your shoulder while rushing off in a terrific hurry; then as if deliberating about it, getting the words just right, with plenty of time (duration).

5. Language   Grammar involves sentence patterns. Meaning shifts with grammar and grammar with meaning. Some examples:

As host, Henry turned on the electric barbecue spit. (If "on" is part of the verb "turned on," a delicious meal may be in sight. If it is part of the modifier, the guests may be aghast.)

Little Willie tore up the street.

Mehitable took a tramp in the woods.

Agnes called up the dumb waiter.

Have the students create other examples.

6. Language   Ask students to read a news item and an editorial from their daily newspaper and then make a study of the language differences in these two types of writing.

7. Language   Have students read a novel and a "how-to-do-it" book and then make a study of the language differences between the two.

8. Language   Ask students to listen to a television or radio news report, then to a commercial, and make a study of the differences in language used. The programs may be taped and the differences demonstrated to classmates.

9. Language   Ask students to listen to a speaker and then analyze only the types of language he used.

10. Language and meaning   There are two important ways by which one makes clear the meaning of what he says: (a) by changing the *pitch* or *tone* (inflection) when uttering a word and (b) by *stress*. Have students practice these in class:

> Take the word "well." Say it in as may ways as you can:
> Meaning "Go ahead and tell me more."
> Meaning "I disapprove."
> Meaning "I'm scolding you."

> Take the word "no." Say it in as many ways as you can:
> Meaning "Really."
> Meaning "That's impossible."
> Meaning "I certainly will not."
> Meaning "How funny that is."
> Meaning "That's really revolting."

11. Language and meaning   Have two students give a "Double Word Play." Let a boy and girl using only each other's names talk to each other. Have them make a date, accept the date, keep the date, have a fight, make up, say goodnight, *using only inflection and stress.*

12. Language   Discuss how objects or ideas are given different labels by different groups. Use slang as an example. For instance, have students list as many labels as they can for a college student who has prestige or personal appeal.

13. Language   To compare referents, have two students each draw a chair and compare differences. Not only is the object called chair the referent but also one's concept of chairs as a class. Repeat with other students and other objects.

14. Language   Have students think up a nonsense term and give it meaning by citing its characteristics. For example:

> All smoogles have comcom. In the spring, when the smoogle emerges from hibernation, his comcom is quite inferior in quantity and quality and not of much use to man. If smoogles are given a high protein diet during the spring months, the comcom can be sheared by late May or early June. After shearing, the smoogle can be turned loose until the next spring. The comcom of about fifty smoogles is needed to make a lady's sweater. What do you know about the smoogle and its comcom?

15. Word association   Have the class relax physically and mentally and then speak a word (a noun: smoke, popcorn, rain, picnic, etc.) as emotionally noncommittal as possible, although there should be an idea in your mind. Then call for the first response that comes into students' minds. The differences in responses will be interesting and will prove how listeners react, regardless of what was in the speaker's mind. You may also speak with considerable emotional coloring when you say the word to discover if there is any difference in responses.

16. Symbols and signs   Ask students to identify the symbols and signs they see during a single day.

17. The meaning of words   Select a word and ask each member of the class to write down what the word means to him. Compare the meanings. Do they vary? Why?

18. Stereotyping   Have the class write one word or phrase (the first that comes to mind) that describes each of the following words. Pronounce each word allowing time for the written response.

prostitute	churchgoer
farmer	atheist
artist	teen-ager
football captain	Miss America
Texan	preacher

Have students compare the words or phrases they have written down.

19. Stereotyping   Have the class write definitions of the following:

> WASP
> nigger
> junkie
> Afro-American
> Italian

You may want to add to the list.

KNOWING ONESELF

1. Who are you?   Have each student write on a sheet of paper three key words or phrases denoting who he is. These words or phrases should refer to dimensions of himself that class members may not know. The sheet is then pinned on the front of the student. All the students then circulate, but they may *not* speak for five minues. Then, for ten to fifteen minutes, they may talk to anyone to become better acquainted. Following this informal, getting-better-acquainted period, a discussion may be held, or individual papers written, to consider the effect this exercise will have on subsequent communication of the group.

2. Knowing oneself   One's real self is composed of many subselves. Below are listed some of the major types of selves that most Americans have.

a. *A physical self:* American girls place a premium on the cosmetic self; boys place it on the athletic self. Being beautiful is terribly important to most American women; and being well-built and on the "team" is deeply important to young men.

b. *An intellectual self:* Many people take pride in their intelligence. Good grades and other signs of intellectual achievement are important to them. A speech is always a situation in which the intellectual self is being demonstrated, weighed, and tested.

c. *A spiritual self:* Some people think of themselves as being a religious person whose life's work is the spiritual helping of others.

d. *A moral-ethical self:* Most Americans think of themselves as being honest, prompt, reliable, hard-working, patriotic.

e. *A social self:* Most people want to belong. Being a member of a club or dating, going with the gang, being "in the know," is important. Having a self that gets along with others is vital to most people.

f. *An economic self:* To most Americans nothing is more important than being a "success": having a job with prestige, making money, etc. Men have selves which say: "A man's job is work; bringing home the paycheck; supporting the family."

Have each student write in specific terms what he wants to be someday for each self.

3. Knowing oneself   Have each student prepare and tell a story in which one of the characters is himself. After each story is told, discuss the characters and their relationships. See if the listeners can detect which character is the author.

4. Self-awareness   Ask each student to do the following: Construct a personal profile. Identify yourself, your likes, dislikes, prejudices, talents, strong individual characteristics, heroes, events that influenced your life. Analyze your personality socially, intellectually, emotionally, morally, religiously, economically, and politically.

5. Knowing oneself   Since we come to know ourselves by the decisions we make, have students carefully think out in advance the following two-minute speaking assignments:

a. Rank the following six factors in order of their importance first, second, and so on, and give your reasons for so doing: (1) friends, (2) education, (3) family, (4) money, (5) religion, (6) health.

b. Rank the following six professions and occupations on the basis of which has contributed most to civilization: (1) preacher, (2) farmer, (3) politician, (4) scientist, (5) artisan, (6) teacher.

c. You must give up the following six modern conveniences. Decide what to give up first, second, and so on and explain your reasons: (1) telephone, (2) radio and television, (3) automobile, (4) refrigerator, (5) bathroom, (6) washing machine.

d. Ten people are stranded in a desert, and your rescue helicopter can save only five; the other five must be left to perish. The people are: (1) an Army captain, (2) Miss America, (3) a 12-year-old boy, (4) a wealthy society woman, (5) a noted scientist, (6) a preacher or priest, (7) a college president, (8) a college football player, (9) a bricklayer, (10) a medical doctor. You are the helicopter pilot. Whom would you save and why?

6. Knowing oneself   Have students relate an event which they consider to be one of the most important ones in their lives. These speeches will not be criticized.

7. Knowing oneself   Assign students a speech in which they are to describe some very important event which made them grow. It might be emotional growth, intellectual growth, growth in self-awareness.

8. Knowing oneself   Ask each student to bring to class something which he holds to be of value and have him tell the others why he so regards it.

9. Knowing oneself   Have each student select a personal problem that faces him and write out a possible solution to this problem, step by step.

10. Self-concept   Have each member of the class identify a public figure whom he perceives as resembling himself. Let the class discuss and identify the traits held in common by the student and the public figure. The student can later identify the traits he had in mind.

11. Self-concept   Have each student select an animal that he perceives as resembling himself and follow the directions given in assignment 10.

12. Self-disclosure   Have each student list five things that he would tell about himself to almost anyone but that are not generally known to his classmates.

VALUES, ATTITUDES, AND GOALS

Ask students to do the following:

1. Goals   List three goals which your parents have set for your family. List three similar goals you might want for a family of your own.

2. Motive appeals   Collect some advertising. Try to decide what motives are appealed to. Are there also attempts to create dissonance which might be resolved by buying the product?

3. Values and beliefs   List four beliefs that are very important to you. Then share your beliefs with the class.

4. Values and beliefs   List five beliefs of your parents and indicate whether or not you have the same beliefs.

5. Values and defensiveness   Describe the feelings you had when someone said something threatening to one of your values or beliefs. How did you feel toward the person? How did you behave in that communication situation?

FEEDBACK

1. One-way and two-way communication   Select five students and ask each of them to draw on a sheet of paper a design according to oral directions given by a sender. No questions are allowed. The sender will stand with his back to the five receivers, and the receivers should be seated so that they cannot see each other's papers. Other class members may observe the drawings, but no one may speak except the sender; the communication is to be one-way. The sender may use any group of figures he has created, such as:

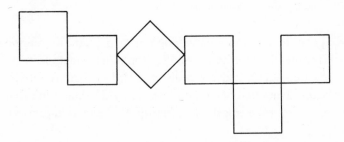

After the sender completes his directions, the drawings are shown to the class along with the drawing described by the sender.

Then the same group of five receivers will draw a different design following the instructions of the sender, but this time the receivers may ask questions and the sender will answer them so that two-way communication occurs. Again, the drawings are then compared and shown to the class.

2. Feedback   You can demonstrate different forms of feedback by asking one student to make a statement to a second student. The second student will have been handed a card indicating the type of feedback he is to give, i.e., verbal positive, verbal negative, nonverbal positive, and nonverbal negative.

3. Feedback   Have two students discuss a subject that is controversial to them observing *one rule:* every statement made must be paraphrased by the receiver until the sender is satisfied with the understanding the receiver has of the statement.

4. Feedback   Have students observe the ways in which different racial groups provide feedback to each other. Are there differences?

5. Feedback   Have students observe a cross-cultural communication situation. What feedback is provided?

NONVERBAL COMMUNICATION

1. Nonverbal communication   Play some classical music that is not too familiar to most of the class members. Ask class to describe, either verbally or in writing, their emotional responses. Choose music in which the composer was describing something: Smetana's "On the Moldau," Tchaikovsky's "Swan Lake," etc.

2. Nonverbal communication   Have popular or brilliant march music playing as class enters. When roll is taken, stop music, begin lecturing about listening immediately and rapidly in a rather formal, intellectual manner. Class discovers that one mood was set by the music and that it is difficult to switch from the emotional situation to the mental process.

3. Nonverbal communication   Demonstrate to the class the way in which a piece of music, a painting, and a speech convey a common idea. (For example: The 1812 Overture, a battle scene painting, and Churchill's "Their Finest Hour" speech.) Ask the class to evaluate the relative effectiveness of each medium.

4. Nonverbal communication   Have teams of students compete in listing nonverbal messages on the chalkboard (i.e., car honking, traffic light, train whistle, etc.).

5. Nonverbal communication   Ask students to observe and list the nonverbal messages sent by two different instructors they have.

6. Nonverbal messages in verbal communication Divide students into pairs and have each pair enact an argument between (A) a girl friend and boy friend, or (B) a teacher and a student, etc. They may use only the words "Strawberries taste better with sugar."

7. Nonverbal communication From the following list of emotions and feelings, have each student choose one to express nonverbally to the class:

fright	sadness
joy	anxiety
failure	pride
hate	rejection
love	acceptance

INTERVIEWING

1. Interviewing Have each student describe and analyze an interview in which he participated.

2. Business interview Each student applies for a job as a grass cutter, babysitter, dishwasher, or clerk in store, etc. The teacher or another student acts as the employer. Business letters requesting an interview and stating qualifications are written and application blanks filled out.

3. Interviewing Students are sent out to interview someone in the community for information. They determine a reason for the interview in advance, and an introductory letter is either sent or given by them to the person being interviewed. A written or oral report or a news story is used to follow up.

4. Interviewing Have a personnel worker or an employer from a local business speak to the class on interviewing.

CONVERSATION

1. Introductions Of what use are introductions to good conversation? Have students, in groups of three, make the following introductions:

Your parents and a teacher
One of your present classmates and a former classmate who is now attending another school

Your older sister and the older brother of a friend

Your son to a businessman

Your minister to the principal of your school

The President of the Student Council and the Mayor

2. Conversation   Distribute and perform Ring Lardner's essay "On Conversation." Have students identify the stereotyped phrases. In contrast to the problems revealed in the essay, list some outstanding characteristics of good conversation.

3. Conversation   Have students listen to and analyze excerpts of conversation from recorded plays such as:

St. Joan (G. B. Shaw)

The Family Reunion (T. S. Eliot)

Death of a Salesman (Arthur Miller)

Under Milkwood (Dylan Thomas)

4. Conversation   Chain conversation. Each student in class takes his turn in carrying the conversation forward. He must stick to the subject for a certain length of time.

SMALL-GROUP COMMUNICATION

1. Small group   Ask students to do the following: Interview your parents, a teacher, and one businessman. Find out how many groups each interviewee belongs to which require him to participate in group discussions. What problems does he see in the groups as they engage in discussion?

2. No-leader discussion   Divide the class into four groups of five students each with one student designated as the observer. Have each group discuss a selected problem for fifteen minutes. Set a goal of consensus for the groups. Have each group, through a spokesman, report the decision reached by the group. With the help of the observers, discuss such things as: Did leadership emerge? What patterns of participation could be observed? Why was the number 5 selected for group size? How did group norms affect participation and the decisions reached?

3. Discussion Divide the class into four groups randomly and have each group designate a leader and a spokesman. Have the groups discuss a problem for twenty-five minutes. After the discussions have each group evaluate and report its ideas and feelings. Have the students again comment upon the process involved in their deliberations. Did the designation of a leader enhance activity? Did everyone take part? Why did different groups arrive at differing viewpoints on the same problem?

4. Small group Have small groups discuss real school problems that may have been brought before the Student Council.

LISTENING

1. Listening Have each student make a list of "loaded" words that he hears during a three-day period and share the list with his classmates.

2. Listening training passage[1]

To the instructor: Be certain each student has paper and pencil. Discuss the following information with the class before reading the passage to the class: One important job in listening is to identify the structure of what has been said. This task includes figuring out what the speaker's purpose is, what his main point is, how he supports his main contention, etc. His main point may be, "I think you ought to start a tree-planting program in this corner of the country." He may use three arguments to support his main point. Or he may use three examples, instead. You as a listener should make sure that the examples or arguments serve only to support his main point; don't get lost in them. You should also be able to recognize his purpose, hidden though it may be in examples, apologies, humor, etc.

Read aloud: At this time I am going to read to you a short speech by Bruce Barton entitled "Spare Time." Do not take notes. Just listen carefully. I will ask you some questions about it later. Your job will be to identify the structure of this speech. Are you ready?

"Last month a man in Chicago refused a million dollars for an invention he had evolved in *his spare time.*

"You are interested in this because it confronts you with the possibilities of your spare time. Did you ever stop to think that most of the world's great men have achieved their true life, not in the course of their needful occupations, but—in their spare time?

[1]Contributed by Ralph G. Nichols.

"A tired-out railsplitter crouched over his tattered books by candlelight or fire-glow, at the day's end, preparing for his future, instead of snoring or sky-larking like his coworkers. Lincoln cut out his path to later immortality . . . in his spare time.

"An underpaid and overworked telegraph clerk stole hours from sleep or from play at night, trying to crystallize into realities certain fantastic dreams in which he had faith. Today, the whole world benefits by what Edison did . . . in his spare time.

"A down-at-the-heels instructor in an obscure college varied the drudgery he hated by spending his evenings and holidays tinkering with a queer device of his, at which fellow teachers laughed. But Bell invented the telephone . . . in his spare time.

"Gentlemen, you, too, have spare time. The man who says, 'I would do such and such a great thing, if I only had the time' would do nothing if he had all the time on the calendar. There is always time . . . spare time . . . at the disposal of every human being who has the energy to use it."

This is the end of the speech by Bruce Barton. I will now read ten questions to you. After each question I will pause. During the pause, answer the question with a yes or no or with a one- or two-word answer. Do not answer aloud, but write your answers on a piece of paper. I will not repeat any questions, so concentrate on listening while I read the questions.

To the instructor: Pause after each question to give the students time to write an answer. Do not repeat any questions. Do not read the answers until all the questions have been answered.

Question	Answer
a. The speaker's main point was that most great men have achieved their true life in their spare time.	Yes
b. To support his main point, the speaker used four examples.	No
c. Who was mentioned in the first example?	Lincoln
d. Who was mentioned in the second example?	Edison
e. Who was mentioned in the third example?	Bell
f. Does the author use restatement?	Yes
g. What one invention is named?	Telephone
h. The speaker's purpose was to inform?	No
i. The speaker's purpose was to get us to act?	Yes
j. The speaker feels that many of us do not have spare time.	No

3. Conversation Send five people from the room. Tell the remaining group a story. Invite the five back into the room one at a time. Have one member of the control group relate the story. Each listener will then in turn relate the story as he heard it to the next person entering the room.

4. Listening comprehension test[2]

> *Read aloud:* This test consists of a description of a scavenger hunt. Do not take notes. Just listen carefully. I will ask you some questions about it later. Are you ready?

> "Orville, Maine, and Lexington, Maine, are neighboring towns. In order to visualize the situation clearly, imagine the capital letter 'H.' The left vertical line is a typical street covering a two-block area in Orville, called Maple Street. The right vertical line represents another typical street in Lexington, called Elm Street. The horizontal bar—the cross-bar—is a bridge connecting the two towns.

> "One Saturday, three students, who were having a committee meeting at the Wilson home, located at the foot of the right vertical line, decided to plan a scavenger hunt for a week from Sunday. Sunday came and fourteen young scholars met at the Wilson home to begin the hunt. The group was divided into two teams, A and B, each consisting of seven people. The rules were announced: everyone must be back in forty-five minutes; the first group returning with all five articles would be the winner, or the team that had the most articles would win. Following the rules, the first clue was read: Proceed across the bridge to the wishing well at the end of the bridge.

> "Scurrying across the bridge first, Team B found one of the lists and proceeded north of the bridge to the Greens', the second house in the block. However, after searching, the Greens were not able to find any of the items on the list.

> "Team A finally found the other list and traveled across the bridge into the other town. Turning left, they went to Rev. Flynn's house and secured three of the items on the list.

> "In the meantime, Team B had found one of the articles, a dictionary with a 1939 copyright, at the Browns' at the foot of the left vertical line. Then proceeding north to the field in the upper half of the 'H,' they easily found the four-leaf clover. They next approached the bridge from the Orville side and midway along the bridge found the multicolored stone they were looking for.

> "Coming into Lexington, Team B looked at their watch and discovered that the forty-five minutes were up. As they started back

[2]Contributed by Ralph G. Nichols.

for the Wilsons' house they met Team A. Upon seeing each other, they raced back to the Wilsons' only to discover upon arrival that both teams had three articles each. It was a tie!

This is the end of the description of a scavenger hunt.

To the instructor: Pass out answer sheets now.

Read aloud: I will read ten questions to you at this time. After each question I will pause. During the pause, you should examine the several suggestions listed as possible answers for each question and pick the letter identifying the correct answer. Place this letter in the blank space beside the number of the question just read.

To the instructor: Read the following questions after the students have been given the answer sheets. Pause after each question to give the students time to choose their answers and record their choices. Don't read them the answers until all questions have been answered.

Question	Answer
a. Who had the scavenger hunt?	2
b. When was the scavenger hunt held?	4
c. How many committee members planned the event?	2
d. How many people were on each team?	3
e. In what state did the scavenger hunt take place?	2
f. Where was the wishing well located?	2
g. What was the location of the Brown's house, where the dictionary was found?	4
h. Where did Rev. Flynn live?	2
i. What was the copyright on the dictionary?	2
j. Where was the our-leaf clover found?	3

Answer sheet

_____a. 1. The scavengers
       2. A church youth group
       3. A group of scholars
       4. None of these

_____b. 1. On a Saturday
       2. The day after the committee meeting
       3. In the afternoon
       4. A week after the committee meeting

_____c. 1. Two
2. Three
3. Seven
4. Fourteen

_____d. 1. Five
2. Six
3. Seven
4. Eight

_____e. 1. Massachusetts
2. Maine
3. Connecticut
4. Kentucky

_____f. 1. In the upper half of the "H"
2. In Orville
3. Midway along Elm Street
4. At the foot of the left vertical line

_____g. 1. In Lexington
2. On Elm Street
3. At the top of the left vertical line
4. At the foot of the left vertical line

_____h. 1. At the foot of the right vertical line
2. In Lexington
3. Close to the wishing well
4. At the top of the right vertical line

_____i. 1. A 1933 copyright
2. A 1939 copyright
3. A 1941 copyright
4. A 1949 copyright

_____j. 1. Outside Rev. Flynn's house
2. Along the bridge
3. In the "U" area of the "H"
4. By the wishing well

5. Having a purpose for listening   Before reading a paragraph or selection, give the students one or more specific purposes. One might be to determine the mood of the piece or the character of the person described. The purposes should include recall of facts, making interpretations, and evaluating information.

6. Finding main ideas and important details   Have students listen to a short selection and suggest a title.

7. Finding main ideas and important details   Read a short story to the group, and ask the students to tell what happened in a one-sentence summary.

8. Classifying   As students listen to you read a list of items, perhaps types of food, have them classify the items and write them in appropriate spaces on a previously prepared outline form.

9. Making comparisons Have students listen as you read the names of a number of objects. For example: muffin, cake, spoon, cookie. Then have them select those that are alike in function or category or perhaps the one that is different.

10. Making comparisons Students listen as you read short paragraphs which compare people, places, or events. From memory, they then attempt to recall likenesses and differences.

11. Making comparisons Students listen to the reading of a selection which contains information that they are to categorize or put into chart form. After listening to the selection the first time, they are given a prepared worksheet containing the basic structure of the chart. The selection is then read again, sentence by sentence, allowing time for the students to fill in the chart.

12. Listening critically Ask students to listen to political speeches and lectures or discussions in which the speakers have strong opinions or views, and as they listen, to keep the following questions in mind:

a. What is the speaker's motive?

b. What emotionally toned words or phrases does he use to sway his listeners?

c. Are his views based on fact or opinion?

d. Does he sell his points by the use of propaganda techniques or by logic?

e. Do his statements agree or conflict with my experience?

f. What is the importance of his speech to others and to me?

13. Listening critically Read aloud: You live in a world filled with *persuaders* and not all of them are ethical. Many persuaders deliberately seek to hide the truth, present only one side of the picture, distort facts, and prey upon your emotions. Your job as a listener is to be aware of the unethical persuader.

Then have the students listen to a public speech and ask themselves the following questions:

a. What is the real purpose of this speaker?

b. Is the problem as real and important as he says?

c. Is the evidence presented sufficient to warrant the conclusion the speaker asks me to accept?

d. Is there evidence which has not been presented?

e. Does the speaker give the source of his data?

f. Does this problem really affect me? (Assume you are a member of the make-believe group.)

g. Is the speaker covering up the main issue by unimportant jokes, stories, examples, details?

h. Does the speaker appear *sincere?*

i. Does the speaker have a reputation for honesty?

j. Is the speaker using *good logic?*

Write your report to be handed in at the next class session.

14. Listening   Send five students out of the room and read a report to the rest of the class. Call back one of the five who left the room, and ask a student who heard the report to repeat it to him. Call back another of the five and have the first returnee repeat the report to him. The second should repeat it to the third, the third to the fourth, and the fourth to the fifth. The other students should note how the message changes as it is passed along. Following the exercise, discuss why the changes occurred. Discuss the implications of rumor. Repeat the exercise with another group.

15. Listening test   Have five students each prepare a three-minute inform- ative speech and a six-question recall test on the speech. Following each speech, compute the average listening score of the class and discuss with the students why they missed certain questions and answered others correctly. Compute the overall average listening score of the class following the last speech, as well as the total score on the five tests for each student.

PROTEST COMMUNICATION

1. Protest communication   Have students read about a demonstration or riot and make an oral report to the class.

2. Violence   Some protest communication has utilized violence. Ask students the questions: How does this cut off communication and inten- sify the problem? To what extent is violence "effective" communication?

3. Protest communication   Ask each student to describe as accurately as he can an illegal protest communication incident he has observed, or, if he has observed none, to talk with someone who has observed one and record his description.

COMMUNICATION BREAKDOWNS

1. Communication breakdown analysis   The study of communication should benefit from a careful analysis of a comunicative event as it occurs in a natural context. Hence the following assignment for students: Remain alert for a breakdown in communication in some specific situation in which you participate. Then prepare a four-part paper that (a) gives enough description and detail to establish the context in which the breakdown occurred, (b) describes what happened that could be classified as a communication breakdown, (c) pinpoints where and why the breakdown occurred, and (d) suggests what might have prevented it.

2. Communication breakdowns   In speech communication there are actually three messages: the intended one, the actual one, and the received one. Ask students whether they have had any experiences recently that support this view and if so, to describe the experiences. What difference did such experiences make, if any?

IMPROVING THINKING AND PROBLEM SOLVING

1. Making inferences and drawing conclusions   A series of paragraphs or selections may be read to students, with concluding statements to be completed by them. For example:

The air was crisp and clear. I was so preoccupied with the beauty of the day that I didn't see the ice in my path and came down with a bump on the sidewalk.

The season is_____.

The speaker lives in the_____.

2. Improving thinking   Bring in samples of good and poor logic found in newspapers. Have students take materials to the floor, show or read to class, and explain the example.

3. Improving thinking   Have students bring in examples of advertisements and editorials which are kinds of propaganda. Have them show and explain these to the class.

4. Improving thinking   Pair students and have each pair choose a controversial subject. Each pair then prepares a short, short speech on opposite sides of the topic. Allow each student a short rebuttal period also. Have class analyze the thinking presented.

5. Improving thinking   Write an essay using every device of crooked thinking possible. In the margin, number each device. Prepare a key to these numbers on a separate sheet of paper. Give the essay to another student. Either the student or the writer keeps the key. The evaluator prepares another key. Compare the writer's key with the evaluator's.

6. Improving thinking

Story A. Read aloud the following story to the class:

> As you step onto your front porch from your living room, you see a delivery truck approaching along the street. You also see that your next-door neighbor is backing her car from her garage into the street in the path of the approaching truck. You see the truck swerve, climb over the curbing, and come to a stop against a tree, which crumples one of its front fenders.

Now *read aloud* the following statements about the story to the class and have each student respond by judging the statement to be true, false, or doubtful.

a. Your next-door neighbor was backing her car into the street in the path of the approaching truck. T   F   ?

b. The delivery truck was traveling at a reasonable speed. T   F   ?

c. The only damage resulting from the incident was to the truck's fender. T   F   ?

d. You saw the truck swerve and climb over the curbing. T   F   ?

e. Your neighbor across the street was backing her car out of the garage. T   F   ?

f. The truck suffered no damage. T   F   ?

g. You saw the truck approaching as you stepped onto your front porch from your living room. T   F   ?

h. The man who drove the delivery truck swerved and ran his truck up over a curbing.   T F ?

i. The delivery truckdriver swerved in order to miss a child playing in the street.   T F ?

Story B. Read aloud:

A man, his wife, and his sons, ages eleven and fourteen, drove across the country on a vacation trip in their three-year-old automobile. They started the trip on a Friday the thirteenth. The wife said she did not like the idea of leaving on that day, and the man laughed at her statement. In the course of the trip the following mishaps occurred:

The automobile radiator sprang a leak.

The eleven-year-old boy became car-sick for the first time in his life.

The wife was badly sunburned.

The man lost his fishing rod.

Statements about Story B:

a. There were fewer than two children in the family.   T F ?

b. The sedan's radiator sprang a leak.   T F ?

c. The wife really didn't mind leaving on Friday the thirteenth.   T F ?

d. A fishing reel was lost.   T F ?

e. The family's trip began on Friday the thirteenth.   T F ?

f. The eleven-year-old lost his fishing rod.   T F ?

g. The story mentions the name of the family taking the trip.   T F ?

h. The make of the automobile in which the family made the trip was not mentioned in the story.   T F ?

i. The man laughed at his wife's fears of Friday the thirteenth.   T F ?

Story C. Read aloud:

John and Betty Smith are awakened in the middle of the night by a noise coming from the direction of their living room. Smith investigates and finds that the door opening into the garden, which he thought he had locked before going to bed, is standing wide open. Books and papers are scattered all over the floor, around the desk in one corner of the room.

Statements about Story C:

a. Mrs. Smith was awakened in the middle of the night.	T	F	?
b. Smith locked the door from his living room to his garden before going to bed.	T	F	?
c. The books and papers were scattered between the time Mr. Smith went to bed and the time he was awakened.	T	F	?
d. Smith found that the door opening onto the garden was shut.	T	F	?
e. Mr. Smith did not lock the garden door.	T	F	?
f. John Smith was not awakened by a noise.	T	F	?
g. Nothing was missing from the room.	T	F	?
h. Mrs. Smith was sleeping when she and Mr. Smith were awakened.	T	F	?
i. The noise did not come from their garden.	T	F	?
j. Smith saw no burglar in the living room.	T	F	?
k. Mr. and Mrs. Smith were awakened in the middle of the night by a noise.	T	F	?

Answers for Story A:

a. T—That's what the story says.

b. ?—Story doesn't say.

c. ?—Tree, grass, and other parts of truck may have been damaged but not necessarily.

d. T—That's what the story says.

e. ?—Story says only that next-door neighbor was backing car but does not preclude this possibility.

f. F—Story states the contrary.

g. T—That's what the story says.

h. ?—Story doesn't say whether truckdriver was a man.

i. ?—Story does not preclude this possibility.

Answers for Story B:

a. F—Story says there were two children.

b. ?—Car could have been a sedan, could have been a station wagon or some other type.

c. ?—Story states only that she said she did not like the idea.

d. ?—Story doesn't preclude this.

e. T—That's what the story says.

f. ?—Story doesn't preclude this.

g. F—Story contains no such mention.

h. T—Story contains no such mention.

i. ?—Story says that he laughed at her statement that she didn't want to leave on "that day"—but does not preclude possibility that she had some other reason than fear of Friday the thirteenth. Maybe she had a party planned.

Answers for Story C:

a. ?—Betty is not necessarily John's wife nor even a "Mrs."

b. ?—Story does not say that he did.

c. ?—Story doesn't say—it could be that John or Betty left them scattered on retiring.

d. F—Story states the contrary.

e. ?—Story doesn't say.

f. F—Story states the contrary.

g. ?—Story doesn't say.

h. ?—Story doesn't say that Betty Smith was a Mrs.

i. ?—Garden could be in same direction as living room but not necessarily.

j. ?—Story doesn't say whether or not he saw a burglar.

k. ?—Story doesn't say that Betty Smith was a Mrs.

7. Making inferences and drawing conclusions   Read narrative paragraphs and have the students write a sentence for each one to indicate what might happen next. For example:

It was Nancy's birthday. All during school, Nancy noticed that her friends were smiling and whispering to each other. After school, Nancy couldn't find anyone to walk home with, so she went by herself. She walked into the house, planning to spend a quiet afternoon reading, _____
_____.

8. Problem-solving exercise

NASA Exercise Individual Worksheet—Instructions to Students:
You are a member of a space crew originally scheduled to rendezvous with a mother ship on the lighted surface of the moon. Due to mechanical difficulties, however, your ship was forced to land at a spot some two hundred miles from the rendezvous point. During the landing, much of the equipment aboard was damaged, and since survival depends on reaching the mother ship, the most critical items available must be chosen for the two hundred-mile trip. Below are listed the fifteen items left intact and undamaged after landing. Your task is to rank order them in terms of their importance in enabling your crew to reach the rendezvous point. Place the number 1 by the most important item, 2 by the second most important item, and so on through 15, the least important.

You have fifteen minutes for this phase of the exercise.

_____Box of matches

_____Food concentrate

_____Fifty feet of nylon rope

_____Parachute silk

_____Portable heating unit

_____Two .45-calibre pistols

_____One case of dehydrated Pet milk

_____Two 100-pound tanks of oxygen

_____Stellar map (of the moon's constellation)

_____Life raft

_____Magnetic compass

_____Five gallons of water

_____Signal flares

_____First-aid kit containing injection needles

_____Solar-powered FM receiver-transmitter

NASA Exercise Direction Sheet for Scoring:

a. Score the net difference between each answer and the correct answer as indicated on the answer sheet. For example, if the answer you gave was 9 and the correct one was 12, the net difference is 3, your score for that particular item.

b. Total these scores for your individual score. See the rating chart below.

c. The group recorder then totals all individual scores and divides by the number of participants to arrive at the average individual score.

d. The group recorder scores the net difference between the group worksheet answers and the correct answers.

e. Total these scores for a group score.

f. Compare the average individual score with the group score.

Ratings:

0–19	Excellent
20–29	Good
30–39	Average
40–49	Fair
50 and over	Poor

NASA Exercise Answer Sheet:

Rationale	*Correct Number*	
No oxygen.	15	Box of matches
Can live quite awhile without food.	4	Food concentrate
For travel over rough terrain.	6	Fifty feet of nylon rope
For carrying.	8	Parachute silk
Lighted side of moon is hot.	13	Portable heating unit
Some use for propulsion.	11	Two .45-calibre pistols
Needs H_2O to work.	12	Dehydrated Pet milk
No air on moon.	1	Two 100-pound oxygen tanks
Needed for navigation.	3	Stellar map
Some value for shelter or carrying.	9	Life raft
Moon's magnetic field different from earth's.	14	Magnetic compass
You can't live long without this.	2	Five gallons of water

No oxygen.

Kit might be needed but needles are useless.

Communication with mother ship or earth.

<u> 10 </u> Signal flares

<u> 7 </u> First-aid kit

<u> 5 </u> Solar-powered FM receiver-transmitter

9. Problem-solving exercise: Riot grievances[3]   [Note: The following exercise is designed to deal with the communication implications of the current racial situation in the United States. In other words, this exercise is useful both in the integrated classroom and in a white classroom.]

Riot Grievances Sheet

Instructions: You are a member of a team sent to measure the present attitudes of people in the riot cities as precisely as possible. Before gathering the specific data, you want to draw some tentative conclusions based upon your own experience and that of your colleagues. How would you rank the following as major grievances? Your task *now* is to rank these twelve items according to the highest level of intensity. Place 1 by the most important item, 2 by the second most important, and so on through 12, the least important.

<u> 3[4] </u> Inadequate housing

<u> 9 </u> Inadequacy of federal programs

<u> 2 </u> Unemployment and underemployment

<u> 12 </u> Inadequate welfare programs

<u> 10 </u> Inadequacy of municipal services

<u> 5 </u> Poor recreation facilities and programs

<u> 11 </u> Discriminatory consumer and credit practices

<u> 6 </u> Ineffectiveness of the political structure and grievance mechanisms

<u> 1 </u> Police practices

<u> 7 </u> Disrespectful white attitudes

[3]Developed by Judy Carter, graduate student at The University of Kansas, and Dr. Robert Williams, Colorado State University, Fort Collins.
[4]These are correct answers and would not usually be printed on the instruction sheet.

___8___ Discriminatory administration of justice

___4___ Inadequate education

This is an exercise in group decision making. Arrange the class into several small groups. Ask each student to fill out the Riot Grievances Sheet without consulting others.

Now each group is to come to agreement about a group ranking on the Riot Grievances Sheet. Decisions should be made on a logical basis; "conflict reducing" techniques such as a majority vote, averaging, or trading should not be used; differences of opinion should be viewed as a help rather than a hindrance to decision making.

After about twenty minutes of discussion, ask the students to record their individual and group predictions on the Group Summary Sheet. A recorder for each group can then do the following.

a. Score the net difference between each individual's answers and the correct answers. For example, if the answer was 9 and the correct answer was 12, the net difference is 3, the score for that particular item.
b. Total these scores for each individual.
c. Total all individual scores and divide by the average number of participants to arrive at an average individual score.
d. Score the net difference between the group's predictions and the correct answers.
e. Total these scores for a group score.
f. Compare the average individual score with that of the group.

Ratings:

0–19	Excellent
20–29	Good
30–39	Average
40–49	Fair
over 50	Poor

Generally, group scores will be lower (more accurate) than the individual scores. This fact could lead to a discussion of the values of the group process. Racial differences in the class may, however, alter this usual finding; such a result should also be discussed. Most important, for discussion, is the process by which decisions were made in each group.

Group Summary Sheet

Individual Predictions	1	2	3	4	5	6	7	8	9	10	11	12	Group Predictions
Inadequate housing													
Inadequacy of federal programs													
Unemployment and underemployment													
Inadequate welfare programs													
Inadequacy of municipal services													
Poor recreation facilities and programs													
Discriminatory consumer and credit practices													
Ineffectiveness of the political structure and grievance mechanisms													
Police practices													
Disrespectful white attitudes													
Discriminatory administration of Justice													
Inadequate education													

Group _____

PARLIAMENTARY PROCEDURE

1. Decision making   Hold a mock trial involving either a hypothetical or real situation. Ask students to role play lawyers, witnesses, jury members, etc.

2. Legislative assembly   Divide the class into committees which have responsibilities in a legislative assembly organized while studying parliamentary procedure. One small group may serve as a Constitution Committee, another may select domestic issues to debate, and a third small group may choose international issues to debate. Have each member of each committee prepare a written report assessing the effectiveness of the interactions in his group.

3. Parliamentary procedure   Have members of the class organize a club, elect officers, and plan for the next club meeting. Announce that this club will hold future meetings periodically (one every two weeks, every month) for a specified time, practicing the methods used in parliamentary procedure. Each meeting should have a different chairman.

4. Mock political assembly   Have students form a mock political assembly consisting of opposition parties. Have the class choose an issue to debate and begin researching the topic. A series of debates will follow.

5. Parliamentary procedure   As students conduct business in a mock political assembly they have created, give slips of paper with orders like those given below to various members:

a. Postpone a motion indefinitely.

b. Postpone a motion definitely.

c. Make a motion to lay the main motion on the table.

d. Make a motion to reconsider the question.

e. Make a motion to refer a question to a committee.

f. Introduce a motion and then amend it.

g. Rise to a point of order.

h. Ask for a division of the assembly.

6. Parliamentary procedure   As students become more skillful in applying the rules of parliamentary procedure, your directives might become more general.

a. See if you can terminate debate and settle the issue within ten minutes.

b. Render this motion unacceptable.

c. Find a way of killing further debate.

FAMILY COMMUNICATION

1. Family communication: The car and the kid

John and Patricia Conley were apparently no more or less perplexed by the generation gap than any other parents of a teen-age girl. Julie, their sixteen-year-old daughter, was a good student, reliable, known for her quick smile and friendly manner. She rarely caused her parents any great problems, though they had long since given up trying to make any sense out of the exuberant and slang-filled speech she constantly used.

Julie was an only child and her parents were often quite restrictive as to where she went and whom she went with. Julie naturally complained occasionally, but there were never any major problems until one warm June evening. School had just been dismissed for the summer, and Julie was given the family car for the evening to go to a girl friend's party. She was given careful instructions that she was to be home by 12 o'clock.

The all-girl party was a great success, and the happy teen-agers were so engrossed in talk that the hours slipped by quickly. Someone finally pointed out that it was almost 1 a.m. Julie gasped with surprise and quickly told her hostess that she had to leave. Several of her friends quickly asked for rides home. Julie knew she was already late so why would a few extra minutes matter?

As she drove down the street toward where the first girl lived, one of the other girls in the car spotted two boys she knew walking down the street and asked Julie to stop and give them a ride. Julie knew neither of them but stopped anyway to pick them up. At the next intersection Julie's car was hit broadside by a man who failed to stop at the traffic light. No one was hurt but the car was inoperable. Police, after questioning all of them, took Julie home in a squad car. Both worried parents came running out of the house to see what had happened. In the turmoil of Julie's excited efforts to explain, all her father heard was, "We were riding around with a couple of guys, and some old man hit us." Visions of his daughter roaming the streets late at night in a car with boys she didn't even know combined with the built-up tensions in Mr. Conley, and he vented his anger by slapping Julie so hard that she fell to the pavement. The patrolman attempted to intervene, and Mr. Conley hit him, breaking his nose.

Julie spent ten days in a hospital with a concussion, the officer needed emergency treatment, and Mr. Conley was fined $300 and given a suspended sentence for striking an officer of the law. It was months before father and daughter could even begin to talk to each other without anger, and three years later there is still bitterness between them.

Study Questions:

a. Who was the sender and who the receiver of the fateful communication?

b. What effect did the time, place, and circumstances have on Mr. Conley's actions?

c. Did Julie's choice of words have any effect on Mr. Conley's action?

d. What effect did the emotions of both Julie and her father have?

e. Were both Julie and her father attempting to communicate? Were they listening to each other?

f. Was the "punishment" by Mr. Conley related more to what Julie did or what she said?

g. What roles did values play in this incident? What were the possible differences in orientation between Mr. Conley and Julie?

h. How do Julie and her father perceive each other? Does the generation gap have any effect?

i. Did Mr. Conley show any sensitivity to Julie's needs?

j. How could this incident have been prevented?

k. What sort of interference was there on the communication channel?

l. Was Mr. Conley reacting logically or emotionally to the content of what Julie said?

m. Did Mr. Conley's perception of himself and/or Julie color his judgment?

2. A generation gap From *Newsweek*, February 19, 1968

Nervously fingering a pink Kleenex, primly smoothing a pair of white gloves in her lap, Mrs. Dorothy Ault sat in the witness chair of an antiquated Phoenix courtroom and told her grisly tale.

The tragedy began, said Mrs. Ault, when she and her husband

had awakened early the previous Saturday morning to find their daughter, Linda, still not home from a Friday night at the movies. They searched in vain for the girl throughout nearby Tempe, Arizona, where pretty, auburn-haired Linda was a sophomore studying accounting at Arizona State University. Hours later the girl returned home, her mother said, and cheerfully admitted she had spent the night with an Air Force officer she knew. "She said she was 21 and what might be wrong for us was all right for her."

SWITCH: Naturally, her parents couldn't see it that way. First, Mrs. Ault snatched a mesquite switch from the desert ground and lashed the girl's head. Later that day the Aults withdrew her from the university. Still she was not properly contrite, her mother felt. "I told Linda that after all she had put so many people through and wasn't sorry, maybe she would suffer over an animal," she said. "She loved animals."

And so, next morning, an eerie procession filed out of the modest house on South Mountain to a cactus-dotted gully. With Mr. and Mrs. Ault were Linda and her pet mongrel dog, Judy. After they ordered Linda to dig a shallow grave, Mrs. Ault testified, they handed her a newly purchased pistol. "I held the dog and told her 'The best way is through the head.' Linda brought the gun down. Then the gun went back up—I didn't see it any more—and I heard a shot."

Linda Ault died of a gunshot wound in the head. The inquest officially ruled Linda's death a suicide, and stunned authorities at first decided the only charge against the parents could be that of cruelty to animals. But then at the weekend they arrested the elder Aults on the charge of involuntary manslaughter. At least, said police Sgt. John Fields, the parents "knew the emotional state of their daughter when they furnished her with a loaded pistol."

Study Questions:

a. What effect did the time between early Saturday morning and hours later have on the communication between Linda and her parents? Is it possible that the parents' reaction might have been different if the initial communication had taken place early Saturday morning?

b. Was Linda's action out of context with the time in which the act occurred?

c. Who was the sender? Who was the receiver?

d. Was there a cultural difference between Linda and her parents?

e. What role did values play in this drama? What was the point of orientation of Linda? Of her parents? What is your point of orientation? Do you think it colors your perception of the incident?

f. How did sender and receiver perceive each other? What might be their perception of the world? Of the subjects?

g. Did either party understand what Linda did? Was there any indication that her parents attempted to understand *why* Linda committed the act with the Air Force officer?

h. What was the emotional state of Linda when she revealed the act? Of Linda when she shot herself? What was the emotional state of her parents between early Saturday morning and hours later? Of the parents after Linda revealed her act? Did the emotional state of either party have any bearing on their attempts to communicate?

i. Were the two parties attempting to communicate? Did they want to listen to each other?

j. From the report, which parent seems to have been more upset over Linda's act? Why?

k. Did age play a role in this drama?

l. Did either party seem sensitive to the needs or "rights" of the other party? Were the parties concerned about themselves or about each other?

m. Was the punishment related to the initial act? What did each party expect of the other in terms of communication? What did the parents want Linda to say? Why? Why didn't Linda say it?

n. Was Linda ethical in telling the truth?

o. Suppose Linda's initial act could not be retracted; how might the suicide have been avoided, in terms of communication? Was the problem really one of generation gap? Did Linda select the best channel? Did the parents know "the emotional state of their daughter when they furnished her with a loaded pistol"? What are your views on gun control?

3. Family communication Have five students, narrator, and four players read to the class the following scene from *Blue Denim* by James Leo Herlihy and William Noble. Time: 1958, an early May evening. Scene: The Bartley house, one of the thousands of six-room frame houses built in Detroit during the industrial boom of the nineteen twenties. Visible to the audience are a part of the main floor and a part of the basement. These levels are joined by rough wooden steps which lead from an upstairs landing to the basement. Another set of steps, the old-fashioned, cellar-door type, leads up through a slanted hatch to a narrow corner of the backyard, where a few bushes, a doghouse, and a crucifix-shaped clothesline pole can be seen. Characters:

Arthur Bartley, tall, thin, 15, rather serious. He wears the current high school uniform—blue denims and an old sweat shirt.

Major Bartley, Arthur's father. One might guess from his appearance that he has spent much of his life sleeping too much, overeating and perhaps —though he is not a drunk—overdrinking. Concentration is difficult for the Major, and there is a vague hint of wildness in his eyes and in his manner. He has a game leg and walks with a noticeable limp; but this does not impede his ability to move about rapidly.

Jessie Bartley, Arthur's mother. A thin and pretty woman, somewhere in her forties. She seldom loses her temper—instead, through most minor crises, she maintains an infuriating calm.

Lillian Bartley, Arthur's sister, is in her early twenties, not unattractive, but a little tired-looking.

(At the opening of the scene the backyard is seen in late evening sunlight. The Bartley family is seated at the table in the dining room. After a tense pause, like the aftermath of a family quarrel, Arthur rises abruptly and drops his napkin on his chair.)

Arthur Excuse me. (*He goes through the hallway into the kitchen.*)

Major Jess, I'm going out there and talk turkey to that boy. (*He follows Arthur into the kitchen.*)

Jessie (*Gathering the dishes*) Oh, dear!

Lillian (*Helping with the dishes*) Mother, doesn't Dad realize Arthur was only three the Christmas we got that dog? It's only natural he should feel this way.

Jessie I suppose so. (*Lillian starts into the kitchen.*) Look, he didn't even touch his jello. (*She follows Lillian into the kitchen. Arthur enters the backyard and sits dejectedly on the ground, facing the doghouse. After a moment, the Major approaches him.*)

Major Son . . .

Arthur Yeah, Dad.

Major We're all going to miss Hector, son.

Arthur Sure. Only why did you have to do it while I was at school?

Major You heard what the vet said. Hector was an old dog—old and sick and suffering.

Arthur It was probably right, what you and Mom did. I know. It's just—you get up in the morning, you got a dog—you come home, no dog. For Pete's sake, you want to say good-bye, at least.

Major We were trying to spare you that good-bye.

Arthur Sure.

Major (*Annoyed*) Sure? What does that mean, sure?

Arthur Nothing.

Major Look, Arthur, you're nearly sixteen years old. When I was your age, my dad did a lot of things I didn't understand. But looking back, I . . .

Arthur Sure, I know. (*He turns away.*) Look, Dad, I want to clean up all this stuff—his things and all.

Major Don't turn your back on me. I'm talking to you!

Arthur Sorry, Dad. (*There is an uncomfortable pause. The Major, not able to understand his son's attitude, turns and exits into the house.*)

Have the class describe the communication behavior of the father and of the son. What principles relative to family communication are illustrated in this scene?

4. Family communication   Have two students read to the class the following scene from Part I, Scene 1 of *Summer and Smoke* by Tennessee Williams:

John Do you have a chill?

Alma Why, no!—no. Why?

John You're shaking.

Alma Am I?

John Don't you feel it!

Alma I have a touch of malaria lingering on.

John You have malaria? (*Grins at her*)

Alma Never severely, never really severely. I just have touches of it that come and go. (*Laughs airily*)

John Why do you laugh that way? (*With a gentle grin*)

Alma What way? (*John imitates her laugh. Alma laughs again in embarrassment.*)

John (*Laughing, rises and moves L., facing her*) Yeah. That way.

Alma I do declare, you haven't changed in the slightest. It used to delight you to embarrass me, and it still does.

John   I guess I shouldn't tell you this, but I heard an imitation of you at a party.

Alma   Imitation? Of What?

John   You.

Alma   I—I? Why, *what* did they imitate?

John   You singing at a wedding.

Alma   My voice?

John   Your gestures and facial expression!

Alma   How mystifying!

John   No, I shouldn't have told you. You're upset about it.

Alma   I am not in the least upset. I am just mystified.

John   Don't you know that you have a reputation for putting on airs a little—for gilding the lily a bit?

Alma   I have no idea what you are talking about.

John   Well, some people seem to have gotten the idea that you are just a little bit affected!

Alma   Well, well, well, well. (*Tries to conceal her hurt.*) That may be so, it may seem to some people. But since I am innocent of any attempt at affectation, I really don't know what I can do about it.

John   You have a rather fancy way of talking.

Alma   Have I?

John   "Pyrotechnical display" instead of "fireworks," and that sort of thing.

Alma   So?

John   And how about that accent?

Alma   Accent? This leaves me quite speechless! I have sometimes been accused of having a put-on accent by people who disapprove of good diction. My father was a Rhodes Scholar at Oxford, and while over there he fell into the natural habit of using the long A where it is correct to use it. I suppose I must have picked it up from him, but it's entirely unconscious. Who gave this imitation at this party you spoke of?

John   (*Grinning*) I don't think she'd want that told.

Alma   Oh, it was a *she,* then?

John   You don't think a man could do it?

Alma   No, and I don't think a lady would do it either!

John   I didn't think it would have made you so mad, or I wouldn't have brought it up.

Alma   Oh, I'm not mad, I'm just mystified and amazed as I always am by unprovoked malice in people. I don't understand it when it's directed at me—

Study Questions:

a. What caused the hurt feeling in the communication?

b. Was John really at fault?

c. Could John have employed more tact?

d. Did John mean to hurt Alma's feelings?

e. What other means or method of communication might John have used to give the same message?

f. What differences between John and Alma socially could be the cause of the gap?

g. Were both John and Alma trying to communicate?

5. Family communication: An incident

Beverly was a tall girl (5'9"); she had a marvelous figure, attractive face, and blonde hair. She wore her hair in a frowsy fashion. Her vocal quality had a definite touch of baby talk; not that her articulation was bad, but her tone quality was thin and her melody patterns childish. By her own admission, she presented a "dumb broad" image.

She was a sophomore in college and was dissatisfied with the level of her achievement in her art courses. She was doing A work and was winning awards; yet on her own value scale she was "lousy." She felt that she was being rewarded for mediocre work and no more was expected of her. She felt that she had the potential to be very good but school was strangling her. Professors kept her so busy turning out worthless projects that she had no time to develop herself to the depth she felt capable of. She wanted to stop taking the "Mickey Mouse" courses, and, with the guidance of a professor who wholeheartedly supported her, concentrate on developing her aesthetic convictions.

Excited about her future in art, she made her decision to drop out of regular university activities for a semester and concentrate on art. Late one night she leaped to the telephone, called her mother, and unleashed what turned out to be a bombshell in her relations with her mother: "Mom, I want to quit school and get a studio and maybe take only three hours of painting and three hours of drawing next semester, just freak out for a while." Her mother, although regarded by most people as a very fine, stable person, almost immediately became hysterical. She made Beverly promise to see a psychiatrist soon and urged her to "be sure and call anytime . . . we're here to talk to, you know." Relations between the mother and daughter had always been good prior to this phone call. But Beverly's communication with her mother in this instance obviously went awry. Why?

6. Family communication "Does He or Doesn't He?" condensed from *Empire*, reprinted in *Reader's Digest*, October, 1968, by James L. Collier.

Over the years, the shocks that I have endured have begun to blend into one long, steady hammering, and perhaps that is why I don't remember a worse jolt than the one I got the other morning when I poked my head into the bathroom. What I wanted was five minutes alone in which to scrape my face free of barnacles. What I got instead was the sight of my 16-year-old boy putting on his make-up. He began by rubbing skin cream into his face. He followed with lipstick, and topped it all off by splashing on some perfume.

At this point he spotted me. "Do you want to get in here, Dad?"

I cleared my throat. "I, ah, the perfume and lipstick. I know times have changed, and all, but—"

"Oh, come on, Dad, this isn't perfume. It's after-shave lotion."

"After-shave lotion? You haven't shaved since Monday. Now explain about the lipstick."

"That's Chap Stick. I got a windburn sailing last week."

"Chap Stick is white. That stuff's red."

"Natural lip color. Who wants to go around with white lips all day?"

"And the face cream?" I began to lose my temper the way I do when called upon to adjust to the modern world. "That's for windburn, too?"

"No, no, that's just bronzer. You know, to give you a tan."

"I see," I said. But that was a lie—I didn't see.

Study Questions:

a. How ethical should communication be? Don't parents and children owe it to each other to be truthful, or does it really matter as long as communication takes place?

b. Was the father justified in saying that he understood when he didn't? Should he have pursued the discussion further?

7. Family communication   Appoint five people to engage in an impromptu discussion before the class on the subject "The Problem with My Family as a Small Group."

8. Role playing   Select students to role-play communication situations on selected problems (teacher-student-parent, parent-child, and student-student) problems.

9. Stereotyping   Have students prepare presentations on certain stereotypes in characterization and values that are presented in the mass media (i.e., the role of father in situation comedies, killing on adventure series, teen-agers). Ask others in group to defend or challenge the value presented.

RESOURCE MATERIALS

BOOKS

Barbara, Dominick A. *The Art of Listening.* Springfield, Ill.: Charles C. Thomas, 1958.

Barnlund, Dean C. *Interpersonal Communication: Survey and Studies.* Boston: Houghton Mifflin, 1968.

Berman, Sanford I. *Understanding and Being Understood.* San Diego, Calif.: International Communication Institute, 1965.

Berne, Eric. *Games People Play.* New York: Grove Press, 1964.

Brooks, William D. *Speech Communication.* Dubuque, Iowa: Wm. C. Brown, 1971.

Brown, James I., and Carlsen, G. Robert. *Brown-Carlsen Listening Comprehension Test.* Chicago: World Book, 1955.

Chase, Stuart. *Guides to Straight Thinking.* New York: Harper & Bros., 1956.

Condon, John C., Jr. *Semantics and Communication.* New York: Macmillan, 1966.

Giffin, Kim, and Bobby R. Patton. *Basic Readings in Interpersonal Communication.* New York: Harper & Row, 1971.

Giffin, Kim, and Bobby R. Patton. *Fundamentals of Interpersonal Communication*. New York: Harper & Row, 1971.

Grant, Joanne. *Black Protest*. Greenwich, Conn.: Fawcett Publications 1968.

Hall, Edward T. *The Silent Language*. New York: Doubleday, 1959.

Harnack, R. Victor, and Thorrel B. Fest. *Group Discussion: Theory and Technique*. New York: Appleton-Century-Crofts, 1964.

Homans, George C. *The Human Group*. New York: Harcourt, Brace & World, 1950.

Jourard, S. M. *The Transparent Self*. Princeton, N. J.: Van Nostrand, 1964.

Kahn, Robert L., and Charles F. Cannell. *The Dynamics of Interviewing*. New York: John Wiley, 1957.

Knapp, Mark L. *Nonverbal Communication in Human Interaction*. New York: Holt, Rinehart and Winston, 1972.

McCroskey, James C.; Mark L. Knapp; and Carl Larson. *Introduction to Interpersonal Communication*. Englewood Cliffs, N. J.: Prentice-Hall, 1971.

Nadeau, Ray E. *Speech Communication: A Modern Approach*. Reading, Mass.: Addison-Wesley, 1973.

Nichols, Ralph G., and Leonard A. Stevens. *Are you Listening?* New York: McGraw-Hill, 1957.

Phillips, Gerald M. *Communication and the Small Group*. New York: Bobbs-Merrill, 1966.

Reusch, Jurgen, and Weldon Kees. *Nonverbal Communication*. Berkeley: University of California Press, 1956.

Smith, Alfred G., ed. *Communication and Culture*. New York: Holt, Rinehart and Winston, 1966.

Walker, Daniel. *Rights in Conflict*. New York: Bantam Books, 1958.

FILMS

All I Need Is a Conference. Strauss (28 minutes). Depicts a serious industrial problem and its solution by the conference method.

A Time for Burning. McGraw-Hill Text Films (50 minutes).

A World to Perceive. NET (29 minutes). Emphasizes the role of perception in communication.

Build Your Vocabulary. Coronet (11 minutes).

Communications. McGraw-Hill (12 minutes). Shows examples of communication tools in action and emphasizes the need for effective communication in business, industry, and organizations.

Communications Primer. CFD, or Audio Visual Center, Purdue University (23 minutes). Fits all types of personal and impersonal communications into a conceptual framework, using a model which includes source, coding, channel, receiver, decoding, and destination. The importance of past experiences of the recipient is pointed out as determining the meanings "read into" messages.

Communications Revolution. OSUMPO, or Audio Visual Center, Purdue University (21 minutes). A conversation of Edgar Dale, Marshall McLuhan, Gilbert Seldes, and Keith Tyler on communication.

Developing Imagination. Coronet (10 minutes). Can be tied in well with invention and creativity in communication.

Developing Leadership. Coronet (10 minutes). Especially applicable to the discussion unit.

Discussion in a Democracy. Coronet (11 minutes). Gives an extensive view of the use and role of discussion in a democratic society.

Do You Know How to Make a Statement of Fact? NET (30 minutes). Applicable to the semantics and language unit.

The Ears and Hearing. EBF (11 minutes).

Effective Listening. McGraw-Hill (15 minutes).

English Language: Story of Its Development. Coronet (11 minutes).

Everyday Courtesy. Coronet (10 minutes).

The Eye of the Beholder. REYP (25 minutes). Series of dramatic events culminating in a view of a girl lying on a couch in the studio of an artist with a red-stained knife at her side. The film illustrates what different people see and how it depends on their own conditioning.

The Griper. McGraw-Hill (11 minutes). Focuses on the constant griper and the trouble he creates in his interpersonal relations.

High Wall. McGraw-Hill (30 minutes).

How to Conduct a Discussion. Encyclopaedia Britannica (24 minutes). Shows the responsibilities of the discussion leader and participants, and explains how members of a group can evaluate themselves.

How to Say What You Mean. NET (30 minutes). Deals with communication breakdowns.

Is There Communication When You Speak? McGraw-Hill (22 minutes). Emphasizes the need for the speaker to focus on the receiver and to use the best skills available to impart a more accurate understanding of the message sent.

Just What Is General Semantics? NET (30 minutes). Introduction to general semantics.

Language and Meaning. NET (30 minutes).

Leo Beuerman. Centron (16 minutes).

The Man Who Knows It All. NET (30 minutes). Excellent study in frozen evaluations and closed-mindedness.

More Than Words. Strauss (15 minutes). Focuses on nonverbal messages that contradict or undermine the meaning of verbal messages.

The Nature of Language. TFC, or Audio Visual Center, Purdue University (32 minutes). Illustrates how language is learned and compares oral language with written language.

On the Difference Between Words and Things. NET (30 minutes). Focuses on language and general semantics.

Perception. McGraw-Hill (17 minutes). Explains the process of perception.

Picture in Your Mind. IFF, or Audio Visual Center, Purdue University (16 minutes). Deals with intergroup relations and the origins of prejudice. Excellent for the interracial and conflict communication units.

Room for Discussion. Encyclopaedia Britannica (25 minutes).

Say What You Mean. McGraw-Hill (20 minutes). Deals with language and general semantics.

Social Courtesy. Coronet (11 minutes).

Speech: Conversation. YAF (12 minutes).

Speech: Group Discussion. YAF (12 minutes). Defines the basic types of group discussion and discusses the responsibilities of participants and of the discussion leader.

Strange Interview. General Motors (55 minutes). Deals with interpersonal relations. Shows that the attitudes one has toward others are important factors in getting along with others.

Talking Sense. NET (30 minutes). Six kinescope films dealing with the topics Why people misunderstand each other, What is a good observer? and Allness orientations.

The Task of the Listener. NET (30 minutes).

Telephone Courtesy. Bell Telephone (20 minutes).

Thanks for Listening. Bell Telephone (20 minutes).

Thinking Machines. Horizon of Science Films, or Audio Visual Center, Purdue University (20 minutes). Claude Shannon of MIT and Leon Harmon of Bell Laboratories discuss experiments in machine intelligence.

The Thinking Machine. Carousel Film (54 minutes). Computers write plays, play checkers, etc. Scientists discuss whether or not computers can be creative.

Visual Perception. ETS (20 minutes). Presents the work of Cantril and his experiments in distortions in visual perception—the distorted room, rotating trapezoid, balloons which appear to move, etc.

Ways to Better Conversation. Coronet (10 minutes).

What Is a Good Observer? NET (30 minutes). Deals with perception and the process of observation.

Who Makes Words? Coronet (11 minutes).

Why do People Misunderstand Each Other? NET (30 minutes).

Why Man Creates. Kaiser Aluminum (20 minutes).

FILM COMPANIES

Alturas Films
Box 1211
Santa Barbara, California 95803

Audio-Visual Center
Purdue University
Lafayette, Indiana 47906

Bell Telephone Company
Your local office

Carousel Films
1501 Broadway
New York, New York 10036

Centron Corporation
West 9th at Avalon
Lawrence, Kansas 66044

Classroom Film Distributors
5620 Hollywood Blvd.
Los Angeles, California 90028

Coronet Films
65 East South Water Street
Chicago, Illinois 60601

Educational Films
690 Market Street
San Francisco, California 94111

Educational Testing Service
Cooperative Testing Division
20 Nassau Street
Princeton, New Jersey 08540

Encyclopaedia Britannica Films
1150 Wilmette Avenue
Wilmette, Illinois 60611

General Motors Corporation
Public Relations Staff—
    Film Library
General Motors Building
Detroit, Michigan 48202

Henry Strauss and Company
31 West 53rd Street
New York, New York 10010

Horizon Productions
301 West 73rd Street
Kansas City, Missouri 64114

International Film Foundation
475 Fifth Avenue, Suite 916
New York, New York 10017

Kaiser Aluminum and
    Chemical Corporation
Room 864
300 Lakeside Drive
Oakland, California 94604

McGraw-Hill Text Films
330 West 42nd Street
New York, New York 10036

National Educational Media, Inc.
3518 Cahuenga Boulevard
Hollywood, California 90028

Ohio State University Motion
    Picture Division
Ohio State University
Columbus, Ohio 43210

Teaching Film Custodians
25 West 43rd Street
New York, New York 10036

Young America Films, Inc.
18 E. 41st Street
New York, New York 10017

TWELVE

PUBLIC SPEAKING:
ASSIGNMENTS AND
RESOURCE MATERIALS

Public speaking has traditionally constituted a major portion of the basic communication course in the secondary school, and it is currently a significant area of study in the basic course. In many secondary schools public speaking is offered as a second advanced course in communication. Although this resource chapter, like Chapter 13, is not an all-inclusive listing, it does present a wide range of assignments and materials that have been used effectively by secondary school speech teachers.

ASSIGNMENTS

AUDIENCE ANALYSIS AND SPEECH ANALYSIS

1. Audience analysis   Assign each student to a specific group in the community. He is to analyze that group as a prospective audience for himself as a speaker giving a speech on a specific topic. You may wish to provide a set of questions to be answered in the audience analysis.

2. Audience analysis   Have students complete the following audience analysis form for their next speech. There are eleven questions or items of concern.

ASSIGNMENT AREAS

Audience analysis and speech analysis

Being a critic or consumer of public communication

Introductory assignments

Self-confidence and speech anxiety

Speech preparation and components of effective speeches

Delivery

Types of speeches

Audience Analysis

Name_____

Date_____

_____
Title of Speech

1. Specific group I'm addressing:_____

_____

2. Specific purpose of my speech:_____

_____

3. Number of people in audience:_____

4. Sex of audience:_____

5. Average age of audience:_____

6. Educational background of audience:_____

_____

7. My membership in this group is:
   a. Elected   _____
   b. Voluntary   _____
   c. Compulsory   _____

8. Attitude of audience toward me:
   a. They respect me. _____
   b. They know me well. _____
   c. They don't like me. _____
   d. They dislike me. _____
   e. I don't know. _____

9. My attitude toward the audience:
   a. I like most of them. _____
   b. I know most of them. _____
   c. I don't know most of them. _____
   d. I have no attitude. _____

10. Interests of audience:
    a. They like to save money. _____
    b. They are interested in change. _____
    c. They don't like to change. _____
    d. They have little interest in group. _____
    e. They are aware they have a problem. _____

11. Place of speaking: _____
    a. There will be a speaker's stand. _____
    b. The audience will be comfortable. _____
    c. The acoustics will be good. _____
    d. There will be a public address system. _____

3. Speech analysis and criticism Ask each student to prepare a written critical analysis of a speech in print. He may find the text in *Vital Speeches, Representative American Speeches,* a newspaper, or an anthology of speeches. Limit the topics of study to elements of speech emphasized in the speech course. The following might be principal concerns of the paper:

Preliminary concerns
  a. Speaker
    (1) His biography (brief)
    (2) His speaking experience
  b. Audience
    (1) Its make-up
    (2) Its point of view toward the speaker
  c. Subject
    (1) Its relationship to the audience
    (2) Its relationship to the speaker

   d. Occasion
      (1) Its significance to the audience
      (2) Its significance to the speaker

Analysis and criticism of subject
   a. Appropriateness
   b. Formulation of purpose
   c. Organization
   d. Adequacy of introduction and conclusion
   e. Use of transition
   f. Development of ideas
   g. Use of strengthening aids, for example, repetition and restatement, definition, and explanation
   h. Delivery
   i. Effectiveness, immediate and long-range

4. Logical, ethical, and emotional proof Play a recording of a speech of your choice. Have students identify proof types used and evaluate their effectiveness.

5. Evaluating speeches Play a recording of a political convention keynote address. Have students identify and evaluate delivery, idea selection, organization, emotional appeals, and language.

6. Finding examples of rhetorical devices in speeches Have students find passages from speeches which illustrate use of the following rhetorical devices for making speeches more impressive or interesting:

a. The speaker dramatizes a given fact by recasting it into striking contrasts or comparisons.

b. The speaker uses a series of rhetorical questions to emphasize a point.

c. The speaker uses a long story to illustrate a point.

d. The speaker uses restatement or repetition to gain a certain point.

e. The speaker uses a single image for developing his central idea.

f. The speaker uses irony and ridicule to make his point more impressive.

g. The speaker uses language which has a lofty and elevated appeal.

h. The speaker uses an abundance of personal pronouns (I, you, we, etc.) to gain more directness with his audience.

BEING A CRITIC OR CONSUMER OF PUBLIC COMMUNICATION

1. Being a critic of public communication   Ask each student to bring to class one editorial, essay, or speech which denounces a practice, policy, governmental organization (or other organization), or a prominent person. Have the student read the material to the class and convince the class that the point being made in the editorial, essay, or speech is fallacious or ill-founded, in short, that it is an example of untrue and irresponsible public persuasion.

2. Freedom of speech   Have each student bring to class and read aloud accounts of occurrences that bear on freedom of speech, or passages from articles or books that raise questions relative to freedom of speech. Some students should be encouraged or assigned to select passages from George Orwell's novel, *1984* (New York: Harcourt, Brace, 1949), which illustrate the methods by which thought is controlled by the supertotalitarian state.

INTRODUCTORY ASSIGNMENTS

1. Effective-speaker report   Have students give a short oral report on the most effective speaker they have heard, or tell about one of the most interesting platform performers they have heard. Ask them to explain in detail why this performer was interesting.

2. Analyzing a speaking event   Ask students to go to a public speech or view one on television, listen carefully, observe the speech, and answer the following questions:

a. Did the speaker use an organizational pattern that was familiar to you? What was it? What were the major points of his speech?

b. Did the speaker use visual aids? What types did he use?

c. How did the speaker attract and maintain interest and attention?

d. What did you see that you hope to avoid in speech making?

3. Types of speeches   Ask each student to collect five speech samples and to classify each according to purpose.

SELF-CONFIDENCE AND SPEECH ANXIETY

1. Speech anxiety   Divide the class into seven groups and have each group discuss one of the following seven common fallacies:

a. Self-confidence is the same as "not being afraid."
b. Fear is a sign of inferiority.
c. Fear is bad and undesirable.
d. Only cowards are afraid.
e. Proficient performers do not have fear.
f. Self-confidence will come suddenly after enough practice, and then fear will not be known again.
g. Anything painful or unpleasant is undesirable.

2. Self-confidence   Ask each student to write a description of his thoughts, feelings, and behavior when faced recently with a task related to something that really mattered to him.

3. Self-confidence   Have students prepare a two- to three-minute report of a personal experience in which they experienced fear.

4. Fear inventory   Ask each student to list those physical reactions to fear he has experienced. Tabulation can be made for the class as a group. Also, each student may discuss with another student his fear inventories to discover how they experience fear differently.

Fear Inventory

Mouth dries out	_____
Mouth gets wet	_____
Blush	_____
Get red spots (blotches)	_____
Hair stands on end (goose bumps)	_____
Spine tingles	_____
Hands are hot	_____
Hands perspire	_____
Feel warm all over	_____

Perspire all over	————
Voice gets high and tight	————
Voice gets hoarse	————
Nervous	————
Tense	————
Tremble	————
Hands shake	————
Knees tremble	————
Shortness of breath	————
Breathe fast	————
Hands get cold	————
Heart beats more rapidly	————
Cramps	————
Butterflies in the stomach	————
Other (————————)	————

SPEECH PREPARATION AND COMPONENTS OF EFFECTIVE SPEECHES

1. Selecting worthwhile speech topics   Have each student prepare a list of worthwhile speech topics and submit the list for class reaction. Spend one class session in evaluating the topics. At a later time, a mimeographed list of "good" topics can be distributed to the class, along with some indication of the concern or interest the class has in each one.

2. Becoming acquainted with the library   Have a task force make a floor plan of the library and charts of the reference shelves showing where various types of materials are located. The plan may be duplicated and distributed to all members of the class.

3. Organization exercise: Relay race   This exercise help students learn to think logically on their feet. It's also a good way to lead into impromptu speeches. Divide the class into four parts. Have each part of the class write down a speech topic on a piece of paper. Exchange the pieces of paper. At the start, one student from each group runs to the board and writes an introductory statement. Another student from each group then runs up and writes in outline form another point of the speech. The first team to write on the board a complete outline for the speech, in logical order, wins the relay.

4. Organization exercise   Ask students to do the following: Assume that each item in the following list represents an idea in an outline of a speech. Organize the items so that a logical speech outline results. In each blank of the outline form following the items, place the letter of the appropriate item.

Thesis: Elementary school teachers should have speech correction training.

a. Examples of speech defects.

b. Illustration—stutterer sent to playground during recitation.

c. Opening attention—quotation from Wendell Johnson.

d. A trained teacher can give invaluable aid.

e. Illustration—unattended hoarseness became tuberculosis.

f. Examples of teacher reinforcement training.

g. Overview of the speech.

h. Emphasis on American birthright—the education of the whole person.

i. Example of mishandling an articulation problem.

j. Statistics—incidence of defects among children.

k. Many elementary pupils have speech defects.

l. Explanation—role of classroom teacher and speech therapist.

m. Illustration—ten-year-old girl who stuttered was helped.

n. Definition and background of speech correction training.

o. Summary of thesis and main points.

p. An untrained teacher may unknowingly do harm.

q. Quotation from Berry and Eisenson—average age of onset of defects.

r. Examples of teacher referrals.

s. Statistics—inefficiency of untrained teacher referrals.

	Preferred Organization	*Alternative Organization*
Introduction		
A.	c	
B.	n	
C.	g	

Body

    I. <u>k</u>

      A. <u>a</u>

      B. <u>q</u>   j

      C. <u>j</u>   q

   II. <u>p</u>

      A. <u>b</u>   s

      B. <u>i</u>   b

      C <u>s</u>   e

      D. <u>e</u>   i

  III. <u>d</u>

      A. <u>l</u>

      B. <u>f</u>   r

      C. <u>r</u>   f

      D. <u>m</u>

Conclusion

    A. <u>h</u>   o

    B. <u>o</u>   h

5. Organizing the speech   Have each student list on a sheet of paper two topics suitable for each organizational pattern studied. Then have the class members read their topics for each organizational pattern.

6. Organizing the speech   Have each student take one topic and show how it might be organized according to each of the patterns of organization studied.

7. Developing ideas   Have students analyze a printed speech in terms of types of supporting materials used and how the idea was developed.

8. Developing ideas   Ask students to find two examples from written speeches which illustrate each of the following:

a. How the speaker gets the attention of the audience in his introduction

b. How the speaker explains that his subject is important and worthwhile

c. How the speaker prepares the minds of the audience for a clear understanding of his central idea

d. How the speaker concludes his speech

9. Adapting the language   Have students listen to recording of a speech and then identify and evaluate the ways in which the speaker adapted his language to the audience and the occasion.

10. Adapting the language   Have each student invent and write out a figure of speech. Write the speech figures on the board and have the class identify them as simile, metaphor, metonomy, personification, etc.

11. Adapting the language   Assign each student to write for oral presentation a brief descriptive passage. Have the class discuss the speaker's success in using language clearly, forcefully, and beautifully.

12. Writing an introduction to a speech   Have each student write an introduction to a speech in which he establishes audience contact by complimenting the audience on their town, the building, their schools, civic progress, beautiful scenery, etc.

13. Concluding the speech   Provide students with a copy of a speech from which the conclusion has been removed. Ask each student to write a conclusion. Then have the conclusions read to the class.

14. Preparing a speech   Have the class choose a subject for a specific audience and, during a class period, work the speech through the preparation process.

DELIVERY

1. Delivery description   Have students listen to a newscaster or speaker on TV and then write a paragraph describing the delivery used. Ask if it was overplayed, underplayed, or neither. For what purposes did he use the various visible aspects? Was he effective? Have students rate him on delivery.

TYPES OF SPEECHES

1. Biographical speech   Ask each student to talk about some prominent contemporary person. An outline should be submitted with the main sources of the materials indicated.

2. A human interest speech   Have students give a human interest speech four minutes long about the most interesting character they have ever known. The speech should radiate friendliness, humanness, and warmth. It should be personal and real. Encourage students to bring out specific details and the human and likable qualities of the person rather than godlike or idealistic qualities.

3. Speech of exposition   Ask each student to give a four-minute speech of exposition and focus on two things: conciseness and clearness. Have them explain, define, or describe something. This speech should be based on experience. Sample topics: (a) How to get ready to climb a mountain; (b) How to play chess; or (c) Describe a football play. Be as specific and definite as possible.

4. Demonstration and visual aid speech   Assign two-minute speeches in which the visible message is to be strongly emphasized. Have students evaluate each other as to effective facial expression, eye contact, gestures, movement, and use of visual aids.

5. A "pet peeve" speech   Have each student make a minute speech about something that makes him warm under the collar. Tell him to let himself go—to let this be a rough and tumble affair, allowing the audience to interrupt and heckle but controlling the hecklers with a firm hand. The following topics may suggest a speech.

a. Some people I would like to sock on the nose

b. Careless drivers

c. My noisy neighbors

d. Some of my relatives

e. Some things that annoy me at the movies

f. Silly rules in our school

g. Salesmen

h. Grades and examinations

6. Speech of denunciation   Have students give a four-minute speech of denunciation, taking a stand against some institution, movement, cause, or public figure. Encourage students to take some topic on which they have strong feelings. The purpose is to develop force and drive. Require the speakers to find and use at least four of the following eight types of supporting materials in the speech:

a. Popular authority

b. Expert authority

c. Figurative analogies (fictitious for clarifying a point)

d. Literal analogies (citing a real comparable case to prove a point)

e. Logic and reason

f. Concrete examples

g. Explanation and description for making a point clear

h. Pertinent facts to make a point convincing

7. Speech dealing with some civic project   Have students give a speech dealing with some national movement such as National Fire Prevention Week or Community Chest Drive. Make the speech from four to six minutes.

8. Impromptu speaking chain   To begin the chain, select a student to deliver an impromptu speech on any subject of general interest. Then ask the rest of the class, one by one, to speak two to three minutes on the same subject. This assignment should be used late in the term, when the students have developed their speech abilities.

9. Impromptu speech on controversial subjects   Use some popular controversial subjects to draw the students out. Suggest they take a position for or against something. Have them offer their opinions and reasons as best they can. Six or eight simple subjects may be read or written on the board. Several students may take the same subject.

10. Impromptu persuasive speeches   Ask each student to write on a piece of paper some topic for a persuasive speech. Place the topics in a box and have each student draw two topics, select one, and give a persuasive speech of two minutes' duration.

11. A persuasive speech plan   Have students complete the following paper for their persuasive speech and hand it in one week before the speech is to be given.

a. The problem or need
   (1) What evidence is there that the problem exists?
   (2) How is this problem bad? What evils are resulting from this problem?
   (3) How large is the problem? How many people are affected by it?
   (4) What are the causes of this problem?
b. The solution
   (1) What are the possible solutions?
   (2) Which solution is best? Why?

(3) Has this solution been used anywhere successfully?

(4) What will it cost?

(5) Can it be implemented easily?

12. Cooperative persuasive efforts   Have four students, as a team, prepare a case presenting a current serious problem. The four students will sit together before the class, and with one acting as chairman they will in turn present three- to four-minute speeches presenting the problem. They will *not* offer any solutions.

After the class has heard the problem, teams of four students each will be assigned, with each team responsible for presenting *one* specific solution to the problem presented. Each member of the team will make a three- to four-minute speech during the presentation.

Following the presentation of all solutions, a vote can be taken, after discussion and debate, to accept one of the proposed solutions.

RESOURCE MATERIALS

BOOKS

Adams, Harlen M., and Thomas C. Pollock. *Speak Up.* New York: Macmillan, 1964.

Allen, R. R.; Sharol Anderson; and Jere Hough. *Speech in American Society.* Columbus, Ohio: Charles E. Merrill, 1968.

Brandes, Paul D., and William S. Smith. *Building Better Speech.* New York: Noble and Noble, 1964.

Brooks, William D. *Speech Communication.* Dubuque, Iowa: Wm. C. Brown, 1971.

Hedde, Wilhelmina G.; William N. Brigance; and Victor M. Powell. *The New American Speech.* Philadelphia: J. B. Lippincott, 1963.

Hibbs, Paul; Seth A. Fessenden; P. Merville Larson; and Joseph A. Wagner. *Speech for Today.* New York: McGraw-Hill, 1965.

Irwin, John R., and Marjorie Rosenberger. *Modern Speech.* New York: Holt, Rinehart and Winston, 1966.

Nadeau, Ray E. *Speech Communication: A Modern Approach.* Menlo Park, Calif.: Addison-Wesley, 1973.

Robinson, Karl F., and Charlotte Lee. *Speech in Action:* Chicago: Scott, Foresman, 1965.

Weaver, Andrew T.; Gladys L. Borchers; and Donald K. Smith. *Speaking and Listening.* Englewood Cliffs, N. J.: Prentice-Hall, 1956.

FILMS

Articulation and Pronunciation. C-B Educational Films (30 minutes).

Building an Outline. Coronet (10 minutes).

Communication with Voice and Action. Centron (16 minutes).

Find the Information. Coronet (11 minutes).

Fundamentals of Acoustics. Encyclopaedia Britannica (11 minutes).

Fundamentals of Public Speaking. Coronet (10 minutes). Discusses three major elements in preparing a speech—analyzing, planning, delivering.

Getting Yourself Across. McGraw-Hill (21 minutes). Deals with the impact of one's personality, manifest anxiety, dress, manner, and general speaking behavior on the audience

How to Judge Authorities. Coronet (10 minutes).

How to Judge the Facts. Coronet (10 minutes).

Improve Your Pronunciation. Coronet (11 minutes).

Is There Communication When You Speak? McGraw-Hill (17 minutes). Explains the communication process, the importance of choice of purpose, selection of worthwhile thoughts, analysis of the audience, and effective delivery.

Learn to Argue Effectively. Coronet (10 minutes). Clarifies the role of persuasive argument. Contrasts the significant, serious use of argumentation with the use of irrelevant, unsound judgment that is carried on without purpose.

Library Organization. Coronet (11 minutes).

Making Sense with Outlines. Coronet (11 minutes).

Mechanisms of Breathing. Encyclopaedia Britannica (11 minutes).

The Nature of Sound. Coronet (10 minutes).

Planning Your Speech. Young America Films (10 minutes).

Public Speaking: Movement and Gesture. Coronet (12 minutes). Demonstrates techniques that are appropriate and effective in public speaking and suggests ways to develop ease and spontaneity of action.

Sound Waves and Their Sources. Encyclopaedia Britannica (10 minutes).

Speak Up. Alturas Films (13 minutes).

Speech: The Function of Gestures. McGraw-Hill (11 minutes). Explains and demonstrates the importance of gestures.

Speech: Planning Your Talk. Young America Films (11 minutes). Focuses on process of organizing a speech.

Speech: Platform Posture. McGraw-Hill (11 minutes). Explains the importance of platform posture and appearance and demonstrates how good posture and appearance can be achieved.

Speech Preparation. E-B Educational Films (20 minutes).

Speech: Stage Fright. McGraw-Hill (11 minutes). Explains the underlying causes of stage fright and the methods by which it can be overcome.

Speech: Using Your Voice. McGraw-Hill (10 minutes). Demonstrates some of the common voice faults and shows how such faults can be corrected.

Speech: Using Your Voice: Young America Films (11 minutes).

Your Voice. Encyclopaedia Britannica (11 minutes). Describes the four phases of production—respiration, phonation, resonation, and articulation.

Using Visuals in Speech. McGraw-Hill (14 minutes).

Why Study Speech? Young America Films (11 minutes). Explains why and how the study of speech will be useful to the student in school and daily life now and in the future.

NOTE: A list of film companies and their addresses appears at the end of Chapter 11.

THIRTEEN

ORAL INTERPRETATION AND DRAMA: ASSIGNMENTS AND RESOURCE MATERIALS

Although it is not recommended that drama, oral interpretation, and Reader's Theater be included in the basic communication course for secondary school students, oral interpretation *is* often included in the basic course; and, as indicated earlier, drama and interpretation are frequently included as well. In addition, recent surveys show that often the third or fourth speech course in the secondary school is dramatics. For these reasons the authors have included this chapter, which offers resource materials in drama and oral interpretation.

ASSIGNMENTS

ORAL INTERPRETATION: PREPARATION

1. Oral interpretation: Preparation Ask students to choose a poem and list the steps in literary analysis, preparation, presentation and evaluation.

ASSIGNMENT AREAS

Oral interpretation: Preparation
Oral interpretation: Selecting material
Oral interpretation: Performance
Oral interpretation: Criticism
Choral speaking
Reader's Theater
Theater: Introductory assignments
Acting
Voice and articulation
Pantomime
Characterization
Responding to sense perception
Putting skills together
Appreciating theater
Theater criticism
Writing for theater

2. Oral interpretation: Preparation   Have each student prepare an introduction to an oral interpretation selection. The introduction should help the listener find the idea, the information, and the inspiration the author intended.

3. Oral interpretation: Preparation   Have each student select a variety of types of material to interpret. For each piece selected, the student should write a paragraph that analyzes the piece in terms of feeling, meaning, and content. Each student should select one of each of the following:

a. Descriptive prose passage from a novel

b. A dramatic scene from a play

c. A child's short story

d. A passage from the Bible

e. A humorous prose selection

f. A narrative poem

4. Oral interpretation: Preparation In oral interpretation we use the senses. Bring a paper bag into class filled with all sorts of different objects; have each student close his eyes and then hand him one of the objects. He is to clearly describe the object, using the senses of taste, smell, touch. The sense of sight cannot be used. As the student describes the object, the other students, with eyes closed, can try to guess what it is.

5. Oral interpretation: Preparation Teach students to use systems of marking to indicate how material will be read, making duplicate copies of their speeches, which they hand to you as they rise to read. Examples of such markings are:

a. A curved line or "rocker" *connecting groups of words which should be read* without stopping: "I pledge allegiance to the flag. . . ."

b. A diagonal line between words to show pause. The number of lines will indicate the length of the pause: "We have realized a generous measure of America's purpose, / a miraculous measure for one century. / / / But America is not yet what we prayed it might be."

c. An arrow to indicate the continuation of a thought from one line or phrase to the next:

> I think that I shall never see ⟶
> A poem as lovely as a tree.

d. Broken lines to show they are read at a faster pace:
And in your hands, driving the way you did last night, your car is a murder weapon.

6. Oral interpretation: Preparation Have students practice eliminating substandard dialect by reading aloud together selections containing troublesome sounds:

a. Are our cars here?

b. I bet with my net I can get those things yet.

c. Many a wit is not a whit wittier than Whittier.

d. Piper wrote on the paper, "I am a pauper."

ORAL INTERPRETATION: SELECTING MATERIAL

1. Selecting material for oral interpretation   Select three suitable pieces of literature for reading to each of the following age groups: primary grades, upper elementary grades, junior high school, senior high school, and men's service club.

ORAL INTERPRETATION: PERFORMANCE

1. Oral interpretation: Performance   Have each student prepare a twenty-minute oral interpretation of literature program based on the works of one author.

2. Oral interpretation: Performance   Have each student prepare a twenty-minute oral interpretation of literature program based on a theme.

ORAL INTERPRETATION: CRITICISM

1. Oral interpretation: Criticism   Ask students to attend an oral interpretation event or Reader's Theater presentation and write a critique based on literary worth, audience analysis and audience response, and artistry of presentation.

2. Oral interpretation: Criticism   In order to perfect voice and diction, have students, identifying themselves only by an assigned number, tape the reading of familiar material, such as "The American's Creed." These recordings are then exchanged with another class which has taped the same material. Each listener, having provided himself with as many slips of paper as there are recorded voices, writes a critical evaluation of each, giving attention to voice and diction. These criticisms are returned to the individual students.

3. Oral interpretation: Criticism   In class, and again in small groups, have students tape their prepared reading of some short selections and listen by groups to instant playback. Have students criticize the readings in terms of the standards set up and then retape, striving to make corrections. Save these tapes for comparison with later tapings.

CHORAL SPEAKING

1. Choral speaking Have each student select and arrange a piece of literature for choral speaking, make copies for his classmates, and conduct them as a speaking chorus.

2. Choral reading Selections suggested for use with the different forms of choral speaking are:

a. *The refrain form:*

"Lord Randal"	Scottish folk ballad
"America the Beautiful"	Katherine Lee Bates
"Jesse James"	William Rose Benét
"A Negro Sermon: Simon Legree"	Vachel Lindsay
"Port of Many Ships"	John Masefield
"Two Red Roses Across the Moon"	William Morris
"For the rain it raineth every day," *Twelfth Night*, Act V, Sc. 1, lines 400–416	William Shakespeare

b. *The antiphonal form:*

"John Brown's Body"	Stephen Vincent Benét
"The Beatitudes"	Matthew 5
"The Lovely Shall be Choosers"	Robert Frost
"Ballad of the Oysterman"	Oliver Wendell Holmes
"Waiting for the Birdie"	Ogden Nash
"Jazz Fantasia"	Carl Sandburg
"Four Little Foxes"	Lew Sarett

c. *The cumulative form:*

"Announcement to the Shepherds"	Luke 2: 8–14
"Psalm 23"	Bible
"As Imperceptibly as Grief"	Emily Dickinson
"The Creation"	James Weldon Johnson
"Chicago"	Carl Sandburg
"When I Heard the Learned Astronomer"	Walt Whitman

d. *The unison form:*

"The Road Not Taken"	Robert Frost
"Unmanifest Destiny"	Richard Hovey
"Abou Ben Adhem"	Leigh Hunt
"Quangle Wangle's Hat"	Edward Lear
"I Have a Rendezvous with Death"	Alan Seegar
"Berter"	Sara Teasdale
"Let It Be Forgotten"	Sara Teasdale

READER'S THEATER

1. Reader's Theater   Have students prepare a thirty-minute Reader's Theater program, using a narrator. Also have them describe the staging, lighting, and props they would use.

INTRODUCTION TO THEATER

1. Theater terms   Ask students to describe the use of the following:

roll drop	rotary stage
sky drop	jackknife stage
box set	cut-out drop
leg drop	wagon stage
scrim	traveler track

2. Theater personnel   Have students write job descriptions for the following: stage manager, costume manager, assistant director, publicity manager, property manager, and sound man.

3. Stage and backstage   Take students on a tour of the stage and backstage areas. The proscenium stage is commonly divided into nine specific playing areas, identified by their relative positions. All directions regarding movement on this type of stage are given from the actor's point of view as he faces downstage toward the audience. Explain stage directions and playing areas to your students, using a diagram of a proscenium stage. Discuss the strengths and weaknesses of the various areas and the way stage directions are abbreviated. Also, point out that directions and areas for arena staging differ. Have students take turns responding to directions as they walk around the stage.

ACTING

1. Body positions   Have students assume any one of five basic body positions as requested. They can explain and demonstrate the full-front, one-quarter, profile, three-quarter, and full-back positions and discuss their uses.

2. Moving on stage   When moving on stage, the actor should normally begin his cross with the upstage foot. To avoid awkward adjustments of body position after a cross is terminated, the actor will frequently make a curved approach. Have students demonstrate these movements, reiterating the values of keeping open to the audience. Have all students practice a straight and a curved cross to particular points on stage. Discuss whether crosses to and from certain areas are better made as straight or curved lines.

3. Characterization   Ask each student to observe at least three of each of the following types of persons and activities and to re-create what he observed.

a. A man smoking a pipe

b. A woman shopping with two young children

c. An older person eating

d. A heavy-set person sitting

e. An old man walking

4. Working with another actor   Stage area and the actor's positions are two primary factors influencing attention of the audience. Since the actor rarely works alone and since maximum effectiveness in a scene requires a high degree of interaction, it is important that students realize their positions on stage must be relative to those of the other actors. Use various members of the class to demonstrate the strengths and weaknesses of different areas and positions. Show what is meant by "upstaging" and how actors may inadvertently upstage themselves. Explain and demonstrate what is meant by "cheating" and "countering." Have your students do the following exercises:

Two Actors (Center Stage)

a. Share a scene equally so both are open.
b. Staging relatively equal, adjust for a long speech by one actor. Adjust again for a long speech by the other actor.
c. "Give" a scene to the other actor.
d. "Take" the scene from the other actor.

Three Actors (Center Stage)

a. From full-front positions let actors 1 and 2 give the scene to 3.
b. 3 and 1 give the scene to 2.
c. 3 and 2 give the scene to 1.
d. 3 focuses on 1 and 2, who share the scene.
e. 1 focuses on 2 and 3, who share the scene.
f. 2 focuses on 1 and 3, who share the scene.

5. Blocking a scene After your students have grasped the fundamentals of stage movement and positioning and how each contributes to dramatic effect, try the following: Select several scenes from available plays that require a considerable amount of movement. Assign the scenes to your class so that each student is required to prepare a blocking plan for each scene. Have various students direct each scene in class and defend their blocking in an open discussion.

VOICE AND ARTICULATION

Good acting obviously requires the actor to make effective use of his voice in expressing the emotional and intellectual content of the dialogue. While a detailed study of the voice cannot be undertaken here, it is important that beginning actors understand that a good stage voice is both intelligible and flexible.

Proper projection of the voice is a function of controlled exhalation, proper phonation and resonation, and articulation. Explain and demonstrate these aspects of speech, stressing the importance of diaphragmatic breathing, relaxation of the throat, and proper use of the articulators. Have students do the following exercises as needed:

1. Relaxation

a. In a standing position, tense all the muscles of your body as tightly as possible and hold for fifteen seconds. Suddenly release the tension and let the body relax. Try this also in a seated position.

b. Let the head fall forward, rotate heavily over the right shoulder, hang loosely over the back letting the jaw fall open, rotate over the left shoulder, then up. Repeat.

c. Allow the jaw to fall open and say: Yah, Yah, Yah, Fah, Fah, Fah, Mah, Mah, Mah, etc.

d. Yawn. Come out of the yawn with a clear, open ah; with a round open oh.

e. Tense the neck and throat as much as possible and read a speech from a play. Relax the throat and read the same speech. (If possible, have students try this with a tape recorder so they can hear the difference.)

2. Breathing

a. Lie down on your back, place your hands at the base of your rib cage, and relax. Note the way you are breathing. (This is proper, diaphragmatic breathing.)

b. Standing with hands on hips (thumbs and forefingers at base of ribs) quickly draw in the breath through the mouth as if frightened. Notice the action of the breathing muscles. Exhale slowly and easily, noting movement of rib cage.

c. Exhale suddenly on "puh."

d. Take a deep breath and count from one to five; to ten; to twenty. See how far you can count without strain.

e. Sustain a tone of comfortable pitch, starting it moderately loud and gradually decreasing the volume until the tone becomes very soft. The quality of tones should not alter with the change of volume and should be smoothly and easily produced throughout the exercise.

f. Same as preceding exercise, but start the tone softly, and gradually increase the volume.

g. Begin a tone softly, gradually increase in volume until the tone is loud; then gradually decrease or diminish the volume.

3. Resonance

a. Drop the jaw as in yawning. The throat should feel relaxed and freely open. Direct the tone toward the front of the mouth, and say: day, day, day; hah, hah, hah; see, see, see. Avoid constricting or pouting the lips.

b. Whisper ah; my; thy; by. Now speak and intone the same syllables.

c. Drop the jaw loosely for each syllable and speak, then sing, yah, bah, lah; yay, bay, lay; yee, bee, lee; yoh, boh, loh.

d. Speak, then sing, zee zee; zoo zoo; zay zay; zah zah; zoh zoh; zee zoo zee zoo; zay zah zay zah. Prolong and emphasize the consonant sound before going to the vowel.

e. Select the most comfortable pitch of the speaking voice. With lips loosely closed, gently and easily say hm. Repeat several times. Repeat and sustain the sound. Vibration should be felt in the front of the mouth, face, and nose. After vibration is sensed, try humming on other pitches lying well within the speaking range of the voice.

f. To make the tone darker and deeper drop the jaw with flexibly rounded lips and practice exercises with vowel sounds aw, oh, and oo.

g. To make the tone bright and brilliant your mouth should be comfortably open with the lips flexibly spread. Practice exercises with ay, ee, ah, and ai.

4. Articulation

a. With closed teeth, form wee-woo-wee-woo, repeatedly moving the lips vigorously away from the teeth.

b. Open the mouth wide as for ah, then round the lips as for oo, protruding them somewhat and keeping the mouth wide open (so that the mouth has somewhat the shape of a trumpet); then stretch the lips as for ee; return to the unrounded position for ah. Thus: ah-oo-ee-oo-ah-oo-ee-oo. Repeat ten times. Continue, using other lip consonants before the vowels; pah-poo-pee-poo; bab-boo-bee-boo; mah-moo-mee-moo. Repeat ten times.

c. Repeat with exaggerated lip action for w and with wide-open mouth for ah: twah-twoo-twee-twoo, etc. Repeat ten times.

d. Say bah-bay-bee-boh-boo-bwah, letting the lower jaw rise and fall for each syllable. Repeat ten times.

e. Thrust the tongue out straight; point tip downward, then upward. Repeat, pointing tongue first upward then downward, five times.

f. Open the mouth, lips in smile position. Keeping chin and lips motionless, touch lightly first one corner of the mouth, then the other, with the pointed tongue. Repeat five times, slowly, rhythmically.

g. Repeat the syllable lee as rapidly as can be done with distinctness. The tip of the tongue should tap the upper teeth or teeth ridge for each syllable.

h. NOTE: Practically all Gilbert and Sullivan song lyrics provide excellent articulation exercises when read aloud.

5. Flexibility

a. Sustain a hum for four counts on various pitches lying within a comfortable range of voice and follow it by open vowel sounds as: hm-ah; hm-ay; hm-ee; ho-oh; hm-oo.

b. Ask and answer questions, carefully noting inflection of voice: "Where are you going?" "I'm going home." "Will you write this letter for me?" "Certainly, I shall be glad to write it."

c. Contrast the inflection used when saying in an expressive manner, "The day was dark and cold and dreary" with that used in saying, "Pitter, patter fell the rain."

d. Say "No, no! Don't do that" in a cross, determined tone of voice. Note the pitches used. Make the same statement as if joking, using a laughing inflection. Say the same as if speaking to a very small child. Does the inflection vary with mood?

e. Use inflections adapted to the meaning of the following exclamations. "Ship ahoy!" "Halt! Who goes there?" "All aboard!" "Play ball!" "Hello there!" "Fire! Fire!" "Hush, hush!" "Be still!"

f. Count from 1 to 8, and let the size of the number indicate the degree of loudness.

g. Repeat, using the alphabet from A through H.

h. Vary the pitch and intensity as you count from 1 to 8. Raise, then lower, the pitch and the degree of loudness.

i. Vary the intensity and rate as you count from 1 to 8.

j. Vary the pitch and rate as you count from 1 to 8.

k. Vary the pitch, intensity, and rate as you count from 1 to 8.

l. How many different meanings can you give the word "no" by varying the way you say it? Make a list of meanings. How many different interpretations can you give to the sentence "I want to go to the dance tonight"?

PANTOMIME

1. Stage pantomime   Bodily action has been called language in another form. In contemporary theater it probably ranks with the actor's voice as a means of expression. The actor must realize that good stage pantomime is selective, unified, heightened and projected. Explain why the actor must selectively simplify the realities of life in order to communicate them effectively. Demonstrate how excessive detail clutters meaning. Explain why all stage movement must be purposeful. Discuss and demonstrate the problems of enlarging actions for the sake of projection. Have students apply these principles to the following classroom demonstrations. After each pantomime, have the students show what would have been normal actions in the situation and how they were modified for the exercise. Invite all students to participate in the discussion of each presentation.

a. Chase a small pig on, off, and on the stage and catch it.

b. Set the table for a formal dinner, breaking a dish in the process.

c. Peel and eat an apple.

d. Look up a telephone number, dial it, get a busy signal, and hang up.

e. Disrobe, put on pajamas, and get into bed.

f. Get out of bed and get dressed.

g. Using a knife, stalk and murder a person who is working at a desk.

2. Pantomiming scenes   Have students select short scenes from plays known to the class and present them in pantomime without dialogue props. See if the class can recognize the scenes. In the discussion preceding this exercise, emphasize the differences between acting a scene and playing charades.

3. Exaggerated movement   Have students look for examples of selective and exaggerated movement in a local play or movie. Discuss the effectiveness of such movement.

CHARACTERIZATION

1. Learning characterization   A central function of the actor is to embody a character as fully and vividly as possible within the scope of the playwright's basic style and purpose. The actor's obligation to "flesh out" a role must be tempered by the playwright's intention and the director's interpretative design. Discuss play analysis with emphasis on theme, tone or atmosphere, style, plot, and function of characters. Explain "beats," or units of action. Have students categorize characters from the following types of plays as either "individuals," "types," or "shadows:"

a. A contemporary serious drama

b. A contemporary comedy

c. A Shakespearean play

d. A Restoration comedy

2. Learning characterization   An analysis of a role requires extensive study of the script, utilizing the actor's experience and powers of observation. Explain to students how an actor derives cues to character from:

a. The description and comments of the playwright

b. The character's manner of speech

c. What other characters in the play say about him

d. Business suggested by the playwright

e. Major attitude changes by the character throughout the play

Have students write detailed analyses of characters from plays of your choice. It will be most helpful if this exercise can be structured around a local production viewed by the class *after* they have completed their written analyses and *before* the assignment is discussed in class.

3. Learning characterization   Actors must learn to use their powers of observation in ways that will contribute to their work on stage. Explain how movement, gesture, posture, and speech differentiate individuals. Assign students the responsibility of observing three people of widely differing types, and record their observations. Using the mannerisms of the people observed, have the students do the following exercises in class:

a. Make a sandwich and eat it.

b. Straighten a room, hanging up loose articles of clothing.

c. Mix a drink, using ice.

d. Put on and tie your shoes.

e. Pack a suitcase.

RESPONDING TO SENSE PERCEPTIONS

1. Responding physically   Have students practice showing physical response as they read material about sense perceptions. Examples:

a. It was a cold, dark, damp day.

b. It's so hot and sticky and humid, I can't study.

c. "And the silken, sad, uncertain rustling of each purple curtain thrilled me— filled me with fantastic terrors never felt before."

d. Say—listen—If you could only take a bath in moonlight!

2. Showing moods vocally   Have students use practice material to achieve appropriate physical responsiveness in oral reading, i.e., exaggeration in farce; ease in humor; tension in melodrama; "freezing" to point a line; subtle change in eye expression; posture; head emphasis and other gestures. Practice material to show changes of mood in reading include:

a. "He was my friend, faithful and just to me.
   But Brutus says he was ambitious;
   And Brutus is an honorable man."
b. "Then spake the bride's father, his hand on his sword,
   For the poor, craven bridegroom said never a word."
c. "Hollyhocks! Hollyhocks! Stiff as starch!
   Oh, fix your bayonets! Forward march!"

PUTTING SKILLS TOGETHER

1. Improvisations   All the projects up to this time have concentrated on various aspects of acting technique. In this exercise have the student concentrate on putting all the skills together. Discuss and call upon members of the class to demonstrate the way movement and voice are affected not only by character but by plot, locale, mood, and period. Have your students do improvisations in class based on any combination of character, locale and time, and situation listed below. (Note: Time can be interpreted either as contemporary realism or as a period requiring a certain style of acting. It is suggested that you use both interpretations to give students some exposure to period style.)

Character

a. The leader of a teen-age street gang
b. An elderly janitor
c. A sophisticated thirty-five-year-old lawyer
d. A professional athlete or dancer
e. A schoolteacher, any age

Locale and Time

a. A swank apartment (present-day New York or sixteenth-century London)

b. A deserted waterfront warehouse (San Francisco today or in 1900)

c. A native hut in the Congo (today or in the year 1890)

d. An Indian lodge in the Artic Circle (today or in the year 1820)

e. A bus on a mountain road (today in West Virginia or in Mexico in 1935)

Situation

a. You are awakened by a strange noise and discover the body of a murdered man. You wish to sound an alarm but sense that the murderer is still in the vicinity.

b. You enter to meet your fiancée, who has left a note saying that she will return in a few minutes. While waiting you discover something that has fallen from her pocket which indicates that the object of your affections is already married. Decide what you are going to do when your fiancée returns.

e. You enter to meet a man who has promised to introduce you into a high-paying but illegal activity. You wait for a few minutes, lose your nerve, and try to leave but find the door is locked.

d. You enter to look for an article that you had left behind. In the course of searching for it, you find a purse containing $10,000. Decide what to do with the money before you leave.

e. You enter just after falling and hitting your head. Temporary amnesia causes you to forget your identity. After awhile you discover something that restores your memory.

APPRECIATING THEATER

1. Reports   Everything the student learns about the stage contributes to his knowledge of theater and theoretically to his ability to appreciate the efforts of those who work in the field. However, all the preceding strategies in this section were designed to teach various aspects of acting, which, after all, is only one part of theater. The following exercises are an attempt to introduce the student to dramatic criticism and to help him realize that there is more to theater than acting.

Discuss the fact that theater criticism exists on at least three levels: the literary, the theatrical, and the practical. Explain that people disagree on what is good in theater just as they disagree on what is good in other areas. The important thing is that the student should *have some reason for his belief*. Have students prepare reports describing (a) the finest bit of acting, (b) the finest play, or (c) the best movie or television program they have seen. Ask them to tell in detail why they consider it the finest.

2. Ranking best-liked plays Have each student rank a list of familiar plays from best to worst. Discuss the ratings in class, requiring students to give reasons for their decisions. Be sure to differentiate between good dramatic criticism and popular acclaim while at the same time pointing out that the two need not be in opposition.

3. Directing a scene Have each student prepare a brief scene from a play that will be produced in your vicinity. The student should prepare an analysis of the play as a whole along with a detailed production plan for the scene, complete with blocking, technical notes (staging, costuming, and lighting), and the subtext for the actors. After the play has been presented, discuss the performance in class, comparing it to the production plans developed by the students. If time permits, let each student direct his version of the scene in class to illustrate his arguments. Let the class discuss the relative merits of the results.

THEATER CRITICISM

1. Attending a play Have your students attend a play and look for violations of the "rules" that have been established for movement and positioning. Discuss these in class. Were the "violations" effective? If so, why? If not, why did the rule violations occur?

WRITING FOR THEATER

1. Puppet scene Have each student write a puppet scene three to five minutes long. Make the puppets and present a series of the best scenes in an elementary school classroom.

RESOURCE MATERIALS

BOOKS

Aggertt, Otis J., and Elbert R. Borven. *Communicative Reading,* 2d ed. New York: Macmillan, 1963.

Albright, H. D.; W. P. Halstead; and Lee Mitchell. *Principles of Theatre Art,* 2d ed. Boston: Houghton Mifflin, 1968.

Armstrong, Chloe, and Paul D. Brandes. *The Oral Interpretation of Literature.* New York: McGraw-Hill, 1963.

Bacon, Wallace A. *The Art of Interpretation.* New York: Holt, Rinehart and Winston, 1966.

Batcheller, David R., ed. *Films for Use in Teaching Theatre.* Washington, D. C.: American Educational Theatre Association, 1967.

Cobin, Martin. *Theory and Technique of Interpretation.* Englewood Cliffs, N. J., Prentice-Hall, 1959.

Cole, Toby, ed. *Directing the Play.* Indianapolis: Bobbs-Merrill, 1953.

Collier, Gaylan Jane. *Assignments in Acting.* New York: Harper & Row, 1966.

Dean, Alexander, and Lawrence Carra. *Fundamentals of Play Directing.* New York: Holt, Rinehart and Winston, 1965.

Fernandez, Thomas L., ed. *Oral Interpretation and the Teaching of English.* Champaign, Ill.: National Council of Teachers of English, 1969.

Kahan, Stanley. *Introduction to Acting.* New York: Harcourt, Brace and World, 1962.

Lee, Charlotte, *Oral Interpretation,* 4th ed. Boston: Houghton Mifflin, 1970.

Litto, Frederic M., ed. *Directory of Useful Addresses.* Washington, D. C.: American Educational Theatre Association, 1966.

Lynch, Gladys E., and Harold C. Crain, *Projects in Oral Interpretation.* New York: Holt, Rinehart and Winston, 1959.

Ommanney, Katharine. *The Stage and the School.* New York: McGraw-Hill, 1960.

Parrish, W. Maxfield. *Reading Aloud,* 4th ed. New York: Ronald Press, 1966.

Roach, Helen. *Spoken Records.* New York: Scarecrow Press, 1963.

Seldon, Samuel, and Hunton D. Sellman. *Stage Scenery and Lighting,* 3d ed. New York: Appleton-Century-Crofts, 1959.

Seltzer, Daniel, ed. *The Modern Theatre.* Boston: Little, Brown, 1967.

Sievers, W. David. *Directing for the Theatre.* Dubuque, Iowa: Wm. C. Brown, 1965.

Veilleux, Jeré. *Oral Interpretation: The Recreation of Literature.* New York: Harper & Row, 1967.

Woolbert, C., and S. Nelson. *The Art of Interpretive Speech.* New York: Appleton-Century-Crofts, 1968.

FILMS

Athens: The Golden Age. Encyclopaedia Britannica (30 minutes).

Basic Principles of Stage Costuming. Olesen Company. Six 35-mm. color filmstrips.

Part I	—	General Organization of Script
Part II	—	Application of General Design Principles
Part III	—	Sketches and Use of Textiles
Part IV	—	Workroom Facilities and Basic Sewing Techniques
Part V	—	Patterns and Fitting
Part VI	—	Special Problems

Basic Techniques of Scenery Painting. Olesen Company. Six 35-mm. color filmstrips.

Part I	—	Material and Equipment
Part II	—	Prime and Base Coat Techniques
Part III	—	Overlase Coat Techniques I
Part IV	—	Overlase Coat Techniques II
Part V	—	Special Techniques
Part VI	—	Painting the Drop and the Scrim

Creative Drama—The First Steps. NWU (29 minutes).

Directing a Play. IFB (10 minutes).

Elementary Set Design. Olesen Company. Five 35-mm. color filmstrips.

Part I	—	The Physical Stage and Basic Set Design
Part II	—	Basic Elements of Design
Part III	—	Drafting for the Proscenium Stage

Part IV — Styles of Scenery
Part V — Special Types of Settings

Elementary Stage Makeup. Olesen Company. Four 35-mm. color filmstrips.
Part I — Straight Makeup for Men
Part II — Straight Makeup for Women
Part III — Making Up Youth for Old Age
Part IV — Use of False Hair and Nose Putty

Film for Film Analysis. Audio-Visual Center, Purdue (16 minutes).

Greek and Roman Theatres of the Ancient World. Olesen Company.
Five 35-mm. color filmstrips.
Part I — Ancient Greek Theatre of Epidauros
Part II — Theatre of Dionysus I
Part III — Theatre of Dionysus II
Part IV — Hellenistic Theatre of Priene
Part V — Roman Theatre of Orange

Hamlet: The Age of Elizabeth. Encyclopaedia Britannica (30 minutes).

Lighting for the Theatre. Olesen Company. Three 35-mm. color filmstrips.
Part I — Basic Stage Lighting Equipment
Part II — Area Lighting
Part III — Back, Side, and Full Lighting

Macbeth: The Themes of Macbeth. Encyclopaedia Britannica (28 minutes).

Roman Circuses, Naumachiae and Amphitheatres. Olesen Company.
35-mm. color filmstrips.

Scenery Construction. Olesen Company. Seven 35-mm. color filmstrips.
Part I — The Simple Flat
Part II — Complex Flats
Part III — Handling Flats
Part IV — Platforms
Part V — Parallels
Part VI — Stairs
Part VII — Ramps

Sophocles' Electra. Olesen Company. 35-mm. color filmstrip.

The Age of Sophocles. Encyclopaedia Britannica (30 minutes).

The American Theatre. Olesen Company. Two 35-mm. color filmstrips.
Part I — The Late Eighteenth-Century and Early Nineteenth-Century American Theatre
Part II — The Nineteenth-Century American Theatre: 1826–1950

The Final Performance of Sara Bernhardt. Young America Films
(27 minutes).

The History of the Physical Theatre. Olesen Company. Four 35-mm.
color filmstrips.

Part I	—	The Ancient Greek, Roman, Medieval, Spanish, and Italian Renaissance Theatres
Part II	—	The Elizabethan and Seventeenth-Century French Theatres
Part III	—	English, European, and American Theatres of the Eighteenth and Nineteenth Centuries
Part IV	—	Twentieth-Century Theatres.

The Theatre: One of the Humanities. Encyclopaedia Britannica (30 minutes).

What Happens in Hamlet? Encyclopaedia Britannica (30 minutes).

Working Aids for the Theatre Technician. Olesen Company. Three
35-mm. color filmstrips.

Part I	—	Stage Machinery and Equipment
Part II	—	Stage Hardware
Part III	—	Shop Machinery and Tools

Yesterday's Actors. Olesen Company (30 minutes).

EQUIPMENT SUPPLIERS

LIGHTING EQUIPMENT

American Stage Lighting
1331 North Avenue
New Rochelle, New York 10804

Century Lighting, Inc.
3 Entin Road
Clifton, New York 10036

Electro Controls
2975 South Second West
Salt Lake City, Utah 84104

Electronics Diversified
0626 S.W. Florida Street
Portland, Oregon 97219

Gothic Color Company
90 Ninth Avenue
New York, New York 10011

Hub Electric Company
2255 West Grande Avenue
Chicago, Illinois 60612

Kliegl Brothers
32–32 48th Avenue
Long Island City, New York 11101

Little Stage Lighting
10507 Harry Hines Boulevard
Dallas, Texas 75220

Major Corporation
P.O. Box 359
Crystal Lake, Illinois 60014

Olesen Company
1535 Ivan Avenue
Hollywood, California 90028

Paramount Theatrical Supplies
32 West 20th Street
New York, New York 10011

Rosco Laboratories
Harrison, New York 10528

Skirpan Electronics, Inc.
41–43 24th Street
Long Island City, New York 11101

Strong Electric Corp.
87 City Park Avenue
Toledo, Ohio 43602

Superior Electronic Company
2807 Conn Street
Bristol, Connecticut 06010

Theatre Production Services
52 West 46th Street
New York, New York 10036

Times Square Lighting
318 West 47th Street
New York, New York 10036

Costumes and Properties

American Costume Company
810 Broadway
New York, New York 10003

Central Shippee Inc.
24 West 25th Street
New York, New York 10010

Costume Associates, Inc.
68 East 153rd Street
Bronx, New York 10451

Eaves Costume Company, Inc.
151 West 46th Street
New York, New York 10036

Giesen
389 St. Peter
St. Paul, Minnesota 55102

New York Costume Company
10 West Hubbard Street
Chicago, Illinois 60610

The Armoury
2122 Fillmore Street
San Francisco, California 94115

Stage Equipment

Art Draperies Studios
2766 North Lincoln Avenue
Chicago, Illinois 60614

Automatic Devices Company
2121 South 12th Street
Allentown, Pennsylvania 18103

Olesen Company
1535 Ivan Avenue
Hollywood, California 90028

Theatre Production Services
52 West 46th Street
New York, New York 10036

MUSIC AND SOUND EQUIPMENT

Sony
8150 Vineland Avenue
Sun Valley, California 91352

Sound Associates
432 West 45th Street
New York, New York 10036

FOURTEEN

RADIO, TELEVISION, AND FILM: ASSIGNMENTS AND RESOURCE MATERIALS

Among the areas in speech communication in the secondary school that have grown significantly in the last few years are radio, television, and film. Many new secondary schools have well-equipped broadcasting studios, and some offer fairly comprehensive training in broadcasting. Whether these areas are included in the basic communication course or are offered as separate courses, the assignments and resource materials presented in this chapter may be helpful.

ASSIGNMENTS

INTRODUCTORY ASSIGNMENTS

1. Radio and television log At the beginning of this unit, ask students to keep a viewing-listening log for radio and television, including what programs they hear and for approximately how long.

ASSIGNMENT AREAS

Introductory assignments
Writing for radio
Newscasting
Ad-libbing
Criticism
NAB and FCC
Commercials
Programming
Sports
Engineering
Amateur radio
Movie camera
Interviewing
Television
Films

2. Radio and television personalities   Have the students present a "Who am I" program, selecting characters from radio and television. Or you may choose to record the voices of familiar characters on television, radio, and records and have students write their guesses for each voice on a sheet of paper, comparing them afterwards.

3. Radio and television habits   On the first day of discussion, hand out a questionnaire for the students to complete as a basis for tabulating (a) the number of hours spent per day during the school year listening to radio and watching TV, (b) the number of movies seen per month, and (c) the favorite programs of each type.

4. Television habits   Structure questions regarding television entertainment, news offerings, and current newspaper and periodical articles in an effort to determine:

a. Student information-gathering habits
b. Student knowledge on issues
c. Student interest and involvement in current affairs

You could ask these questions in an unannounced, ungraded quiz. You will probably find that students are appallingly unenlightened. Discuss the "finding."

5. Television behind the scenes   Suggest for outside reading about behind-the-scenes television the paperback *Only You, Dick Darling!* by Merle Miller and Evan Rhodes, published by Bantam Books.

6. Broadcasting notebook   Ask each student to read at least one article each week about broadcasting. The article is to be placed in a notebook and a brief note or reaction to it written by the student.

7. Broadcasting notebook   Make sketches or collect pictures showing the broadcast process, step by step. Put them in your notebook.

8. Research topic   Choose a topic for research that is related to radio, television, or film. Plan a three- to five-minute microphone talk on the topic and write a thousand-word paper on it.

9. Vocations   Ask each student to do the following: Begin a chart of possible vocations in the fields of radio and television. Designate page one for radio, page two for television. Draw several vertical lines on each page to make columns. Column one: name of job; two, brief description of work required; three, training required; four, possible salary; five, availability of jobs for men and women; six, brief notes as to your fitness and interest. This project will not be completed until the end of the semester, but keep filling it in as you progress through the semester.

10. Class-conducted survey   Have the class as a whole make a survey of the listening-viewing habits of their friends at school and in their neighborhood or community. Have them block it out so that there is no wasted motion or overlapping of information. A well organized survey can be beneficial in several ways. If it covers a sufficient area of the community or a sufficient number of people to be representative, the school or community newspaper might be interested in the results.

Plan the survey in an orderly manner. Use the whole class, but appoint or ask for volunteers for a planning or steering committee.

Work out the questions to be asked and the introduction to be used. This must be done systematically. Give sufficient information to the person being called or called upon so that he will cooperate with the project, but don't waste his time.

Finally, form a committee to do the analysis. All results must be carefully prepared and presented to the committee; then the committee will tabulate and make conclusions, presenting them in written form to the class.

WRITING FOR RADIO

Ask the students to do the following:

1. Writing continuity   Listen to a radio program. Keep a running time on the sequence of the parts of the program. Can you identify each part? Did the program follow the standard sequence? If it did not, in what sequence were the parts arranged?

2. Writing continuity   Do the same project as in assignment 1 for television.

3. Writing scripts   To practice writing scripts properly, write the following:

a. A twenty-second piece of continuity to introduce a currently popular tune

b. A thirty-second introduction of a recent convocation guest who is now appearing as a guest on the local radio station.

c. A frame for the following types of shows: a news show, a DJ show, a panel show. Your opening and closing should not take more than a total of two minutes; it should include your theme song, the show's title, today's feature, a sponsor's name, product, and tag line but no commercial. Write the continuity for yourself, as the announcer. Keep these frames in your notebook. They will be used during the next several units of study.

4. Writing commercial copy   Write commercials to be used on various occasions by advertisers. Give your commercials over a microphone brought into the classroom.

5. Writing commercial copy   Using the daily newspaper as a guide, write a thirty-second commercial for one of the advertisers.

6. Writing copy   Write a twenty-second piece of continuity to introduce five popular songs.

7. Preparing news copy   If arrangements can be made with the local station to obtain some news copy for several days, practice "stripping the machines." See how rapidly you can identify each segment that comes over the wires and put on the proper hook. Practice reading all these types of copy. Begin with the Spot summary. Edit the five-minute copy to three minutes. Edit the five-minute copy and plan as a show that has a sign-on and sign-off.

8. Writing news   Prepare a spot news announcement concerning an important event that is happening in the high school, city, or state.

NEWSCASTING

1. Analyzing a news commentary   Have the students listen to a straight newscast and then to a news analysis or a commentary on the news. Then ask them to write a paper discussing the difference between interpreting the news and commenting on it.

2. Listening to newscasts   Tape a number of newscasts from different stations on the same day. Play the tape and have the students analyze the programs for content, for treatment of the same news stories, and for slanting of the news.

3. Organizing the news program   Have several students work as a committee with the fifteen-minute news. One newscaster can specialize in the local news; another in state; another in national and international; one in sports, weather, or women's copy. As many as are desired can work on this team. Each one will introduce the next one. Plan your frame for a regular show. Make a copy for your operator; then try running the show several times. Add a commentator if this seems desirable.

4. News commentary   Ask each student to listen to a commentary program and then build an answer to this show or build a show that supports the other side of the question.

5. News commentary   Ask the students to study several commentators in their area and try to identify their points of view and their differences of opinion. Two students may be assigned to plan commentaries that disagree about some local problem, school or community. The class can hear and decide which one makes the more valid presentation, also which one the community would be more likely to accept. Would either one be accepted by a local station?

6. News commentators   Have the students study the biographies of several noted commentators and answer these questions: What experiences led them from straight news work to commentaries? What would you say is the most important aspect of a commentator's training and abilities?

7. Television news   Ask students to view one television news show for at lease five consecutive days and keep a record on these points: Were there any differences in the personality or style of approach on any specific days or in dealing with any segment of the news? Did the newscaster seem to be more at ease in any one segment of the news than any other? Did he keep the same arrangement of categories of news each day?

8. News programs   Ask each student to plan to listen to or watch examples of the basic three types of news shows and to determine in what ways they differ in purpose, value, and production.

9. News programs   Ask students to do the following: Plan to listen to as many news broadcasts as you can in one day from a chosen station. Note what items of the news are repeated. Is the same copy or a rewrite used? Do you detect any other differences? If so, can you explain why?

10. News programs   Appoint a committee of several students to record a number of news shows from different stations on the same day and at the same general news period. An evening news program is recommended. Have them bring these to class and analyze them. What seem to be the differences in the treatment of the day's news? Ask them to explain.

11. News reporting   Ask each student to write and deliver a major news item from the school or community in a sixty-second story.

12. Preparing news copy   Ask each student to do the following: Bring a six- to eight-inch-long news story from your local paper to class. In a pre-fixed time element, such as ten minutes, rewrite the story for broadcast. Set yourself an air-time length, such as forty-five seconds.

13. News programs   In some communities, a radio or television station is owned by the newspaper. If this is true of your community, ask students to study for several evenings the dinner-hour news broadcast and compare it with the evening newspaper. On a specific day, you or a student can record the show, but other members of the class should not listen to it. Instead, have them study the newspaper and plan a broadcast from that day's news. If possible, assign someone to obtain from the station a copy of that evening's script. Now compare the students' script, the newscaster's script, and the recorded show.

AD-LIBBING

1. Analysis of ad-libbing   Ask each student to do the following: Listen to programs containing a special report that is ad-libbed. Sports programs, news events, special community or church affairs, events of particular interest to women are some ideas for such programs. Keep a record of what you hear. Do you note any similarities among such programs? Observe the vocabulary used. Note how the speaker is able to make you think you are there. How does he achieve this illusion? Can you determine how it is done?

2. Ad-libbing practice   Have students practice reporting events ad lib on mike. Some ideas for these practice sessions are:

a. An honor award being given to your school's star athlete at a convocation is being recorded for broadcast over a local station. You are the announcer.

b. Any major event in the community.

c. An event you have never seen but perhaps have read about or have seen on television or in the movies: the launching of an atomic submarine, a missile launching or moon-shot, a fashion show, the laying of a cornerstone for a new public building in your community or state.

3. Ad-libbing commercials   Have each student prepare a wire copy (obtainable from the local station) and ad-lib the commercial. Have the student deliver it in class. After all have finished, have the class analyze them. (An ad-lib commercial is one in which only a few items of importance are given to the announcer, and he must make up the commercial on the spur of the moment.)

CRITICISM

1. Influence of television: Criticism   Have students prepare a list of questions for a poll or a series of interviews they will actually conduct to find out how much the purchasing habits of people in the community are influenced by television (and radio) advertising.

2. Mass media criticism   Have students clip from magazines or periodicals (for Speaker's Resource Packets) critic's columns, reports, or reviews of mass entertainment or educational programs. If possible have them find reviews of shows they've seen themselves and compare their own observations with those of the reviewers.

3. Mass media criticism   Have students write a review of a TV show or a movie as if they were professional critics.

4. Influence of television, radio, and film: Criticism   Have a group of students read Fred W. Friendly's *Due to Circumstances Beyond Our Control* (New York: Random House, 1967) and plan a panel discussion of this criticism of network television. Another group can do the same task using Marshall McLuhan's *Understanding Media* (New York: McGraw-Hill, 1964).

5. Influence of television: Criticism   Have half the class read William J. Lederer's *A Nation of Sheep* (New York: W. W. Norton, 1961) and the other half Vance Packard's *The Hidden Persuaders* (New York: Pocket Books, 1957). Have a discussion of the ideas presented in these books.

NAB AND FCC

1. NAB   Ask students to look up the history and the function of the National Association of Broadcasters, and then pay a visit to a local station to find out its relationship to the NAB.

2. FCC   Have students read the FCC regulations concerning commercials in radio and television and then listen to or watch a news show, paying particular attention to the placement of the commercials and their content. Ask them what changes they would recommend in the FCC regulations.

COMMERCIALS

Ask students to do the following:

1. Analyzing commercials   Collect as many commercials as you can and make a study of them. How many times was the sponsor's name given? If a local firm, how many times were his address and phone number given? How many times was the product mentioned? Can you discover any patterns as to where these items are placed?

2. Analyzing commercials   Listen to and view several commercial programs. What proportion of time was given to commercials and to the program? Were these commercials separated from the program or were they integrated into the program? Which do you prefer? Why? Do you think your preference is the popular preference or not? Can you determine how a sponsor or producer decides on which method to use?

3. Writing commercials   Write and practice delivering the following commercials:

a. Thirty-second action copy for a single voice for a local business and for a national firm.
b. Thirty-second good-will copy for a local firm and a national firm or product.
c. Thirty-second educational copy for a local and national firm.
d. Repeat the above projects in sixty-second copy.

4. Writing news and commercial copy   Using the daily newspaper as a guide, write a three-minute newscast and a sixty-second commercial.

PROGRAMMING

1. Producing a program   Divide the class into groups. Through discussion let each group decide on a fifteen-minute radio broadcast. The program should include call letters, theme, commercials, and a definite format. All members of the group must participate. The programs can take the form of interviews, children's programs, housewives' programs, teen-age variety shows, newscasts, dramatic hours, cultural spots, or any other format. The scripts are to be written and timed. Records can be played but not in their entirety since it takes up too much speaking time. This program can be easily recorded in a separate room using just a tape recorder. It can then be played for the students and evaluated.

2. Programming   Ask each student to collect and put in his notebook, a schedule of programs for a small local station and a large, metropolitan network station. Ask the students what differences they discover in the programs.

3. Audiences   Ask each student to do the following: Select two stations, one small local station and the other a large metropolitan network station. On a map draw an area which represents the coverage of each station. Then write an analysis of the audience make-up for each station and indicate the type of programming you would schedule if you were program director of each station.

SPORTS

1. Sports announcing   Ask those students who are interested in sports announcing to do the following: First, be sure you know the rules and the vocabulary for the game you want to announce. Here are several practice suggestions:

a. Turn the sound off on your television set when there is a game being broadcast. Try to follow and announce it.

b. Obtain a film of some game. Turn the sound off and announce the game. Record yourself. Then play back the recording and the sound track of the film. Compare and then plan your own training program.

c. Tape-record a football or basketball game you attend. Four students can record with each one announcing a quarter of the game. Perhaps your coach, your teacher, or a local sports announcer will audition the playback of your announcing and make suggestions for your training program.

2. Sports announcing   Have students who are interested in sports announcing read several of the references on sports announcing and also collect articles from magazines and newspapers by and about successful sports announcers.

ENGINEERING

1. Engineering staff interviews   Have students visit a radio or television control room and interview the engineering staff, preparing their questions before they go.

AMATEUR RADIO

1. Visiting amateur radio operator   Have students visit an amateur radio operator when he is broadcasting.

MOVIE CAMERA

1. Using a movie camera   If students have access to a movie camera, have them try some television-camera techniques with it.

INTERVIEWING

1. Interviewing practice   Ask students to do the following: Imagine that you have a weekly interview program on a local station. Your guest this week is some high school student who has distinguished himself. Plan your interview. Remember your adult audience does not know this student and your school situation as you do. Can you sustain an interview for ten minutes and keep it interesting and informative?

2. Interviewing practice   Have each student in the class adopt the name of a well-known person living today—someone about whom it is possible to gather information—research the person, and turn in an outline of the person's life. Then have each student write his own name at the top of a card and his adopted name at the bottom. Collect and record the pairs of names. Detach the bottom half of each card with the student's adopted name on it and have each member of the class draw a name from this collection to be his guest on a series of interview shows.

3. Interviewing programs   Have the students do the following: Listen to some interview programs. Note how the interviewer keeps the interviewee doing most of the talking and how he keeps the conversation moving along some planned outline. Can you follow his plan? Note his techniques or methods in asking questions. What does he do with the answer to the question?

TELEVISION

Give the following assignments to students:

1. Visiting a television station   Plan a visit to a television station. Pay close attention to the equipment. Find out if you can talk with the staff personnel. If you can, go prepared to ask questions. Make arrangements to sit in the control room during a production. Pay attention to the commands of the director. If possible, go into the studio and watch a crew set up for a production. After you return, discuss the visit in class. Your teacher may plan some report projects.

2.. Television jobs   Write a report on the individual jobs in the television team.

3. Use of television cameras   Watch a television show involving a group. Analyze its picture composition and use of camera lenses.

4. Use of television cameras   Select a short dramatic sequence from a play which you know well. Try to chart the use of the camera as though you were a director. Can you discover the dramatic possiblities of the camera?

5. Television commercial   Write a one-minute commercial for television in which you make a talk for a product. This is a talk and not a demonstration. Using only one camera, plan how you would use various shots and lenses to make the talk more interesting.

6. Television commercial   Write a one-minute commercial, showing a product's usefulness. Demonstrate the product. Plan the production of this commercial with two cameras. You produce it as though you were the floor director and another student the talent. Then change positions. Can you concentrate on the "take" lens?

7. Television interviewing   Plan a three-minute interview on television. Choose a member of your class and interview him about the tour to the television studio or about your work in this class in television. Use your parents as an audience.

8. Pantomime and television   Plan a pantomime of a children's story. Using musical background or music and sound, integrate these elements for a television production. Use only two cameras. Plan your camera work. Use only one person as talent. Keep your story simple.

9. Dramatic television scene   Plan a two-voice or dramatic sequence for a two-camera show. Keep the scene very short and simple.

FILMS

Give the following assignments to students:

1. Producing a film   Produce a short film (three to four minutes) that demonstrates or teaches. Write the script. Be sure everyone knows time, place, and length of shooting session. Have all properties available.

2. Producing a film   Produce a short commercial film (four to five minutes).

3. Producing a film   Produce a short documentary film (four to five minutes).

4. Producing a film   Produce a one-minute commercial for TV.

5. Producing a film   Produce a short film skit (four to five minutes). Suggested ideas:

a. A chronic deadbeat tries unsuccessfully to borrow money from his "friends."

b. A group of people gather, one by one. They have all been asked to meet by the same friend, but they don't know why. Finally the friend shows up with his birthday cake.

c. Three folk singers with instruments appear to try out individually for a television producer. Individually they are bad, but the idea occurs to the producer that they might go over as a group. They try a song as a group and are a great hit.

You will need a director, cameraman, clapstick boy, boom operator, and recordist. Until you gain experience, take shots in sequence.

6. Basic shooting   Make a hand-held shot in which you "spray the garden." Swing the camera quickly from one object to another. When the film is projected, you will see that such a practice is very undesirable. Then make a pan shot, hand-held, of a static subject (a long building, for example) using a long lens. The combination of hand-holding and long lens should result in a bad pan. Finally, shoot the same pan using a tripod and normal lens.

7. Basic shooting   Shoot a hand-held tilt shot with normal lens and then the same shot with the camera on a tripod.

RESOURCE MATERIALS

BOOKS

Atkins, Jim, Jr., and Leo Willete. *Filming TV News and Documentaries.* Philadelphia: Chilton, 1965.

Barnhart, Lyle D. *Radio and Television Announcing.* Englewood Cliffs, N. J.: Prentice-Hall, 1953.

Becker, Samuel L., and H. Clay Harshbarger. *Television Techniques for Planning and Performance.* New York: Holt, Rinehart and Winston, 1958.

Blum, Daniel. *Pictorial History of Television.* Philadelphia: Chilton, 1950.

Bobker, Lee R. *Elements of the Film.* New York: Harcourt, Brace & World, 1969.

Broadcasting Primer: Evolution of Broadcasting. Washington, D. C.: Federal Communications Commission, Office of Reports and Information, n.d.

Brodbeck, Emil E. *Handbook of Basic Motion Picture Techniques.* New York: McGraw-Hill, 1950.

Chester, Girard; Garnet R. Garrison; and Edgar E. Willis. *Television and Radio,* 3rd ed. New York: Appleton-Century-Crofts, 1963.

Clark, Charles G. *Professional Cinematography.* Hollywood: American Society of Cinematographers, 1964.

Crews, A. R. *Professional Radio Writing.* Boston: Houghton Mifflin, 1946.

Curran, Charles W. *Screen Writing and Production Techniques: The Nontechnical Handbook for TV, Film, and Tape.* New York: Hastings House, 1958.

Duerr, Edwin. *Radio and Television Acting: Criticism, Theory, and Practice.* New York: Holt, Rinehart and Winston, 1950.

Gaskill, Arthur L., and David A. Englander. *How to Shoot a Movie Story: The Technique of Pictorial Continuity*. Hastings-on-Hudson, N. Y.: Morgan & Morgan, 1960.

Head, Sydney W. *Broadcasting in America*, 2d ed. Boston: Houghton Mifflin, 1972.

Hilliard, Robert T. *Writing for Television and Radio*. New York: Hastings House, 1962.

Houston, Penelope. *The Contemporary Cinema*. Harmondsworth, Eng.: Penguin Books, 1963.

Hughes, Robert, ed. *Film: Book 1*. New York: Grove Press, 1959.

Hyde, Stuart W. *Television and Radio Announcing*, 2d ed. Boston: Houghton Mifflin, 1971. Record accompanies text.

Jacobs, Lewis, ed. *Introduction to the Art of the Movies*. New York: Farrar, Straus, 1960.

Klapper, Joseph T. *Effects of Mass Communication*. New York: Free Press, 1960.

Knight, Arthur, *The Liveliest Art*. New York: New American Library of World Literature, 1959.

Lawson, John Howard. *Film: The Creative Process*. New York: Hill & Wang, 1964.

Lawton, Sherman P. *The Modern Broadcaster: The Station Book*. New York: Harper & Row, 1961.

MacCann, Richard Dyer. *Film: A Montage of Theories*. New York: E. P. Dutton, 1966.

Mackey, David R. *Drama on the Air*. New York: Prentice-Hall, 1951.

Manvell, Roger. *Films*. New York: Cambridge University Press, 1950.

Mascelli, Joseph V. *The Five C's of Cinematography*. Hollywood: Cine/Grafic, 1965.

McMahan, Harry Wayne. *Television Production: The Creative Techniques and Language of TV Today*. New York: Hastings House, 1957.

Mercer, John. *An Introduction to Cinematography*. Champaign, Ill.: Stipes, 1967.

Oringel, Robert S. *Audio Control Handbook for Radio and TV Broadcasting*. New York: Hastings House, 1956.

Pincus, Edward. *Guide to Filmmaking*. New York: New American Library, 1969.

Reinsch, J. Leonard, and Elmo Ellis. *Radio Station Management,* 2nd ed. New York: Harper & Row, 1960.

Reisz, Karel. *Technique of Film Editing: Basic Principles for TV.* New York: Farrar, Straus, & Giroux, 1953.

Schramm, Wilbur. *The Effects of Television on Children and Adolescents.* New York: UNESCO Publications Office, 1964.

Settel, Irving. *A Pictorial History of Radio.* New York: Citadel Press, 1960.

Spear, James. *Creating Visuals for TV: A Guide for Educators.* Washington, D. C.: National Education Association, 1962.

Stasheff, Edward, and Rudy Bretz. *The Television Program.* New York: Hill & Wang, 1962.

Talbot, Daniel, ed. *Film: An Anthology.* New York: Simon & Schuster, 1959.

Taylor, John Russell. *Cinema Eye, Cinema Ear.* New York: Hill & Wang, 1965.

The Television Code. Washington, D. C.: National Association of Broadcasters, revised 1966.

Warshow, Robert. *The Immediate Experience.* New York: Doubleday, 1962.

White, Llewellyn. *The American Radio.* Chicago: University of Chicago Press, 1947.

White, Melvin R. *Beginning Radio Production.* New York: Oxford University Press, 1951.

Zettl, Herbert. *Television Production Handbook.* Belmont, Calif.: Wadsworth, 1961.

FILMS

Public Opinion. EBF (11 minutes). An analysis of public opinion in terms of what it is, how it is formed, and what it can accomplish.

Radio Waves. McGraw-Hill (26 minutes). Discusses man-made and natural radio waves.

Television: How it Works. Coronet (11 minutes). Discusses the fundamentals of television broadcasting, including operation of a cathode ray tube, image orthicon tube, electron gun, deflecting coils and a syncgenerator.

The Television System. McGraw-Hill (14 minutes). Discusses basic principles of television broadcasting.

Your Voice. Encyclopaedia Britannica (11 minutes). Demonstrates some of the common voice faults.

PART FOUR

PROFESSIONAL CONCERNS OF THE SPEECH TEACHER

Part Four focuses on three professional concerns of the speech communication teacher: student teaching; professional organizations and publications; and directing the cocurricular speech program. Chapter 15 describes student teaching as a realistic yet protected learning situation and attempts to prepare you for that role. Chapter 16 points out the professional responsibilities of a speech communication teacher and describes the professional organizations you will want to consider joining and the professional publications you will want to consider reading. Finally, Chapter 17 develops a philosophy of cocurricular activities and describes a number of activities that might be included in a good cocurricular speech program.

FIFTEEN

THE STUDENT-TEACHING EXPERIENCE

Student teaching is that portion of the undergraduate teacher education program designed to help the student *learn how to teach* by applying the skills and understanding he has gained from the methods course and other courses and by coping in the real situation with guidance and feedback from a competent supervising teacher. It enables the student to *learn how to teach* in a realistic but protected environment.

Ideally, student teaching provides the opportunity to start at the beginning, to test preparation and skills in very small bits of teaching or with small groups of pupils. As the student demonstrates his ability to handle these short "micro-units," he will learn to plan, analyze, and teach and also to evaluate his teaching—all under the direction of his supervising teacher. As he progresses to more and more extensive and difficult segments, he will inevitably encounter teaching problems, which he also will learn to solve under the direction of the supervising teacher, assisted when desirable by the university coordinator.

It is expected that many teaching, professional, and nonprofessional staff members will have a profound influence on the experiences and learning of the student teacher. It is unlikely that the first teaching position of the newly trained teacher will be exactly like that of his supervising teacher. In fact, in view of the many different administrative patterns in schools, the varying socioeconomic situations in which teaching is done, and the tremendous differences in social interaction among various groups of people, it is *most unlikely* that the initial

1. Describe the typical student-teaching experience.
2. Identify the goals of the student-teaching experience.
3. Describe the roles of the student-teacher, supervising teacher, and university coordinator.
4. Describe the training and entering behaviors expected of the student teacher.
5. Describe the initial experiences in student teaching.
6. Identify selected teaching behaviors the student teacher should be able to demonstrate.
7. Describe the student teacher's expected growth from dependence to independence during student teaching.

teaching assignment will be at all similar to the student-teaching assignment. Many supervising teachers, however, help the student teacher plan a wide variety of experiences not only to enable him to make some judgments about his own interests and competencies in teaching, but also to help him gain some initial experience with widely differing patterns.

The specific purposes of student teaching are the following: (1) to enable the student to test his learnings; (2) to give him an opportunity to try out, to err, and to receive suggestions and guidance that will enable him to improve his ability to teach; (3) to enable him to gain an understanding of the relationships between a *real* school and a *real* community; (4) to widen his understanding of teaching as a profession; (5) to sharpen his perceptions of problems and issues in education as he is confronted with these as a part of his experience; and (6) to help him develop a realistic self-concept as a teacher.

It is hoped that in the student-teaching program the achievement of these objectives will be a truly cooperative endeavor among the entire professional staff. Each student teacher must seek to understand his own personality, his level of competence, his interests, his strengths and weaknesses, and his ability to adapt to new situations. At the same time he needs to examine the requirements and specifications of different teaching positions open to him and to make valid decisions in regard to his ability to fit into them.

THE STUDENT TEACHER'S PREPARATION

The presence of a student teacher requires an adjustment on the part of the pupils in the high school classroom. It is important that they get used to the idea and accept having a student teacher. The primary responsibility for creating a positive set on the part of the pupils rests with the supervising teacher. As a student teacher, however, you will want to talk with the supervising teacher to gain an understanding of the situation and to learn how you will be received.

There is no set formula for preparing pupils to accept a student teacher, but factors such as pupil age, whether or not this is the pupils' first experience in having a student teacher, and what the class is like need to be considered. The pupils should be told that the student teacher is another teacher who is coming to work with them and that they are his first class. It is important that the pupils perceive the student teacher as a qualified member of a teaching *team*—their regular teacher and the student teacher. Pupils should be given the student teacher's name and background. References to the student teacher as a college senior, as a person completing his college training to be a teacher, and as a person embarking on a professional career are appropriate. These steps in preparing the pupils for the student teacher should be carried out, of course, by the supervising teacher. It would be awkward for you, as the student teacher, to try to welcome yourself, to show your credentials, and to define your role to the class on the first day. Nevertheless, you have a stake in this preparation of the class, and you can profit from knowing what preparation has been made.

Second, you will need to acquire some specific materials in orientation visits at the school. *Before* student teaching begins, you should obtain a teacher's handbook or administrative manual, a student handbook, a list of audiovisual aids, an extra set of textbooks, copies of curriculum guides, class lists of students, and a daily schedule of classes.

Third, you will want to gather information from those persons in the school with whom you visit: a brief overview of the community—general makeup and philosophy; schedule of subjects taught; class size, number of boys and girls, and any special problems; ability levels, a brief explanation of classroom guidelines and procedures; textbooks used; a brief explanation of the overall curriculum for the year and where the class will be when your teaching begins; an overview of the curriculum to be covered during the student-teaching period and what units you will teach; and available resources: visual aids, library, and classrooms.

A fourth concern in getting ready to student-teach is learning school policies and procedures. Much of this information will be given to you when you visit the school before student teaching begins, but you may wish to meet with your supervising teacher specifically to obtain this information. Some of the detailed classroom procedures are best learned through observation, but others you will need to know from the start to avoid a serious blunder.

INITIAL EXPERIENCES IN STUDENT TEACHING

WRITTEN UNIT AND LESSON PLANS

Start to prepare for your student teaching by finding out what units you will teach so that you can formulate unit plans as well as lesson plans. You should make out both daily and long-range lesson plans. Always have them checked, corrected, and approved by your supervising teacher before you teach the lesson. It is important that your supervising teacher know what (subject matter) and how (procedures) you plan to teach.

It is not uncommon to find supervising teachers who do not prepare detailed written plans for their own teaching. Like other complex tasks teaching is seldom properly done without a considerable amount of thought and preparation. This is probably true for most teachers, in-service as well as preservice, but the in-service teacher has the advantage of experience upon which to base his thinking. It may be possible for experienced teachers to perform very well in the classroom with little more apparent planning than can be found in a schedule book, but—whatever may be the case for the professionals—student teachers generally need to prepare written plans. Written plans are not so much a burden as an assist in growth toward a professional level of teaching.

The value of preparing written plans prior to each teaching experience is deemed sufficient to justify this requirement as a standard operating procedure. Written plans require thought and organization, they can be examined in advance by coordinators and supervising teachers, they help to assure quality learning experiences for pupils, and the student teacher who has prepared them is apt to undertake his early teaching encounters with more confidence and with greater chances of success. Units vary in length, of course, but they frequently extend for a period of several weeks and provide an excellent opportunity for the student teacher to acquire experience in selecting subject matter, establishing objectives, accumulating background information, selecting and obtaining teaching materials, organizing teacher episodes, preparing student assignments, and arranging for the evaluation of pupil accomplishments.

Within the larger framework of the unit plan there is opportunity for short-term planning by the week and by the day. It is well to think of short-term planning as representing a cycle consisting of planning–performance–evaluation–revision or extension of plans, and so on, until the objectives are either satisfactorily reached or abandoned. Planning and pupil evaluation are necessarily linked in the teaching process, for one step cannot logically proceed without the other. A common weakness found in teaching is the failure of teachers to establish objectives, to teach them, and then to evaluate specifically in terms of attainment. It is the understanding of the planning process as a cycle that the student teacher is expected to gain and to use.

As suggested in this methods book, objectives should be stated in behavioral terms. If the student teacher disciplines himself to write the kind of objectives which require the student to perform either physical or mental behaviors, the other steps in planning will be much easier and more meaningful. When the teaching objectives are unclear, it is probable that the student teacher is relying too much on the outline and problems of a textbook or is simply stating information read from some other source. In addition to the behavioral objectives, the lesson and unit plans will include the instructional strategy and the procedures for evaluating achievement. You should suggest methods, detailed ones, for teaching the selected objectives and justify them on the basis of (1) individual differences among the students, (2) physical facilities, (3) available materials, (4) subject content, and (5) a suitable variety of teaching approaches. It is hoped that as a student teacher you will be able to gain experience in the use of many of the methods which you know. You will want to describe in detail procedures for measuring the attainment of objectives. Following is a set of guidelines for evaluating unit and lesson planning:

1. Selection of content
   a. Has the curriculum guide been consulted?
   b. Are the concepts to be taught adequately justified?
   c. Are the concepts and skills in the proper sequence?

2. Instructional objectives
   a. Are the objectives stated in such a way that their attainment is measurable?
   b. Are they reasonable expectations for the pupils in the class?
   c. Do they provide for learning in the psychomotor, cognitive, and affective domains?

3. Instructional strategy
    a. Do the planned activities specifically fit the stated objectives?
    b. Is a sufficient variety of teaching methods included?
    c. Do the plans provide for the active involvement of all the pupils?
    d. Is provision made for adequate reinforcement of the desired pupil responses?

4. Teaching materials
    a. Have all the sources of teaching materials been checked to determine what materials are available?
    b. Have commercial materials been previewed prior to their inclusion in the plan?
    c. Have any of the materials been prepared or created by the student teacher for specific purposes within the unit?
    d. Will the chosen materials appeal to all or most of the senses?

5. Evaluation
    a. Have evaluation procedures been planned which specifically measure the attainment of the objectives?
    b. Is evaluation a continuous process throughout the unit?
    c. Is systematic observation employed as a means of pupil evaluation?
    d. Is pupil evaluation considered to be a source of feedback from which the teacher may evaluate his own work and revise or extend his teaching plans?
    e. Is self-evaluation, by both the pupils and the teacher, planned?

OBSERVING: TECHNIQUES THE MAIN FOCUS

A second early experience in student teaching is observing the teaching of others. Observation of good teaching can be valuable when one knows what to look for. Some student teachers, however, may hold a rather distorted image of a teacher. They may visualize him as a person standing in front of a classroom with the students seated quietly before him. They may regard the instructor primarily as a conveyer of knowledge. With such an image of teaching, it becomes difficult for the student to grasp the idea that students may be *participants in as well as recipients of learning.* If student teachers do not know what to look for when observing other teachers, they may find themselves becoming absorbed in what is being taught without recognizing what the teacher is doing to create an effective learning situation. It has been the experience of the writers of this book that many student teachers are concerned about their knowledge of subject matter but rarely express concern about their lack of teaching skills. Experienced teachers, of course, recognize that *knowing how to teach is as important as knowing what to teach.* When the student teacher becomes aware of effective teaching techniques, he will not only do a better job of planning his own teaching but will also recognize effective teaching techniques when he observes other teachers.

The following set of guidelines may help the student teacher to focus on teaching behavior as he observes others teaching.

1. Planning
    a. The teacher prepares plans that are clear.
    b. The teacher has pupils participate in planning.
    c. Pupils and the teacher understand the objectives.
    d. The teacher considers students' needs and desires.
    e. The teacher is flexible in carrying out plans.

2. Selecting and using materials
    a. The teacher uses visual aids to stimulate interest.
    b. The teacher uses visual aids to clarify meanings.
    c. The teacher uses visual aids to gain pupil attention.

3. Motivating
    a. The teacher is cheerful and enthusiastic.
    b. The teacher responds overtly to pupils' contributions.
    c. The teacher excites learners by using pupils' past experiences and knowledge.
    d. The teacher introduces material at a level familiar to pupils.
    e. The teacher provides opportunity for pupils to discuss lessons, to participate.

4. Giving directions
    a. The teacher's directions are concise and clear.
    b. Needed clarification is provided by the teacher.
    c. Visual presentations are utilized in giving directions as required.
    d. The teacher defines instructional goals and objectives.

5. Helping learners find meaning
    a. Concept development by the teacher moves from simple to complex.
    b. New information is related to past learnings by the teacher.
    c. Concrete examples, or illustrations, are used by the teacher.
    d. Active participation by the pupils is encouraged by the teacher.

6. Controlling the classroom environment
    a. Pupils' errors in new learnings are accepted by the teacher.

b. The teacher is calm in tense situations.
c. The teacher is considerate of the feelings of pupils.
d. The teacher accepts pupils as unique individuals.
e. Pupil embarrassment is avoided by action of the teacher.

7. Providing for individual differences
    a. The teacher provides individual assistance to all pupils.
    b. The teacher encourages individuality in the pupils.

8. Controlling student behavior.
    a. The teacher circulates among pupils.
    b. The teacher reinforces good behavior with appropriate praise.
    c. The teacher varies the pace and nature of activities.
    d. The teacher discourages excessive noise.
    e. The teacher assists pupils in understanding the reasons for rules.

9. Evaluating
    a. The teacher uses a variety of evaluation techniques.
    b. The teacher encourages pupil self-evaluation.
    c. The teacher helps pupils recognize individual progress.
    d. The teacher rewards pupil achievement.

DISCIPLINE OF STUDENTS

A third concern related to initial teaching experiences is discipline or classroom behavior of pupils. The best way to avoid behavior problems is to have a well-planned lesson, carefully thought out in terms of activities which keep the pupils foremost in mind, activities properly timed in terms of adolescent attention span and executed with steadily increasing skill.

Also, as a student teacher you need to become acquainted with school policies affecting pupil behavior and punishment and to acquire a set of written policies, if they exist in your school. Can you keep pupils after school? When should you refer pupils to other members of the school staff? How do you do this? Can you exclude or dismiss pupils? As emphasized in Chapter 6, classroom control problems are often related to the failure of the student teacher to recognize individual differences among pupils. You may wish to discuss with the supervising teacher the nature of the individual differences you will be likely to encounter in the classes you teach. What you learn from such discussions can be compared with what you learn from direct observation of behavior in your classes and the classes of other teachers in your building. If discipline problems occur, you will find it a good practice to carry on some self-analysis to determine whether you are at fault in creating the situation. Was there some way you might have foreseen a problem developing and prevented it? Following are some guidelines you should follow starting with the first day of teaching:

1. Show a genuine interest in every pupil in the room.
2. Be liberal with *sincere* praise but *do not strive for popularity.*
3. Praise in public, censure in private.
4. Be consistent. Pupils are quick to spot inconsistency.
5. Never punish the entire group for the misbehavior of one pupil.
6. Show confidence in the pupil's ability to develop self-control.
7. Keep pupils who are potential problems interested and busy.
8. Do not create situations that encourage pupils to lie, to challenge your authority, or to test your intentions.
9. Allow pupils to save face when they are in a tight spot.
10. Never punish in anger or to get even.

Many student teachers are determined to be friendly, fascinating teachers, and they find it difficult to believe that a stable classroom climate must be established before effective teaching can begin. Some may have to learn the hard way that the teacher must be the leader who insists on behavior and work standards and that avoidance of this responsibility may have a negative effect. The student teacher should set reasonable goals and postpone the risk of overstimulating the class until routines and work habits are established.

FROM DEPENDENCE TO INDEPENDENCE

When the student teacher enters the teaching experience, he is quite dependent on the supervising teacher and others. Hopefully, he will reach a relatively high level of self-assurance and independence by the time he completes student teaching. It may be best for him to begin with one class or one activity and gradually add more. Some examples of appropriate beginning activities for student teachers are: working with individual pupils, working with small groups, teaching part of a lesson, team teaching with the supervising teacher, participating in homeroom or club activities, taking part in class discussions and planning, giving a demonstration, presenting a short current-events report, and helping with a class project. Student teachers generally are given more responsibility as their teaching effectiveness increases.

The supervising teacher is usually in the classroom most of the time during the first days or weeks the student teacher conducts the class. Gradually, as the student teacher demonstrates increasing confidence, the supervising teacher may increase the length of time he is out of the classroom.

PERSONAL AND PROFESSIONAL ETHICS

Another facet of growth in the process of becoming a professional teacher is personal and professional ethics. The professionally competent teacher develops certain characteristics, among which are an adequate self-concept, security in the teaching role, fairness and objectivity, a sense of humor, an ability to accept criticism, and an involvement in the professional organizations. It is hoped that the student teacher will grow in these ways as a result of the student-teaching experience.

SUMMARY

In summary, student teaching is a realistic yet protected learning situation. It is the focal point toward which the methods course and other professional education courses are directed. It offers the student teacher the opportunity to test his understanding of the process of teaching and learning by applying such understanding to the real situation of teaching. In addition, student teaching provides him the opportunity to observe skilled professionals actively involved in the process of managing a learning system.

This chapter described the goals or purposes of student teaching, as well as the roles played by the student teacher, supervising teacher, and university coordinator. The training and entering behaviors the student teacher is expected to possess have been discussed in detail. Finally, the expected growth of the student teacher from dependence to independence was emphasized. Although no student-teaching experience can be predicted with exactness, the authors have attempted to provide some means of knowing what is generally expected in student teaching.

SIXTEEN

PROFESSIONAL ORGANIZATIONS
AND PUBLICATIONS

Teaching claims to be a profession, but the teacher is not professional unless he actively participates in appropriate professional organizations and reads the journals and other publications of his discipline. It is through these organizations and publications that the teacher is exposed to current developments in education in general as well as to those in his academic field. Both experienced and inexperienced teachers need to be continually engaged in self-education. The effective professional teacher is aware of the latest research findings, resource materials, instructional strategies, and issues in his academic area. Professional speech communication organizations provide such services to speech teachers through their conventions, workshops, available materials, newsletters, and journals.

Although there are dozens of professional organizations, only the largest, most active, and most useful for speech teachers will be identified in this chapter. Each teacher, however, must determine for himself which professional organizations he wishes to join.

National Education Association   The National Education Association has as its objective the general welfare of secondary, elementary, and college teachers; and it has done an effective job of representing the needs and objectives of teachers and public education in general to the people of the United States.

OBJECTIVES

1. Identify relevant professional organizations.
2. Identify and describe the commonly used journals in the discipline of speech communication education.

American Federation of Teachers Another national organization of considerable importance to secondary, elementary, and college teachers is the American Federation of Teachers. Its major influence is probably in metropolitan areas.

State Teachers Association Each state has its teachers association. Like the National Education Association, the state associations are capable of focusing upon the needs and concerns of teachers in general, and to an extent provide services to each academic area. The state associations and the National Education Association, however, cannot provide the attention to materials, objectives, and methodologies peculiar to each academic field as well as can the professional organizations of each academic area. Nevertheless, the influence that state associations have been able to exert in improving the welfare of teachers in general is significant, and the state teachers associations deserve the professional teacher's support.

Speech Communication Association The major professional organization for speech teachers is the Speech Communication Association, known until 1970 as the Speech Association of America. This national organization was founded in 1914 by a group of college speech teachers who felt that speech departments and courses should be independent of English departments. The concerns of the organization soon broadened to include elementary and secondary speech.

The Speech Communication Association draws its members from all areas of speech. It has nine divisions: forensics, mass communication, rhetorical and communication theory, theater, instructional development, public address, speech sciences, interpersonal and small group interaction, and interpretation.

Each year the Speech Communication Association sponsors a national convention, generally in December, when the Legislative Council transacts business and the various divisions sponsor programs and workshops for the general membership. In addition, the Speech Communication Association sponsors a Placement Bureau and provides placement services at the national convention. A file of the credentials of members seeking employment is kept current by the association, and a monthly listing of job vacancies is published and distributed to those subscribing to the placement service.

The Speech Communication Association publishes three journals: The *Quarterly Journal of Speech, Speech Monographs,* and the *Speech Teacher.* The association publishes, also, a *Directory* of its membership, and a *Table of Contents* of articles appearing in the *Quarterly Journal of Speech, Speech Monographs,* and the *Speech Teacher,* and *Spectra,* a newsletter.

The national offices of the Speech Communication Association are located in the Statler Hilton Hotel, New York, New York 10001.

American Educational Theatre Association   Various national speech associations exist that are more specialized than the Speech Communication Association, and one of these is the American Educational Theatre Association. Its objectives are the following: (1) to promote the highest standards in theater practice, teaching, and research; and (2) to create understanding and appreciation of theater. There are three nearly autonomous divisions within the association: (1) the American Community Theatre Association, (2) the Children's Theatre Conference, and (3) the Secondary School Theatre Conference. Each division elects its own officers and governing board, holds its own national convention, and publishes a periodical. The American Educational Theatre Association publishes the *Educational Theatre Journal.* The national headquarters are located at the John F. Kennedy Center for the Performing Arts, 1701 Pennsylvania Avenue, Washington, D. C. 20566.

American Speech and Hearing Association   A speech-related national organization is the American Speech and Hearing Association. Its major objective is to promote the investigation of speech and hearing disorders. The association provides clinical certification for members in either speech pathology or audiology. It publishes three journals regularly: the *Journal of Speech and Hearing Disorders*, the *Journal of Speech and Hearing Research*, and *ASHA*. It also publishes the following on an irregular basis: *ASHA Monograph* and *ASHA Reports*. The national headquarters are located at 9030 Old Georgetown Road, Washington, D. C. 20014.

International Communication Association   The International Communication Association is concerned with the improvement of human communication. It emphasizes business, organizational, and interpersonal communication, and it includes in its membership educators, businessmen, journalists, labor leaders, public relations experts, personnel managers, psychiatrists, engineers, lawyers, medical professionals, ministers, and others who are concerned with the junction of communication in society and its organizations.

The International Communication Association, known before 1969 as the National Society for the Study of Communication, publishes the *Journal of Communication* and sponsors a yearly national convention for the reporting of recent findings and implications of theory and research in human communication and for the conduct of the business of the organization.

American Forensic Association   The objective of the American Forensic Association is to promote excellence in forensics. For the most part, its membership comprises debate teachers and coaches. The *Journal of the American Forensic Association* publishes articles on practical problems in forensics—problems in directing forensic programs, running debate tournaments, case development, etc. The association also supplies standardized debate ballots at low cost to high schools and colleges.

National Forensic League   The National Forensic League is similar to the American Forensic Association in its purposes except that it is primarily for secondary schools rather than colleges. It is the major high school debate organization. The NFL was organized in 1924 with a constituency of twenty high schools and grew to a membership of five hundred high schools by 1936, when the number of chapters was limited to five hundred. In 1960 the limit was raised to one thousand chapters. Even so, the league remains a society of select schools with outstanding debate programs. The NFL uses a system of credit points as the basis for its honors program, awarding Degrees of Honor, Excellence, and Distinction for specified levels of proficiency. It sponsors regional tournaments and a national tournament each year.

International Thespian Society   This well-known dramatics organization is quite popular in secondary schools and of importance to speech educators. Its purpose is the advancement and improvement of dramatic arts programs in secondary schools. Its official publication is *Dramatics*. Like the NFL, the International Thespian Society has a point system for rewarding participation, service, and achievement in dramatic arts.

Regional speech associations   In addition to the national professional speech associations, there are four important regional associations: the Speech Association of the Eastern States, the Southern Speech Communication Association, the Central States Speech Association, and the Western Speech Communication Association. The Speech Association of the Eastern States includes those states within the area bounded by Maryland and Pennsylvania on the south and west and New York and New England on the north. *Today's Speech* is the official journal of this association. The *Southern Speech Journal* is published by the Southern Speech Communication Association, whose territory is bounded by the Ohio River on the north and Texas and Arkansas on the west. The Central States Speech Association includes those states from Ohio in the east to Missouri and Oklahoma on the south and the Dakotas, Nebraska and Kansas on the west. The *Central States Speech Journal* is the official publication of this organization. The remaining states are included in the Western Speech Communication Association, and the association's publication is *Western Speech*.

Most states have a state speech association especially concerned with the needs of secondary school speech teachers and with the secondary schools' speech programs. As a speech teacher in a secondary school, you will want to join and support your particular state speech association.

SUMMARY

As previously indicated, the educational and professional organizations identified in this chapter are not the complete roster. However, these are the major organizations of which a professional teacher of speech should be aware, and theirs are the publications that are most conducive to continuous professional growth. The time has come to dispel the notion that "anyone can teach speech communication." The need today is for truly professional teachers. In addition to being well trained pedagogically and theoretically in speech communication, being professional means keeping abreast of new knowledge and skills and supporting those professional organizations whose objectives are directly related to improving speech communication. This chapter has identified those organizations and their journals.

SEVENTEEN

DIRECTING THE COCURRICULAR
SPEECH PROGRAM

The cocurricular speech program is composed of those speech activities outside the classroom which are related directly to the curricular speech program. These activities are cocurricular, not extracurricular. Extracurricular speech activities are those outside the classroom that are *separated from and unrelated to* the curricular speech program of the school. Today effective speech programs in American secondary schools are an integral part of the total school program and are directly related to the speech communication objectives of the school. The good cocurricular speech program grows out of the curricular program and is consistent with the objectives of that program as well as with the objectives of the school itself. Extracurricular programs, on the other hand, do not grow out of the curricular program and may or may not contribute to the achievement of school objectives. Unfortunately some extracurricular programs sponsored by nonschool groups exist to serve the nonschool organizations' objectives and public relations rather than the school. Hence the first requirement of good out-of-class speech activities is that they constitute a cocurricular program rather than an extracurricular one.

OBJECTIVES

1. Describe an exemplary philosophy of cocurricular speech activities.
2. Identify the goals of the cocurricular speech activities program.
3. Identify and describe the various types of cocurricular speech activities.
4. Explain how to organize a new cocurricular speech program.
5. Describe the typical cocurricular debate program and identify the skills expected of the director of such a program.
6. Explain how to organize and manage an interscholastic debate tournament.
7. Explain how to organize and manage solo speech events, tournaments, or festivals.
8. Explain how to organize and manage discussion contests and festivals.
9. Explain how to organize, direct, and manage a dramatic production.
10. Describe the goals and values of a Readers' Theater program.
11. Explain how to organize and manage a speaker's bureau.

PURPOSE OF THE COCURRICULAR PROGRAM

The general purpose of the cocurricular speech activities program has been defined by the Contest Committee of the North Central Association (1951):

> Such activities give the pupil of special aptitude an opportunity for more intensive and extended experience than is possible either in formal courses or in the general education program.
> Principals and teachers should, therefore, treat the interscholastic speech activities as having educational values identical with those that govern classroom instruction in speech.

The Contest Committee further states that cocurricular activities should be integrated with class instruction, that such activities should be taught by a person whose qualifications are in every sense equal to those of persons teaching speech courses, and that cocurricular activities should be counted in the teaching load. Clearly, this committee of the North Central

Association views interschool speech activities as directly related to the objectives of the curricular speech program but as primarily for the benefit of the exceptionally talented speech student. As is made clear in the next section of this chapter, not all cocurricular speech activities are interscholastic contest activities, and consequently not all of them need to be limited to the few bright students in speech. Hence the objectives of the cocurricular program to which the authors of this text subscribe are (1) to improve the student's oral communication behavior, (2) to improve the student's knowledge and understanding of communication principles through his participation in realistic communication events, and (3) to develop the student's awareness and appreciation of the role of communication outside the classroom.

These purposes are not always recognized in outside-the-class speech activities, and often they are thwarted entirely as other goals come to influence the cocurricular program. When these other goals become prominent, the program usually ceases to be cocurricular and becomes extracurricular in the worst sense of the term. Some common problems and serious weaknesses then emerge. These problems, identified by Johnston (1952, pp. 1–12) are:

1. The existence of an activities program without any real understanding by teachers and pupils of the function it should perform

2. No consistent evaluation of the activities in terms of fundamental objectives

3. Failure to keep the program vitally related to the curriculum

4. Failure to allow students to plan, make decisions, and accept responsibility in the learning activity

5. Participation limited to a few pupils

6. Overemphasis on competitive aspects of the program

7. Devotion of too much energy to the promotion of a national organization

8. Inadequate recognition of teachers' duties in the activity program in considering teachers' loads

The director of the cocurricular speech program needs to play a leadership role in helping the school define the objectives of its program and periodically evaluate the program. He needs to be aware of the problems that can develop in an activities program that has become separated from the curricular program. Most of the adverse criticism of speech education in secondary schools is directed at the out-of-class speech activities programs—programs that are extracurricular rather than cocurricular. Some of the common criticisms include: too much emphasis on winning, gathering of trophies main objective, loss of regular school time, overemphasis on speech activities for a few students, expense out of proportion to the number of students who benefit from the program, inadequate supervision of students on trips away from school, and loss of teacher effectiveness in the classroom as his interest and energy shift to the activities program.

Speech activities programs that have lost sight of their *fundamental educational role* have brought much adverse criticism from speech teachers, students, parents, and school administrators. Among the most severely criticized is interscholastic, competitive debate. Probably the sharpest attack has been made by Moffett (1968, pp. 96–97):

> Although formal debate as practiced by clubs and diplomats may help teach the presenting of evidence, I'm afraid I must take a strong stand against this kind of discourse in education . . . . Formal debate is a game of one-upmanship, an unproductive duel of personalities. The goal is to overwhelm the opposition, not to enlarge one's mind. In my experience, debating societies always include in their membership the most dramatic dogmatic students in a school . . . . I have several other objections to formal debating: both the dualistic format and the yes-or-no wording of topics cast issues in a crude either-or way that militates against relativistic thinking; the two parties often do not talk to the same point because their speeches are prepared; there is no feedback or interaction except in the rebuttal; and the speakers are in effect learning to ignore and talk past each other, an all too common trait of everyday conversation and diplomacy . . . .

The director of the cocurricular speech program and the debate coach need to be keenly aware of the educational objectives that debate and other speech activities can fulfill and to work diligently to keep the program focused on those objectives. Unless such a role is played by the director of the cocurricular speech program, it is likely that the problems identified previously will emerge and that criticism will be forthcoming. There is great value in a soundly conceived cocurricular speech activities program that provides a stimulating opportunity for students to apply speaking skills in real situations.

TYPES OF COCURRICULAR ACTIVITIES

Cocurricular speech activities include plays, discussion, debate, extemporaneous speaking, original oratory, declamation, oral interpretation, dramatic reading, humorous reading, duet acting, Reader's Theater, student senate, legislative assemblies, manuscript reading, impromptu speaking, radio speaking, television speaking, speaker's bureaus, and others. These activities may be conducted either as interschool or intraschool activities. Unfortunately, many high schools and colleges perceive cocurricular speech activities as interscholastic *only,* and often highly competitive at that.

Among the most common interscholastic speech activities are debate tournaments, extemporaneous speaking, oratory, individual events contests or festivals, one-act play contests or festivals, and legislative assemblies. Cocurricular speech activities carried on by a school within its own community include radio and/or television programs, speaker's bureaus, full-length dramatic productions, Reader's Theater, student senate, panel or discussion programs, and legislative assemblies. Some speech activities are both interscholastic and community—for example, oral interpretation, and humorous and dramatic readings. Debate and discussion also can be used in both areas if organized properly. The best cocurricular programs have both interschool and intraschool activities.

ORGANIZING A NEW COCURRICULAR SPEECH PROGRAM

Many speech teachers have faced the problem of organizing a cocurricular speech activities program in a school in which none, or a very limited one, has existed. The following suggestions may prove helpful to the teacher faced with that problem:

1. Join the state's speech association and the secondary schools' forensic association. These organizations usually publish journals, bulletins, or newsletters that list the dates, places, rules, etc., of debate tournaments, solo events contests, drama festivals, and legislative assemblies that are held throughout the state.

2. Through the state organizations, as well as through the professional organizations discussed in Chapter 16, you can order materials for cocurricular speech activities. Join these organizations and use their help.

3. Appraise the needs, interests, abilities, and potentialities of the students and plan a cocurricular program that will meet their needs and develop their abilities. The long-range program should be focused toward an increasingly diversified program that will serve a broad range of students. You may need to begin with a few activities, however.

4. At an early date, organize a speaker's bureau and inform community organizations, clubs, and groups of its objectives and offerings. Students who represent the speaker's bureau should be prepared to offer interesting, relevant, and worthwhile discussions, speeches, readings, skits, and debates. Similarly, the community needs to understand the purposes of the speaker's bureau, i.e., that it is not a showcase *only* in which contest winners participate but a program through which students apply speech in real settings, and a program through which the community profits by considering with youth the real problems of the community.

5. Organize a forensic squad, and/or debate club, and a dramatics club. National organizations of these types are identified and described in Chapter 16.

6. Initiate a public information program so that activities and accomplishments of the students are known to the community. The community should understand the *why* of the entire cocurricular program in speech, *what* it consists of and *how* the community's support of it is important.

7. Take advantage of the speech clinics that are available; or organize with the help of other experienced speech activities directors a clinic for your own students.

The remainder of this chapter will focus specifically on ten of the most common cocurricular activities: debate, discussion, one-act plays and other plays, Reader's Theater, oral interpretation, oratory, extemporaneous speaking, humorous and dramatic reading, radio, and the speaker's bureau. Most of these activities can be either interschool or intraschool, community-oriented activities as already noted.

DEBATE

In today's world the individual finds himself a participant, both as advocate and judge, in day-to-day debate. He must champion his own ideas and evaluate critically the ideas of others. He must engage in personal decision making. He needs to know how to evaluate evidence, to interpret evidence, to reason accurately, to test conclusions, and to relate decisions to values. These skills are learned skills. They constitute the chief goals of education. They also ought to be the specific goals of debate. Debate can also aid in preparing students for practical situations of advocacy in later life. The idea that debate is not practical in today's living is false. From Congress to the smallest committee room, the skills of debate must be applied in situations of advocacy.

There are other values in debate. Some of them, as suggested by debate coaches, debaters, and parents of debaters, are the following: (1) Students learn to do research. (2) They learn in depth about a socially significant problem. (3) They learn to organize. (4) They learn to discipline themselves to study and work. (5) They learn that there are different points of view to be respected.

TYPES OF DEBATE

There are two major types of educational debate: traditional and cross-examination. In traditional debate there are four constructive speeches (each ten minutes in length) and four rebuttal speeches (each five minutes in length). The format is as follows:

First affirmative	Ten-minute constructive speech
First negative	Ten-minute constructive speech
Second affirmative	Ten-minute constructive speech
Second negative	Ten-minute constructive speech
First negative	Five-minute rebuttal speech
First affirmative	Five-minute rebuttal speech
Second negative	Five-minute rebuttal speech
Second affirmative	Five-minute rebuttal speech

The constructive speeches are composed of the prepared arguments of the affirmative and negative. The rebuttal speeches are devoted to attack and defense. No new constructive arguments may be given in the rebuttal speeches. Of course, attack and defense are not limited to the rebuttals but occur also in the constructive speeches as the teams begin to clash on the issues of the debate.

The second type, cross-examination debate, is often used in moot-court debating as a training technique for law students. There are several kinds of cross-examination debate, but perhaps the Oregon Plan is most representative. It allows each debater to participate as both questioner and respondent. The format is as follows:

First affirmative constructive: eight minutes
First negative cross-examination of the first affirmative: four minutes
First negative constructive: eight minutes
Second affirmative cross-examination of the first negative: four minutes
Second affirmative constructive: eight minutes
Second negative cross-examination of the second affirmative: four minutes
Second negative constructive: eight minutes
First affirmative cross-examination of second negative: four minutes
Negative summary by either negative speaker: four minutes
Affirmative summary by either affirmative speaker: four minutes

The skills of traditional debate are used in cross-examination debate. In addition, the student learns to use the skills of cross-examining an advocate. Some suggestions for handling cross-examination are:

1. Ask questions that elicit contradictions or admissions.
2. Ask questions pertaining to the respondent's arguments rather than to your own arguments.
3. In constructive and rebuttal speeches, use the answers to questions.
4. Design each question carefully—that is, have a reason for asking it.
5. Have prepared a list of questions on probable issues.
6. Do not comment on responses or argue the point with the respondent.
7. Be on guard for loaded questions if you are the respondent.
8. Give qualifications to answers before giving the answers.

ANALYZING AND RESEARCHING THE DEBATE PROPOSITION

Perhaps the initial step in preparing to debate is to analyze the debate proposition. And the first step in analyzing a debate proposition is defining what it is. It is not a question. It is not the title of a subject. It is not a phrase. It is a *statement expressing a judgment.*

Propositions are generally classified into three types: propositions of fact, of value, and of policy. Propositions of fact are statements affirming the existence of things, the occurrence of events, or the classification of events or things. They are statements maintaining that a certain thing is true. An example is: Resolved, that James Doe is guilty of murder. Propositions of fact seldom are used in educational debates. They are used, among other places, in courts of law.

Propositions of value are statements of judgments as to the worth of something. Unlike propositions of fact, in which the emphasis is on acquiring the pertinent evidence that will show the statement to be true or false, propositions of value assume the existence of facts and thus place the emphasis on determining the quality of the idea, event, or object. Propositions of value are value judgments. They assert the goodness, badness, usefulness, or uselessness of the idea, event, or object. An example of a proposition of value is: Resolved, that capital punishment is useful to society.

The third type of proposition, the proposition of policy, is a statement of a proposed course of action. Educational debate propositions are predominantly propositions of policy. They are "should be" statements. An example of a proposition of policy is: Resolved, that capital punishment should be prohibited. A proposition of policy that is suitable for debate, possesses certain characteristics:

1. It is an affirmative statement.
2. It is a currently controversial and significant subject.
3. It is specific as to a proposed course of action.
4. It has only one central idea.
5. It places the burden of proof and the presumption correctly.

The second step in analyzing the debate proposition is to define the terms used in it in light of the entire proposition. It is important that a debater understand that a "term" is not necessarily a single word. One might define each word from the dictionary individually and yet not have defined the proposition adequately. Rather, a term may be a single word, a phrase, or a group of words. It is necessary to determine which words should be defined individually and which should be defined in groups. Definitions should be specific, clear-cut, and commonly accepted. The intended and reasonable definition of the proposition should prevail. There should be no trick definitions.

The third step in investigating a debate proposition is to learn the history of the controversy. It is important for a debater to acquire the big picture. He needs to discover the answers to such questions as the following: When did the controversy begin? Has it been steady or spasmodic? What bills have been introduced in national or state legislatures concerning this subject? What were the significant historical developments that sharpened the controversy? Who are the people most involved in the controversy? What names keep reappearing relative to this subject? What are the reasons for the controversy? What is wrong? What do people want in this area? Who is currently engaged in the dialogue of the controversy? What groups are taking stands and communicating to the public at this time on the subject? When the debater has answered these questions specifically and in depth, he is on his way to an understanding of the nature and significance of the issues involved in the proposition.

One way of discovering the specific issues of a proposition is by the "stock issues" route. Stock issues are general issues—categories into which specific issues can be classified. They are found in all propositions of policy. They are: (1) Need—Is there a need? (2) Practicality—Does the proposal solve the need? Can the plan work? (3) Benefits and harms—Will the advantages of the new plan outweigh the disadvantages that might result? It is important for a debater to understand that stock issues are relatively unimportant except as a framework to help him discover specific issues. He will not be able to argue effectively for or against the proposition in terms of stock issues but only in terms of specific issues.

The following questions will guide the debater in discovering specific potential issues:

1. Is there a need?
   a. What are the evils of the status quo?
   b. What are the shortcomings of the status quo?
   c. Are these evils or shortcomings serious enough to warrant a change? How are they serious? What are their consequences?
   d. Are these evils inherent in the status quo?
   e. Can these evils be eliminated by repairs to the status quo?
2. Is the proposed solution practical?
   a. Does the plan solve the problem? Does it meet the need?
   b. Can the plan work? Has it been used elsewhere?
   c. Is the affirmative plan the best method of satisfying the need?
   d. What other plans or solutions are possible?
   e. Does machinery exist that could be used to administer the affirmative plan?
   f. Would any new problems come about if such machinery were used to administer the affirmative plan?

    g. What are possible negative counter plans?
    h. Will the negative counter plan(s) work?
3. Will the benefits outweigh the harms?
    a. What are the new benefits?
    b. What advantages does the affirmative plan have over other plans?
    c. What new evils will the affirmative plan create?
    d. How serious will the new evils be?
    e. Will the counter plan(s) create new evils?
    f. How serious will the new evils created by the counter plans be?

In order to answer such questions, the student must gather information on the topic for debate. There are many sources of information available for research on a debate proposition. The following list is not all-inclusive but gives those sources most commonly used. It is a starting point only; the individual debater can find other sources that are equally good in providing information.

1. Card catalogue: The card catalogue is an excellent starting place for research. Look for headings on the issues you have discovered as a result of your analysis
2. Encyclopedias: Encyclopedias are often helpful in the acquisition of general knowledge on the proposition
3. Reader's Guide
4. New York Times Index
5. Congressional Record
6. The United States Government Publications Monthly Catalogue
7. The Reference Shelf Series
8. The Congressional Digest
9. Black's Law Dictionary
10. The Statistical Abstract
11. The World Almanac

Also, you may write to your Senator or Congressman for information on most debate propositions and to groups or organizations concerned with the problem.

The value of information and evidence for debate is determined by their usability. One may gather reams of information and evidence that are of little value because they cannot be used quickly and efficiently. Debaters, therefore, use various types of filing systems for storing information and evidence. One type is notebooks. These are indexed according to issues, and the information is typed on heavy sheets of paper. This method is criticized by many debate coaches because it is inflexible, inconvenient, and tends toward canned arguments.

A second system is original source materials. This is often an unsatisfactory system because of the bulk of the materials. The debater must transport virtually a rolling library or else debate with a limited supply of evidence.

The filing system used most often in educational debate is the card-file box. Generally, three-by-five-inch cards (sometimes four-by-six-inch cards) are used to record information and evidence. They are classified according to the issue headings in either the affirmative division or the negative division of the box. Following is a list of suggestions for effective note taking for file cards:

1. Clearly label the card.

2. Record only one idea unit on each card.

3. Copy accurately and verbatim the quotations and statistics you wish to use.

4. Write legibly or type the information.

5. Never crowd material.

6. Record full bibliographical information.

BUILDING THE DEBATE CASE

A debate case is the complete set of arguments that the debater presents in support of or against a proposition. Theoretically, a case can be made for or against a proposition with only one argument. In practice, however, most debate cases are constructed of several arguments. An argument is a statement or conclusion with reasons and/or evidence for believing it. A logical argument is composed of three elements: evidence, reasoning, and a conclusion. Reasoning is the process of drawing conclusions from evidence. It is the seeing of connections and relationships among facts that point to particular interpretation or conclusion. The major arguments which a team selects to constitute the case are called contentions. Each contention, or major argument, is usually supported by several minor arguments.

The traditional affirmative case is the need-plan case. It meets the stock issues head on i.e., it shows that there are problems in the status quo, that the proposed course of action can solve the problems, that it can be put into operation and administered efficiently, and that it will be advantageous.

A second type of affirmative case that is receiving considerable attention in tournament debating is the comparative advantage case. In this type of case, no specific or strong indictment of the status quo is made. No *need* arguments, such as serious problems in the present system, are given. Rather, two or three topics, i.e., *advantages,* are selected as major contentions of the case; and then each advantage is strongly developed and established so that the proposed course of action is seen, by comparison, as superior to the status quo.

The negative may use one of several types of cases in order to clash with the affirmative. Five specific types are identified here:

1. *Defense of the status quo.* With this type of case, the negative argue that the status quo is working satisfactorily. A considerable portion of the case is devoted to constructive arguments stressing the accomplishments of the status quo. The major attack is on the affirmative need arguments.

2. *Pure negative or direct-refutation negative.* In this type of case the negative rely mainly not on constructive arguments defending the status quo but on direct attacks on the important affirmative arguments. The negative do not argue constructively for any policy; they simply hold each important affirmative argument up to intensive and critical examination. They show the affirmative arguments to be false or deficient in some manner.

3. *A combination of these two types.* Some debate authorities believe that a combination of direct refutation and defense of the present system is the most powerful position the negative can take.

4. *The repairs case.* This type of case is a defense of the status quo with certain modifications to improve it. Usually the negative team shows that the affirmative team has exaggerated the need and then demonstrates that minor modifications in the status quo will solve any problems that exist. The negative attack is directed rather heavily toward the impracticability of the affirmative proposal and the evils that will result from it.

5. *The counter-plan case.* In this type of case the negative admit the affirmative need and then suggest an alternative proposal. The attack is that the affirmative proposal is impractical and has disadvantages and harms.

REBUTTAL AND REFUTATION

Debates are often won or lost in attack and defense. The best arguments and cases will not prevail unless they can be defended from attack. Similarly, unless the debater can effectively attack arguments, he cannot hope to prevent their acceptance. Skills in attack and defense constitute the heart of effective debating.

Synonyms for the words "attack" and "defense" are "refutation" and "rebuttal." *Refutation* is the process of attacking, tearing down, or destroying the argument of an opponent. *Rebuttal* is the process of defending and rebuilding one's own arguments after they have been attacked by the opposition.

The process of refutation may be included in every speech of the debate except the first affirmative speech. A general rule is that important issues should be challenged and refuted as quickly as possible rather than allowed to stand unchallenged until the end of the debate. The process of rebuttal also occurs in every speech in the debate except the first affirmative one. The term "rebuttal" also denotes the second round of speeches in a debate, but as we have seen rebuttal is not limited to these speeches. Both rebuttal and refutation must take place throughout the entire debate.

Refutation and rebuttal are most effective when they are purposeful and organized. In order to engage in attack and defense in an organized manner, the debater needs to keep a systematic account of the debate. One way of accomplishing this is through the use of the rebuttal flow-sheet. The flow-sheet traces the flow of each argument through the course of the debate.

THE DEBATE TOURNAMENT

Most experience in debate is gained through participation in debate tournaments. The director of the cocurricular speech program needs to be acquainted with the tournament procedures in his state. In some states, interscholastic debate tournaments cannot be held without approval by the State High School Activities Association. In most states the debate coaches association, state forensic association, state speech association, or some similar organization coordinates invitational debate tournaments throughout the state. It is important that any new debate coach become familiar with the state's practices and procedures relevant to speech contests, festivals, and tournaments before he sends students to such events and before he sponsors such an event. If the teacher does desire to sponsor a debate tournament, the following guidelines will be helpful:

1. Select the date of the tournament well in advance. In many states, the scheduling of all debate tournaments throughout the state is done in the spring preceding the school year in which the tournaments wil be held. In other states such scheduling takes place in September or October of the school year in which the tournaments will occur. Again, the person planning to host a debate tournament must familiarize himself with the practices in his area.

2. Send invitations to schools to participate in the tournament two or three months in advance of the tournament. They should include the date of the tournament, a statement of the objective, a statement of eligibility requirements, a schedule, information concerning recognition and awards, information concerning housing and dining accommodations, entrance fee requirements, requirements relative to furnishing judges, and the deadline for entering. A registration form, a sample ballot, and a list of regulations governing the tournament should be included with the letter of invitation and information. A sample letter of invitation and a registration form appear below.

Letter of Invitation

Anytown High School
Anytown, Anystate
September 28, 19—

Dear Director of Debate:

Anytown High School invites you and your debaters to participate in a debate tournament to be held at Anytown High School on Saturday, December 12, 19—.

The purpose of this tournament is to provide an opportunity for students to become increasingly responsible and effective debaters through participation in well-organized, guided debating. The proposition to be debated is:

Resolved: (Insert the proposition for debate recommended by the Committee on Discussion and Debate for the current year.)

Constructive speeches will be ten minutes long and rebuttals, five minutes long.

No school may enter more than four teams. Each school must be represented by the same number of affirmative and negative teams, with two speakers on each team. Alternate debaters may be substituted between rounds on each team. Each school will furnish one competent, impartial judge for each two teams it enters. Extra judges will be furnished by the local tournament manager upon request and payment of a fee of $5.00 per debate. The schedule for the day will be as follows:

9:30–10:30 A.M.	Registration
10:45–11:45	Round I
11:45– 1:00 P.M.	Lunch
1:00– 2:00	Round II
2:30– 3:30	Round III
4:00–	Results announced

Lunch will be served in the school cafeteria at $1.00 per person. Paid reservations must be made by each school by December 5.

Please complete and return the enclosed registration form, together with fees and payment for luncheon reservations, on or before December 5. Fees will be refunded in cases of emergency until December 8.

We look forward to greeting you and your debaters here on the morning of December 12 and trust that you are looking forward to a pleasant and educationally profitable forensic experience at Anytown High School.

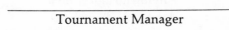

Tournament Manager

Much pretournament planning is required. Committees should be appointed to handle the various jobs: registration (materials and procedures), housing and luncheon arrangements, recruitment and training of chairmen and timekeepers, scheduling of teams and judges, preparation or acquisition of materials (schedules, ballots, instructions to judges and timekeepers, tabulation forms, and signs).

To the novice tournament manager, pairing the teams and assigning judges are the most difficult tasks. The following guidelines are widely accepted:

1. No team should meet another team twice in preliminary rounds.
2. No debate coach should judge his own team in tournament competition.
3. No judge should judge a team twice in the same tournament.

Registration Form

Anytown High School Debate Tournament
December 12, 19___

The following persons will represent _____.
(school)

Affirmative Teams   *Negative Teams*

Team 1: 1. _____   Team 2: 1. _____
         2. _____   2. _____
Team 3: 1. _____   Team 4: 1. _____
         2. _____   2. _____

Judges: _____

Please mail to: _____
(name)

Tournament Manager
Anytown High School
Anytown, Anywhere

Please return by December 5.

One procedure for pairing teams and judges is to use a pairings worksheet. Each participating school is assigned (or draws) a number. Thus all team members from a given school have the same number plus an alphabetical suffix that designates the specific team. Judges from that school have the same number as the teams. The teams are staggered and entered on the sheet, as illustrated on the following sample schedule for Round I.

Sample Schedule

ROUND I

Room Number	Aff.	Neg.	Judge
PMC 122	1A	2B	4
PMC 202	2A	3B	5
PMC 204	3A	4B	6
PMC 207	4A	5B	7
PMC 206	5A	6B	8
PMC 210	6A	7B	9
PMC 212	7A	8B	10
PMC 213	8A	9B	11
PMC 218	9A	10B	12
PMC 302	10A	11B	13
PMC 306	11A	12B	14
PMC 307	12A	13B	15
PMC 310	13A	14B	16
PMC 311	14A	15B	17
PMC 313	15A	16B	18
PMC 314	16A	17B	19
PMC 318	17A	18B	20
PMC 320	18A	19B	21
PMC 322	19A	20B	22
PMU 256	20A	21B	23
PMU 258	21A	22B	24
PMU 204	22A	23B	25
PMU 206	23A	29A	26
PMU 208	24A	30A	27
PMU 213	25A	31A	28
PMU 214	26A	32A	1
PMU 216	27A	33A	2
PMU 217	28A	1B	3

Another procedure for pairing teams is power matching. After two or three preliminary rounds, powerful teams are matched against powerful teams and weak teams against weak teams. Although it is usually not possible for every debate to match teams having exactly equal win-loss records, that is the objective. Power matching, it is argued, "is educationally beneficial in that it provides real challenges—no easy wins or discouraging losses—to all teams. Administratively, however, power matching can be rather difficult and time consuming for the novice tournament director.

When the debaters, debate coaches, timekeepers, and judges arrive at the registration desk, schedules, regulations, and instructions should be distributed to them unless there is to be an opening assembly with formal welcomes, at which time schedules and other materials may be distributed. The schedules and copies of materials should also be posted at convenient places, and the registration-information desk should be manned throughout the tournament. Some tournament directors have students act as hosts, stationing them in each hallway and building to assist debaters and judges in finding rooms and to help make the tournament run smoothly in other ways. Before each round of the tournament, a ballot should be delivered to each judge. Often the timekeeper, acting as chairman, will deliver the ballot, check to see that the correct teams are present, and preside over the debate. The timekeeper will remain with the judge until he or she has completed the ballot and sealed it in the envelope. The timekeeper will then return the ballot to headquarters.

Sample information sheets for judges and timekeepers are shown below.

Information Sheet for Judges

1. Go to the room to which you are assigned for any particular round. Your ballot will be delivered to you there.

2. You may write criticisms on the ballot. Extra sheets of paper will be provided for note taking or criticism.

3. Do not announce the decision at the end of the round. Decisions are to be kept secret either until the end of the tournament or until the end of the preliminary rounds.

4. Return fully completed ballot *with a decision* to the timekeeper.

   Your help and cooperation are greatly appreciated. Thank you.

Information Sheet for Timekeepers

1. After receiving your timecards and ballot, go to your appointment. Greet the debaters and judge, and check to see that they are the correct teams and judge assigned to your room.

2. If after ten minutes past the designated time for a debate to begin a debater, team, or judge is missing, report the fact to

headquarters. Instruct those present in the room to remain until you get back with further instructions.

3. The constructive speeches, the first four speeches in the debate, are each ten minutes long. The rebuttal speeches, the last four speeches in the debate, are each five minutes long.

4. You are to hold in full view of the debater a timecard designating the *amount of time remaining* in the debate speech as each minute expires. At the end of the allotted time for the speech, you are to signal the speaker that his time has expired. (Please stand to signal the end of the time.)

5. You are responsible for the room in which you are officiating. Do not let the students tamper with equipment, bulletin boards, or blackboards. At the end of the tournament, check your room to be sure that everything is in order—chairs, desks, etc.

6. Remember that you are a representative of this high school. Be a courteous host. Your cooperation will help to make the tournament a success.

7. Return the timecards and ballot to headquarters at the close of the debate.
   Your help and cooperation in conducting this tournament are greatly appreciated. Thank you.

The National Forensic League ballots are widely used in tournament debate. Some states have a state-approved or state-recommended ballot for debate. The tournament director should investigate these sources before selecting a ballot for the tournament.

Organizing and managing a debate tournament is not an easy task, but if you plan well in advance, check with an experienced tournament director, and follow the guidelines set forth in this chapter, the tournament can be run smoothly and can be an enjoyable, worthwhile experience for the participants as well as for visitors.

EXTEMPORANEOUS SPEAKING

Interschool speech tournaments which feature individual events nearly always include extemporaneous speaking. The claimed values of extemporaneous speaking are that it fosters the development of the student's organizational skills and his ability to think on his feet.

In extemporaneous speaking contests the participants are given a specified period of time (usually thirty or forty-five minutes) in which to prepare a five- to seven-minute speech on a selected topic. The topics usually deal with current events or with a problem area. The most common practice is to provide topics that have been discussed during the past three months in *Time, Newsweek,* or *U.S. News and World Report.* A pool of topics is prepared by the tournament director before the contest. Thirty or forty-five minutes before a contestant is to speak, he draws randomly three topics from the pool of topics and selects the one on which he wishes to speak. He then goes to the area set aside for preparation and, without outside help or communication and with only the materials provided or allowed, he prepares his speech. In some contests, speakers are permitted to use notes (usually one three-by-five-inch card), but in other contests no notes are allowed. Extensive notes are never permitted. In some contests the speaker is questioned following his speech; in others he is not questioned.

The best preparation for extemporaneous contest speaking is to read widely from the leading news sources, concentrating on current events and significant national and international problems; to develop a note file and bibliography on current topics on which you have read; to learn to analyze problems and to organize your thoughts in response to the problems; and, finally, to practice speaking in order to develop fluency in expressing your ideas and effectiveness in physical and vocal delivery.

The most common faults of extemporaneous speakers in contests are: (1) The speaker fails to speak on the purpose implied in the topic selected. (2) He fails to organize his speech well. (3) He lacks appropriate supporting material.

PURPOSE OF THE SPEECH

The purpose of an extemporaneous speech is either to inform or to persuade. If the topic uses words such as "discuss," "explain," "state," "relate," "describe," or "report," the purpose of the speech is to inform. Also, if the topic uses the verbs "is" or "was" the speech may be treated as informative. If, however, the topic uses "should" or "ought," then the purpose is to persuade; or if the topic requires the speaker to take a stand or to propose a solution, the speech is to persuade. Similarly, if the wording of the topic requires the speaker to compare two ideas, solutions, or values, it should be treated as a persuasive topic. In some contests the topics are single words or phrases (Vietnamization or patriotism, for

example); in such situations the topic may be treated as either informative or persuasive in its purpose.

EFFECTIVE ORGANIZATION AND PROPER SUPPORTING MATERIAL

A well-organized extemporaneous speech has directions and boundaries
that make its plan or framework easily identifiable. The speaker should (1)
plan an introduction, body, and conclusion for the speech, (2) select
three or four main points for the body, and (3) work out clear transitions
from introduction to body, from body to conclusion, and from main
point to main point within the body. If the speech is to inform, the main
points may follow a what, why, how, who, and when procedure or
utilize a topical or chronological order. In the persuasive speech, many
coaches advocate the use of the motivated sequence, a problem-solution
approach consisting of five parts:

1. *Getting attention.* Specific examples, rhetorical questions, shocking
   statements, literary quotation, and humorous stories are examples of
   materials to get attention. Keep in mind that the material must be
   related to the problem.
2. *Presenting the problem.* By using examples, statistics, and testimony, you
   can show the extent of the problem, the effects of the problem, and the
   causes of the problem. The effects of the problem on the listeners can be
   vividly described and directly related to their lives.
3. *Presenting the solution.* Clearly state and explain the best procedure for
   solving the problem. Clarify the cost, time, and administrative procedures.
4. *Visualizing the solution.* Picture in the minds of the audience the
   advantages and the satisfactions to be brought about by the solution
   you propose.
5. *Appealing for audience action.* Appeal directly to the audience's motives:
   their desire to save, to be helpful, to be thought of as intelligent; or to
   their pride in ownership. Ask them to help in the adoption and development of the proposed solution.

Finally, the extemporaneous speech must be delivered effectively. In
almost all instances, the speech is given to a small group. The delivery,
therefore, should be characterized by a conversational style, relaxed body
action, gestures that indicate controlled feelings, and a voice clear and

loud enough to be heard easily. The excited, emotional delivery sometimes found in oratory is inappropriate for the extemporaneous speech.

ORATORY

The orations in most interscholastic oratory contests are original ones, i.e., they consist of the original thoughts of the participant on a topic of current social or political significance. The speech is *carefully* constructed, written in the form of a complete manuscript, and ordinarily delivered from memory. The amount of quoted material that may be used is usually limited to 150 words. Sometimes the limitation is in terms of percentage of total words—for example, 10 or 20 percent. Orations for contest purposes vary in length from seven to ten minutes.

Original oratory should not be confused with declamation (sometimes called oratorial declamation or declaimed oratory), in which the participant memorizes and delivers a speech written by another person. Declamation contests are also held in interschool speech meets but less frequently than contests in original oratory.

Original oratory places emphasis upon careful and complete preparation. Debate and extemporaneous speaking place the participant under some time stresses: in terms of preparation in the case of extemporaneous speaking and in terms of constructing responses in the case of debate. These time stresses are absent from the oratory contest. The effective orator works with his ideas and materials for months before the contest. He continually thinks, plans, and modifies as he constructs the speech. Original oratory also emphasizes the choice of language, the style of the speech. The speech, however, must reflect more than precise expressive wording; it must reveal a commitment to ideas that are meaningful and valued by the participant. In constructing the oration, the student should follow the guidelines on thesis, organization, supportive materials, etc., for persuasive speeches in general.

A final important factor in original oratory is delivery. Unfortunately, orators sometimes acquire a bad habit of delivering the speech in an artificial, noncommunicative manner. Orators sometimes assume overly formal, Napoleonic postures, manipulate the voice in odd ways, and use affected gestures. These delivery characteristics, some argue, are the result of giving memorized speeches. Hence some speech educators believe that the memorized oration has limited value pedagogically, and they argue that the speech should not be delivered from memory. They point out that few memorized speeches are heard in our society. At the very least, we can all agree that the speaker must guard against artificiality in delivering memorized speeches.

DISCUSSION

Many forensic associations include discussion as a contest event, although discussion is generally considered to be a cooperative rather than a competitive activity. Because discussion is recognized as a cooperative venture in problem solving, judges of discussion contests are instructed to rate the individual discussants, the discussion leader, and the product of the functioning of the group as a whole. Individuals are rated against a standard rather than against other discussants. Generally, schools enter individuals in discussion contests, and individuals win the awards that are given. However, in a few contests, *only* groups are evaluated, and the competition, rating, and winning of awards are based on groups rather than on individuals.

The standard procedure in discussion contests is for the director to place the individuals from the various schools into groups of no more than eight students each. Individuals are assigned to groups by chance. The groups discuss the same problem, usually for one hour, and they are judged by one or more judges.

Participants in discussion contests are obligated to prepare carefully just as do contestants in debate, oratory, and interpretation. They should read widely on the discussion topic, become acquainted with the background of the question, carefully analyze the problem, and become familiar with the data (evidence, information, and opinion) relevant to the problem. In addition, they should know what objectives (behaviors) they are attempting to demonstrate as effective discussants. It is important that a number of practice discussions be held before individuals are entered in the discussion contest.

ORAL INTERPRETATION

Oral interpretation, sometimes called poetry reading, prose reading, dramatic interpretation, interpretative reading, or oral reading, is the act of reading prose or poetry to convey the meaning intended by the author to an audience and to elicit from them an appropriate response. The goal in oral interpretation is to enable the audience to comprehend, understand, appreciate, and respond to the meaning of the literature interpreted. Such goals, if they are to be realized by the audience, imply that the interpreter must (1) understand the significance of the work as intended by the author, and (2) communicate that meaning to the audience in a manner that elicits the appropriate response. The primary concern of the interpreter (to communicate the thoughts, emotions, attitudes, and intentions of the author) demands that the interpreter subordinate himself to the literature. The best oral interpretation is that which is communicated with such skill that the audience is caught up in the interpretation (the literature) and hence is almost unaware of the interpreter. Each oral interpretation contest may have its own unique set of rules, and the teacher should study carefully the rules for the particular contest. The following general guidelines are often used, however.

The literature selected must be of high literary merit. An interpreter can be no better than the material he interprets, so the student should avoid the handicap of poor material. The following checklist may help the student select the work he wishes to interpret:

1. What is the author's intention as you perceive it?
2. Is the selection worth your time and effort?
3. Is the theme universal enough to be of general interest?
4. Is the theme too common to be of sufficient interest?
5. Is the narrative thread or the plot line clear?
6. Are the characters fully developed?
7. What is the author's point of view relative to his characters and their actions?
8. Is the style too obvious or too complex for clear oral presentation?
9. Does the story have unity and harmony?
10. Are there sufficient variety and contrast to provide excitement and hold attention?
11. Is there a dynamic progression in the development of the story?
12. What is the crisis or major climax of the story?
13. Does the story hold your interest or excite you? Why?
14. Will it likewise capture the interest of your audience?

15. Does the story have sufficient restraint to maintain an aesthetic balance?

The literature selected should be suitable for oral interpretation. Some literature is too complex for oral interpretation, and other literature may be offensive if read publicly to the usual audience at oral interpretation contests.

The interpreter, in the introduction to the reading, should make clear the audience for whom the author wrote the literature and the particular circumstances. The goal of the interpreter is to present the author's work so that each member of the audience becomes involved in a creative process in which he is stimulated to create his own mental image.

In solo acting and duet acting the objectives are similar to those of the one-act play contest, and the criteria on which evaluation is based are similar to those for one-act plays.

DRAMATIC PRODUCTIONS

One of the most popular cocurricular speech activities in secondary schools today is the one-act play. Many state high school speech associations and leagues include one-act plays in their contests and festivals. Schools with strong speech and drama programs produce three or more major, cocurricular, dramatic productions in addition to the contest or festival one-act plays. In many communities, the junior class presents a play in the fall semester and the senior class produces one in the spring semester. In other schools all the major dramatic productions are all-school affairs.

Whether the play is one act or three acts, most of the following suggestions regarding production and performance apply equally and may be helpful to the novice director.

CHOOSING A PLAY

If experiences in dramatic activities are to be worthwhile educationally to participating students, the plays selected for production must be of high quality. Too many plays are below the standards that ought to be set for such productions. The following standards are those generally considered to be important by directors of high school plays:

1. The high school play should have a worthwhile theme, be sincere and true in its interpretation of life, and accurate in its reflection of customs and manners.

2. It should have literary value—that is, it should be written in acceptable language and in accordance with accepted standards of playwriting, and, as such, it should be emotionally and intellectually stimulating.

3. It should be within the capabilities of the high school pupil to understand and appreciate, taking into consideration the influence of vicarious experience and the pupil's natural interests.

4. It should challenge the highest creative and artistic abilities of all who are associated with its production, thereby affording rich opportunities for study, analysis, and experimentation.

5. It should be good theater, affording opportunities for sincere acting, and be satisfying as entertainment. It should lead rather than follow the community standards of entertainment and appreciation.

6. It should be free of highly sophisticated or advanced roles, vulgarity or profanity, objectionable matter, and sordid, unwholesome presentations of characters and scenes.

The task of selecting the one-act play for contest or festival presentation is made somewhat easier for the novice play director in states which send out a list of acceptable plays from which schools must make their selection. The new speech activities director should check with the state association to learn the requirements for one-act play contests and festivals.

Even with an approved list of acceptable plays, however, the director still has to select a specific play. The following questions may aid him in choosing a play for his school:

1. Is the play likely to challenge the audience and the students—has it a worthwhile theme, convincing and interesting characterizations, a valid interpretation of life?

2. Is the play current, timely, and timeless?

3. Is it suited to the available talent?

4. Can it be staged with the facilities available?
5. Can it be produced within the budget provided?
6. Is it within the experience and limitations of the director?

CASTING THE PLAY

Most experienced directors agree that casting the play is one of the most critical problems in play production. It is a time-consuming and sometimes trying process. Each director must develop a tryout system that works well for him—that encourages interested students to read and that gives him an opportunity to observe and listen to them. It is important that suitable cuttings from the playscript be selected and that copies of the playscript be placed in the school library on reserve so that students may familiarize themselves with the play.

Some directors use tryout forms on which each student trying out for a role writes his name, address, telephone number, height, weight, color of hair, color of eyes, dramatic experience, and out-of-school commitments. This information is valuable to the director for future plays as well as for the play being cast. Most directors use the open tryout system, in which any interested student may come and read for any part. This procedure is time-consuming, but it does foster a wholesome attitude on the part of the students and it often produces some happy surprises.

If the director is to cast the play well, he must have a clear understanding of the requirements of each role and must assess accurately the ability of each actor to fulfill the role to which he is assigned. Voice quality, intelligence, maturity, physical expressiveness, enthusiasm, and physical characteristics are important factors to consider. To help himself fully assess abilities, the director in some schools requires that the student not only read the part but also engage in pantomimes or improvisations. By using these techniques and by requiring students to return for second and third tryouts as the total number of students trying out is reduced, the director can select the best students for the roles.

REHEARSAL SCHEDULE

Once the play has been cast, rehearsals begin. The director will want to prepare a rehearsal schedule and distribute copies to all cast members, technical crew members, parents, the principal, and any others whose cooperation and help are needed in producing the play. A one-act play will require from fifteen to twenty-five rehearsals depending upon the expertise of the director, the experience and ability of the cast, the difficulty of the play, and other factors. Two hours is the optimal length for a rehearsal.

The first meeting should be a general meeting of all persons participating directly in the production of the play. At that time the director's philosophy, as well as the procedures, rules, and duties of various crews and committees, should be explained carefully. Questions concerning production problems, interpretation, and other topics should be handled fully. Following this initial meeting, various types of rehearsals must be called—rehearsals emphasizing reading, blocking, polishing, and mounting. The following rehearsal schedule for a one-act play may serve as a pattern for the novice director to develop his own schedule:

FIRST WEEK

Day	Cast	Crew	Costumes and Props
Monday	Tryouts	Design sets	
Tuesday	Tryouts		
Wednesday	Post cast and distribute scripts		
Thursday	First general meeting		
Friday	First reading		

SECOND WEEK

Monday	Interpretation rehearsal		
Tuesday	Block first half	Recruit crew	Listing of needed props and costumes
Wednesday	Individual work		
Thursday	Block second half		
Friday	Individual work	Start construction of sets	Start construction of props and costumes

THIRD WEEK

Monday	Polish first half	Construction	Construction
Tuesday	Individual problems		
Wednesday	Polish second half		
Thursday	Individual problems		
Friday	Complete run	Assign production duties	

FOURTH WEEK

Monday	Technical rehearsal	Crew rehearsal	Work out problems
Tuesday	Open	Open	
Wednesday	Dress rehearsal		
Thursday	Dress rehearsal		
Friday	Performance		

READER'S THEATER

One of the newest and most rapidly growing cocurricular speech activities is Reader's Theater. Its goal, according to Coger (1967, p. 3), is the following: "To present a literary script with oral readers using their voices and bodies to suggest the intellectual, emotional, and sensory experiences inherent in the literature. The readers may or may not be aided in their interpretive function by lighting, music, sound effects, simple costuming and nonillusory staging." Reader's Theater has been defined by Akin (1962) as "a form of oral interpretation in which all types of literature may be projected by means of characterized readings enhanced by theatrical effects." And Brooks (1962, p. 9) has defined it as "a group activity in which the best of literature is communicated from manuscript to an audience through the oral interpretation approach of vocal and physical suggestion."

Reader's Theater differs from a conventional play in that it emphasizes the aural elements of the literature. The reader expresses the attitudes, feelings, emotions, and actions of the characters by economically using his voice, body, and face to suggest the meaning. He does not distract the audience's attention from the characters, the scene, and the action within the literature. Reader's Theater also demands a type of audience participation different from that elicited by a conventional play. The audience generates its own visualization of the scenery, costumes, action, and physical appearance of the characters, whereas usually these elements are presented tangibly on stage in the conventional play. In Reader's Theater the audience experiences, imagines, and creates.

This new form of theater is growing rapidly as is evidenced by the annual listing of reading theater productions by the Interpretation Interest Group of the Speech Communication Association and the reports of performances in the *Educational Theatre Journal*. It is recommended strongly in the new course of study for high school speech teachers prepared by the American Educational Theatre Association.

Professional examples of Reader's Theater are abundant. In 1951 Charles Boyer, Sir Cedric Hardwicke, Charles Laughton, and Agnes Moorehead read *Don Juan in Hell*. They sat on stools and held scripts (although they had memorized the material), and sometimes shifted their positions on the stools. In 1952 Raymond Massey, Judith Anderson, and Tyrone Power, accompanied by a chorus, read *John Brown's Body*. Lighting and music were used effectively in this Reader's Theater production. In these professional productions, as well as in high school productions for the community or for interschool contests, the entire emphasis is on the aural appeal, and the audience's attention is on the literature. Reader's Theater is not a substitute for conventional plays but is a new form that focuses on the written word.

As Reader's Theater is used in contest events, it is normally restricted to twenty or thirty minutes. Because it is a new activity, the teacher should check with his state activities association or state speech association for specific rules they have adopted.

SPEAKER'S BUREAU

A final activity that should be considered by the director of the cocurricular program in speech is the speaker's bureau. Perhaps no other cocurricular speech activity better unites out-of-class activity with the objectives of the curricular program. Not only does this activity afford a large number of

students the opportunity to participate, but it also offers them the opportunity of applying the various types of speeches in a *real* situation. In
addition, the speaker's bureau performs a service function for the
community and, if administered wisely, also performs an educational
function. Speakers and programs are furnished to community organizations
free of charge. Because of the numerous community groups seeking
programs, there is usually considerable demand for the services. The
challenge is one of organizing the speaker's bureau and of maintaining
high-quality performance.

The director of the speaker's bureau will want to identify those
students who have speaking capabilities and who are interested in
putting these abilities to use. When the speeches, panels, debates, and
other programs are prepared, local organizations should be advised of the
offerings available. It is important to insist that requests for programs be
made two or three weeks in advance. A well-organized, quality-controlled
speaker's bureau can be an asset to the school, the speech program, and
the community.

SUMMARY

This chapter has focused on the cocurricular speech activities program.
Philosophical issues such as the relationship of the speech activities
program to the school's credit courses in speech communication and to the
school's overall objectives have been considered. The goals of the total
cocurricular program, as well as those of each particular speech activity,
have been identified. Guidelines and specific directions have been provided for organizing a debate squad, establishing a speaker's bureau,
producing a play, and managing tournaments or festivals.

REFERENCES

Akin, Johnnye. Brochure announcing a contest for Reader's Theater
scripts. University of Denver, 1962.

Brooks, Keith. "Reader's Theatre: Some Questions and Answers."
Dramatics 34 (1962): 9.

Brooks, William D. *Introduction to Debate.* New York: University-
Exposition Press, 1966.

Faules, Don F., and Richard D. Rieke. *Directing Forensics: Debate and Contest Speaking*. Scranton, Pa.: International Textbook, 1968.

Coger, Leslie Irene. *Reader's Theatre: Handbook*. Glenview, Ill.: Scott, Foresman, 1967.

Johnston, Edgar G. "Critical Problems in the Administration of Student Activities." *The Bulletin of the National Association of Secondary School Principals* 36 (1952): 1–12.

Klopf, Donald W., and Carroll P. Lehman. *Coaching and Directing Forensics*. Skokie, Ill.: National Textbook, 1967.

Moffett, James. *Teaching the Universe of Discourse*, pp. 96–97. Boston: Houghton Mifflin, 1968.

North Central Association. "A Program of Speech Education: The North Central Association." *The Quarterly Journal of Speech* 37 (1951): 347–358.

INDEX TO AUTHORS CITED

INDEX TO TOPICS